Ultimate Dad Stuff

Ultimate Dad Stuff

Shedloads of ideas
for dads

by Steve Caplin and Simon Rose

**SIMON &
SCHUSTER**

London · New York · Sydney · Toronto · New Delhi

A CBS COMPANY

First published in Great Britain by Simon & Schuster UK Ltd, 2014
A CBS company

Dad Stuff first published in Great Britain by Simon & Schuster UK Ltd, 2005

More Dad Stuff first published in Great Britain by Simon & Schuster UK Ltd, 2007

3 5 7 9 10 8 6 4 2

Simon & Schuster UK Ltd
1st Floor
222 Gray's Inn Road
London WC1X 8HB

www.simonandschuster.co.uk

Simon & Schuster Australia, Sydne

Simon & Schuster India, New Delh

A CIP catalogue record for this book is available from the British Library

Hardback ISBN: 978-1-47113-664-1
eBook ISBN: 978-1-47113-665-8
The author and publishers have made all reasonable efforts
to contact copyright-holders for permission, and apologise
for any omissions or errors in the form of credits given.
Corrections may be made to future printings.

Typeset in the UK by Steve Caplin
Printed in the UK by CPI Group (UK) Ltd, Croydon, CR0 4YY

Contents

This book is dedicated to our children: Joseph, Izzy and Connie Rose, Freddy and Joe Caplin. And, of course, to their mothers, Jane and Carol, without whom they'd probably be filthy, unclothed and starving.

Thanks to all those who offered their expertise, in particular: Martin Ball, Andy Best, Margaret Lawrence, Steph Lawrence, Shawn Sorrell, Catherine Christof, Robin Welch, Roger Jackson, all the Gallimores, Simon Trevor-Roberts, Fiona Tracey, Paul Caplin.

Introduction

WHEN STEVE'S FIRST CHILD was born, a friend gave him a mug inscribed *Anyone can be a FATHER, but it takes someone special to be a DAD.* This slushy, saccharine sentiment mystified him at the time. When you're up to your armpits in a sea of disposable nappies, pushchairs and bottle sterilizers, and everything reeks of baby oil and vomit, it's hard enough just to keep going – let alone contemplate the forthcoming joys of fatherhood.

But as your children evolve from babies into kids, they cease seeing you merely as a supplier of powdered milk and poopless Pampers and acquire an interest in your bottomless fund of knowledge and experience. Almost from the moment they begin to talk, kids are asking questions. Questions to which you, no longer just their father but now their Dad, are expected to have instant, accurate, relevant and entertaining answers.

And this is the problem. When our kids expect us to know everything, we really can't disappoint them. That can wait until their late teenage years, when they'll come to believe that everything we ever told them was either misguided nonsense or a cunningly constructed farrago of mistruths calculated to repress their freedom of expression.

Until that fateful day, we have their full attention. We owe it to them, as well as to the whole of Dadkind, to preserve the myth that Dads are infallible, all-knowing and as near omnipotent as a mortal can be.

We need to be able to fix their toys when they break, cheer them up when they're down, entertain them when they're bored, educate them when they're curious and enlighten them when they're confused. We need to be able to juggle, to tie knots, to identify trees and to do magic. We need to know why the sky is blue, why you can't dig a hole right through the Earth, and what to do in a thunderstorm.

Above all, Dads need to be able to make childhood *fun*. Whether it's keeping them going on car journeys or organizing games to play in the park, a Dad should be an endless resource of ideas and inspiration.

None of us are perfect Dads, much as we'd like to be. And while Mums have an established tradition of comparing notes, medical histories and intimate details of their relationships, Dads – by nature reserved and tight-lipped – have no such support group. We need a book to help us become the paragons to whom we all aspire. Until we find it, this one will have to do.

Steve Caplin and Simon Rose, London, 2014

Anyone can be a
FATHER
but it takes someone special
to be a
DAD

1 Fun with everyday objects

PAPER BAGS, STRAWS, EGGS, BALLOONS, bowler hats, ping pong balls, empty loo roll tubes. A treasure trove of tools to be used by the resourceful Dad to amuse, entertain and instruct even the most world-weary of internet-age children.

When they're younger, kids will probably use this detritus to build fantasy castles and spaceships. As they become more inquisitive, it's Dad's turn to show them the true potential of these mundane cast-offs.

These activities don't require complex construction or whole afternoons spent knee-deep in modelling clay, polystyrene and sticky-back plastic. (There's plenty of that in a later chapter.) Some are spur of the moment tricks and games. Others require just a little preparation – the chances, for instance, of happening upon four loo roll holders just when you need them are, at best, slight; it's wise to start saving these items for a rainy day whenever you come across them.

The ball you can't pick up

You walk towards a ball and reach down for it. But, every time, just as your hand is about to touch the ball, it flies off ahead of you as if it's trying to escape. It looks impressive, but is terribly simple.

As you walk towards the ball, pretend to try to grab it at the very moment your foot kicks it away. And if you don't have a ball, use a can.

Kick the ball as you reach to pick it up

No more than seven folds

It's almost impossible to fold a piece of paper in half more than seven times, no matter how big or thin it is. Naturally no child takes this piece of knowledge on trust. They are usually convinced that somehow they will be able to prove the rest of the world wrong with a sheet torn roughly from an exercise book and a firm press or two of a ruler.

As they will soon find, repeated doubling over of the paper means that, generally around the seventh fold, the paper becomes too thick to fold over any more.

Previous generations of children simply accepted this, much as they might accept that the Earth revolves around the Sun. More recently, inquisitive minds have discovered that, using enormous sheets of thin paper, seven folds can be bettered.

Indeed, one precocious American schoolkid, Britney Gallivan, studied the problem as a maths project and found a way to fold paper 12 times. It involves some seriously complicated equations so we'll have to take her word for it.

FASCINATING FACT

If you were able to fold a piece of paper a hundredth of an inch thick in half 50 times, it would be so thick that it would reach from here to the Sun!

The hole in your head hat trick

Don't worry, we're not going to suggest a spot of do-it-yourself trepanning. But you *can* convince smaller kids (and exceptionally gullible bigger ones) that you have a hole in the top of your head.

You need a hat with a hard brim. Something like a bowler, a top hat or a fireman's helmet would work well. So too should a bike helmet, though you may need to reverse it.

Stand against a wall with the brim of the hat touching it. Put your finger in your mouth and inflate your cheeks as if you're blowing hard. As you do so, push your head back slightly so that the brim of the hat is pressing gently against the wall. The front of the hat will rise.

After a moment, take out your finger, let the hat drop back and pretend to be really puffed with the exertion. Then do it again. You can even let your audience examine your head for signs of the hole.

We are very nearly amused

Say 'cheese', Your Majesty

Want to make the Queen smile or frown at your command? Take any British banknote and fold it backwards vertically at the midpoint of the Queen's mouth. Fold it forwards at each end of her mouth, making a small inverted V the full width of the note.

Without the V needing to be particularly pronounced, if you tilt the top of the banknote towards you, the Queen will smirk. Tip it away and she is definitely not amused. Sadly, this doesn't work nearly as well for Charles Darwin, on the back of the £10 note, as his facial hair gets in the way. Nor, sadly, can you do it with Euros as they don't have any faces on them.

If you worry about exposing your children to temptation by handing them your hard-earned money, this trick can be done with pretty much any photo.

As strong as an egg

An egg? Strong? Indeed it is, amazingly so. Any architect would tell you how strong arches are and that domes are stronger still, which is why they're used in a variety of buildings from igloos to cathedrals.

And what is an egg, if not two domes joined together? Given the ease with which eggs break, you may be sceptical.

So try it. Place an uncooked egg upright into something soft and pliable, such as Plasticine or a bunched-up tea towel. Put two piles of books of the same height nearby. Use them and the egg as a tripod on which to rest a light but solid sheet, such as a thin baking tray.

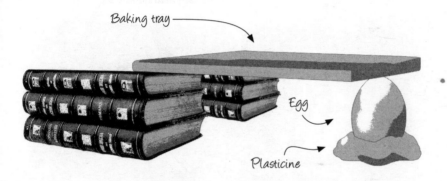

Baking tray

Egg

Plasticine

Gently place a thick book, then another, then another onto the tray. You and the kids will be surprised just how much weight the egg can bear before giving up the ghost. That's because the dome-like egg distributes the pressure evenly around its shell.

Another surprising example of an egg's strength is to wrap your fingers around one lengthways and squeeze it as hard as you can. If you're of a nervous disposition, you may prefer to do this outside or over the sink. Providing you remove any rings that could fracture the shell, the chances are that you won't be able to break the egg, no matter how hard you try. You can even get one or more children to squash your closed hand with all their might.

It worked for us, but bear in mind that we write and draw for a living, hardly occupations renowned for building up muscle strength. You won't find us of an evening tearing up telephone directories. If you've just returned from dragging a sledge to the North Pole, you may succeed where we failed.

The great egg trick

It was all so much easier in the olden days. Children were seen and not heard, called their father 'Sir' and prefaced other adults' names with 'Uncle' or 'Auntie'. How much trickier it is these days for Dads to keep their air of authority and superiority in this been there, done that, got-the-T-shirt-and-bundled-it-dirty-under-the-bed era.

If anything's going to restore the Dads of the world to mythic status in the eyes of their children, it's *The Great Egg Trick*. It isn't easy. In fact, it's fiendishly difficult. The chances are that you will fail. Totally, massively and messily.

But the failure will be so spectacular that your children are likely to talk about it for weeks to come. Make your attempt on *The Great Egg Trick* an annual event and your kids may bring their mates along to witness you getting egg on your face – and elsewhere.

Should you actually succeed in bringing it off, however, you will become a Dad among Dads, spoken of in hushed tones in parks and playgrounds. Other parents may approach you for your autograph, saying it's not for them but their little one. All you need is four eggs, four glasses, four tubes to hold the eggs, and a tray.

Practise with hard-boiled eggs by all means, but when you perform *The Great Egg Trick* in earnest they must be raw.

Place four tumblers or cups half full of water on a table, in a rectangular pattern. Place a tray with a lip onto the glasses or cups. If you're right-handed, have the tray protrude a little to the right (and vice versa).

You need something to hold the eggs. The outer part of matchboxes squashed into a more circular shape would do, or rolled-up index cards held together with rubber bands. Whatever you choose, it shouldn't be much shorter than the egg; the eggs should sit comfortably enough that they won't fall off if somebody breathes too heavily, but not so snugly that they'd still be there after a minor earthquake.

Examine these egg holders from all angles to ensure that they are positioned exactly above the tumblers and then carefully place the eggs onto them, as shown in the illustration.

You are now going to hit the tray out of the way, relying on inertia to keep the eggs in place long enough to plop down into the water. You can whack the tray with the flat of your hand or use a heavy book. Whatever your preferred method, you must give it enough of a knock that the tray flies clear. A quick, clean blow without a follow-through is what is needed, first ensuring that nobody is in the tray's flight path.

Get it right and you've nothing worse than four splashes of water to clear up. Get it wrong, and… well, there's always next time.

The broken egg on the head

We realize that most people must know this one, but there has to be a first time for every child. Place your hand, splayed, on the top of your child's head and tap your wrist with the fingers of the other hand. Inside the victim's head, it sounds exactly like an egg breaking.

Follow it by trailing your fingers lightly down the sides of their head, barely touching their hair. The whole effect is greatly enhanced if they see you holding an egg beforehand.

Other uses for eggs

We're told, on fairly reliable authority, that eggs can also be cooked and eaten. Seems like a waste of a good trick to us.

Balloon games

Wonderful things, balloons. You can fart with them, make electricity with them, juggle with them and even skewer them without bursting them. And best of all, you've probably already got some in a kitchen drawer.

Balloon whoopee

Farting always seems good for a laugh, not only with children, but most adult males too. Unless you're blessed with the melodic talents of France's one-time Moulin Rouge star Le Pétomane (or 'The Fartiste'), you may need to improvise. While nothing can match the rich, deep rasping of manufactured whoopee cushions (except, of course, the real thing), you can still have a merry time with an ordinary balloon.

Simply snip off the ribbed end, keeping as much of the tube as you can. Blowing up the balloon is much harder without it but it can still be managed. Try, if it isn't too disgusting, to get plenty of moisture into the tube. Let the balloon go down, holding the tube between your thumb and index finger with varying pressure until you get a 'note' that you like. Once the tube gets really wet and adhesive, you may not even need to hold it at all.

Do bear in mind, though, that it will need much more well-developed lungs than usual to inflate the balloon, so this may be one trick better left to Dads. 'But the kids told me to do it' will no doubt be your perfectly reasonable excuse later on.

Balloon power

If you've got a spare fluorescent bulb (either the new energy-saving bulbs or the old-style strip lights) try this experiment, which needs to be conducted in pretty dark conditions.

Charge up a balloon by rubbing it on a jumper, and bring it towards the bulb. As it gets close, you should see it light up. With energy-saving bulbs, if you rapidly move the balloon towards and away from the bulb you can get them to stay alight, albeit very dimly.

A fluorescent tube is full of mercury vapour. When electrons are supplied to the bulb with electricity, they cause the mercury vapour to emit invisible ultraviolet light. The white coating on the inside of the tube is composed of phosphors, fluorescent chemicals, which turn the ultraviolet light into visible light. Rubbing a balloon charges it up with electrons and it is these that the mercury vapour in the fluorescent tube are reacting to.

Another neat thing you can do with statically charged balloons is to attract bubbles. Blow them in the normal way and bring the balloon close to one and the bubble will change direction towards the balloon. You have to be very nimble or it will simply crash into the balloon and burst.

Piercing balloons (1)

Shove something sharp into an inflated balloon and you'd expect it to go bang. But if you put a bit of sticky tape on it first, you can insert a wooden barbecue skewer or pointy knitting needle without mishap. In fact, you can insert several, although the air will begin leaking out.

Stick another bit of tape on the other side of the balloon and with care you can even pass the skewer or needle all the way through.

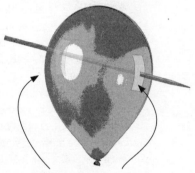

Tape both sides prevents
skewers bursting the balloon

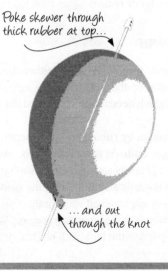

Poke skewer through
thick rubber at top...

...and out
through the knot

Piercing balloons (2)

After we wrote the first edition of this book, one of our readers pointed out that there's an alternative method – that doesn't require any sticky tape.

Don't inflate the balloon fully, but make sure there's still a dark area opposite the mouth of the balloon. The fabric of the balloon is thicker here, and under less pressure; it should be possible to get a skewer through if you proceed with caution. Poking it back out through the knot should cause no problem.

Balloon power

Many people know that if you rub an inflated balloon vigorously against your hair or wool clothing it will pick up static electricity and can then be stuck in place on a wall, ceiling, TV or even a face. The action of rubbing the balloon gives it extra negatively charged electrons. Other electrically neutral objects, such as a tin can, are more positively charged than the balloon, and because opposites attract, the two pull together.

You can get so much more fun from a statically charged balloon than simply sticking it on something. Hold it above your head, for instance, and your hair will

Bring a charged balloon near an empty can...

...and the can will roll towards it as if by magic!

stand up, with each positively charged, upstanding strand trying its hardest to get away from its neighbour. Hold it above a plate of salt, sugar or breakfast cereal and watch the stuff jump onto the balloon.

Even better, the charged balloon will attract water. Turn a tap on so there's a gentle trickle of water. Hold your balloon near it and the flow of water will bend towards the balloon, a neat way of enlivening bathtime.

Cooler still, the balloon will attract an empty drinks can strongly enough to get it to roll along a hard floor, pulling it in either direction. Get a couple of cans and you can have a race.

FASCINATING FACT

Static electricity helps explain lightning and has even powered a spaceship. Printers and photocopiers depend on it for fixing images. No doubt their inventors spent far too much time as kids sticking balloons to walls.

Balloon football

Watching football is endlessly tedious, as most Mums will tell you. The only good bits are the action replays in slow motion. So here's your chance to relive that winning goal: a balloon will naturally move in slow motion. If you and your kids do likewise, you can bring grandstand action into your living room.

Balloon juggling

It's easy to make your own juggling balls. Cut the top and neck off six balloons and fill three of them with sand. Stretch the remaining three over these, so the holes end up opposite the holes in the originals. Bingo! Juggle away!

Standing on balloons without bursting them

Challenge your kids to see if they can stand on ordinary, inflated balloons without bursting them. Naturally, after a bout of noisy experimentation, they'll claim that it's impossible.

Not so, at least not if you use more than one balloon and spread your weight. Turn a tray upside down and use its ridge to secure the balloons beneath it.

Stand near something you can hold onto, such as a table or chair. While your children wince in expectation of four bangs, gingerly put first one foot onto the tray, then a little more weight and finally the other foot. You should be able to straighten up so that you are standing unaided on the tray.

Lip holds balloons in place

Going quackers

Flatten a plastic straw at one end. Cut a little away at both sides of the flattened end so that the straw has a V-shaped point. Put the straw a little way into your mouth, blow gently and, after a little practice, you should be rewarded with a satisfying duck sound.

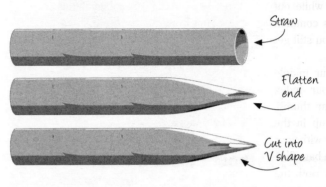

Straw

Flatten end

Cut into V shape

Push another straw into the other end and, although harder to blow, you should be able to produce a much lower note, more moose than mallard.

When service in a fast-food joint isn't quite as speedy as you'd like, getting your whole party to quack together in unison (using the straws thoughtfully provided for this purpose) should do wonders for speeding up your order.

The jumping paperclips

Fold a banknote in three so that, edge on, it looks like a Z. Place one paperclip half an inch or so in from the left end, fastening it to the middle section and front; fasten another half an inch in from the right, fixed to the back and middle sections. (If you place the paperclips on the wrong sections, it won't work.) You should push both paperclips right down – they're only left sticking up in the illustration so you can see where they are better.

Grasp the two side ends of the note and pull. The paperclips will spring off. No surprise there. But when you retrieve them, you'll discover that they are magically linked together.

In the bag

Paper bags are great for catching all manner of invisible things. Hang onto any you get while out shopping. They aren't as common as they once were, but you still get them occasionally.

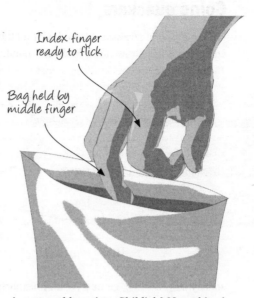

Index finger ready to flick

Bag held by middle finger

Hold the bag with your middle finger inside it and your index finger held back by your thumb. Throw the whateveritis up in the air, following its trajectory with your eyes. As it drops into the bag, flick it with your index finger. Both the noise and the sudden movement will make it seem as if something really has fallen into the bag.

Paper bags are also brilliant for blowing up and bursting. Childish? Not a bit of it. It's an excellent demonstration of how thunder occurs.

I see no ships

The hole in the hand

Hold an empty loo roll tube to one eye and look straight ahead at something in the distance.

Bring your free hand up towards your other eye. As it comes alongside the tube, it should look as if there's a round hole in your hand, through which you can see whatever you were looking at.

If you don't have an empty loo roll tube, then either empty one (see page 112 for a great reason to do this), or else use a sheet of paper rolled up and kept circular with the hand.

Forever blowing bubbles

Children needn't despair if they lose the plastic bubble wand that came with their bubbles, or have run out of bubble solution. Both are easy to replace. You can make your own liquid from one part washing-up liquid to about twelve parts of water. You'll get even better bubbles if you mix a little sugar in, though the water will need to be warm to dissolve it.

Putting the mixture into a clean bowl (dirt is bad for bubbles) makes everything so much easier. You can press umpteen handy objects into service as bubble-makers; bent wire (experiment with shapes), straws (use paperclips to fasten them together into shapes), a fly swatter, plastic strawberry punnets, the plastic bit holding your six-pack of beer together.

You can even use your hands. Overlap your thumbs with your index fingers touching to make a triangle. It's dryness rather than sharpness that pops bubbles, so make sure you soak your hands in the solution. This way you can also hold bubbles *on* your hands without them bursting.

If you're after giant bubbles then make a bubble loop. Slip a couple of straws onto a length of string and tie it into a loop, concealing the knot in one of the straws. Holding the straws, make a rectangular shape, dip it into your solution and gently waft it through the air. A length of fabric tape about six feet long, weighed down with something like a nut or a washer, is another good way of making a bubble loop – though it'll need two of you to open the loop.

If you've a paddling pool and a hula hoop, put the hoop over something in the middle a child can stand on. When they're in position, bring up the hoop and the child will be in the middle of a giant bubble!

Nut to weigh down fabric tape

2 Batteries not required

'DAD, I'M BORED.' Once, those words would have struck terror into your heart. No more. After all, you now have drawers bursting with ping pong balls, balloons, paperclips, straws, sticky tape, old newspapers, empty loo roll tubes, rubber bands and more. You are as prepared as a forward-thinking Dad can be.

But what if you aren't at home when they're getting restless? Don't panic. Resourceful as you are, you still retain the ability to divert, instruct and amuse with nothing more than the body Nature gave you. It may not be the trim, slick, model of perfection it once was, but as an entertainer of children it has no equal.

Here is a range of games and pastimes requiring no preparation or props whatsoever, yet which will still amaze and delight even the most jaded of childish imaginations. Some are educational, some amusing, many are downright daft. Some were favourites of our playground days, ready to be dusted off and re-released to an entirely new generation. All should be part of your ever-expanding arsenal of activities to counter boredom.

Going up

Press down hard (but not *too* hard) on someone's head for 10 seconds. Ask them to shut their eyes while you put your hands under their arms and make as if you're lifting them into the air. Without actually trying to bear their weight, they will get the impression that they have been lifted clear of the ground.

Similarly, pin their arms by their sides while they try hard to push outwards. After 10 seconds, tell them to stop. When you let go, their arms will involuntarily float up into the air.

The incredible shrinking arm (1)

Who can resist the seemingly impossible challenge of lengthening their own limbs? Unlike expensive plastic surgery, this method's 'armless – and the effect is, mercifully, temporary.

Hold your arms out horizontally in front of you, palms touching. As our arms tend to be the same length, your two middle fingers should be the same distance away from you. With one hand, vigorously rub the upper part of the arm still outstretched for four or five seconds. Now hold the two arms out together.

Suddenly the one you've rubbed is longer than the other. Or is it that the other one is now shorter?

You can expect your rubbed arm to be about an inch longer!

The incredible shrinking arm (2)

Here's an interesting variation on the same trick. Stand facing a wall with both arms stretched out, palms flat against the wall.

Now make a sweeping circular motion with one arm, swinging it backwards over your head and back to its starting position. This hand will no longer reach the wall!

Mind the gap!

Blinkety blink

That hallowed time-waster, seeing who can hold off blinking for longest, has actually now become a sport. There are staring face-off competitions with proper rules and giant video screens that project the contestants' faces to the audience.

Set up your own domestic championship. Each competing pair rests their elbows on the table and stares into each other's eyes. At the bell (or tambourine, squeaky mouse or whatever's to hand), they must refrain from touching, talking, laughing, yawning, moving suddenly or even smiling. The first to blink is the loser.

Astoundingly, the record for not blinking is currently over 22 minutes. So get your kids practising now. It surely can't be long before it's an Olympic sport, along with *Thumb Wars* and *Rock, Paper, Scissors*.

The invisible bonds

Get your victim to put their hands together. Then tell them that you are tying their hands together and mime winding string around their hands, around and around and around. As you do it, tell them that their hands are being forced ever more tightly together.

Round and round you go, until you finally tie off the string. Then say you're going to set them free. Mime cutting the string with scissors. If it has worked, they should find it oddly difficult to pull their hands apart.

A related piece of weirdness is to get someone to hold out their arms with their hands six inches or so apart. With your index finger extended, circle their outstretched hands with one of yours, getting faster and faster. They will find it very difficult not to bring their hands ever closer together.

The comedy trip

'Beware of the invisible rope,' you warn, either indoors or out. The kids search for it, but naturally can't find it. Yet, whenever you pass the spot, it trips you up.

It's pretty easy to do. Simply walk normally. As you get to the chosen spot, knock the foot that's coming forward into the heel of the other foot. You will trip convincingly, but with little danger of falling flat on your face. It's pretty hard to spot how it's done, so you can repeat it for ages before, if you're so inclined, letting them in on the secret.

Rock, paper, scissors... gun

Bang! is a shooting variation on *Rock, Paper, Scissors* that has an element of subtlety and tension that's absent from the original game: it can also be played by more than two players.

From two to five players sit in a circle. Tapping their hands on their knees, they all count 1–2–3 then raise their hands in one of three gun positions, aiming at one of the other players. Both hands pointing forwards means Shoot; crossed across the chest means Shield; raised to the shoulders means Reload.

If you shoot someone who's reloading or shooting someone else, you win a point. If you shoot someone who's shielding, there's no score; if you shoot someone who's shooting you, both players' scores are reduced to zero.

You must reload each time before you can shoot but if you reload twice you will get two consecutive shots. The game gets quicker as the players get accustomed to it, and is won by the first player to get five points.

If you're sitting around a table, *Bang!* can be played by rapping closed knuckles on the table during the count.

Tap three times on your knees

Shield

Shoot   Reload

Sofa my next trick...

Who said mimes aren't funny? The sofa

Forbid the kids from going into the secret cellar, located behind the sofa or settee, or whatever you call that long piece of furniture you doze on after a good lunch. When you go behind it into the cellar, simply walk behind it, getting lower in jumpy stages as if you're descending steps. Once you've completely disappeared from sight, turn round and come back up again.

Why this should be such a source of wonderment to young minds remains a mystery, but it's there for Dads to take advantage of. You can even install an escalator to make your journey that much smoother. Try canoeing along a hidden river, too, jerking forward as you dig your paddle in.

Who said mimes aren't funny? The lift

If you encounter a frosted glass door with a solid bottom half then, with your audience on the other side, press the imaginary down button. By bending your knees you can appear to be slowly 'descending' to another floor.

You can mime the lift getting stuck between floors and jiggling you up and down as the machine struggles to free itself. As the *pièce de résistance*, press the button again and, with a bemused expression, find yourself being bizarrely carried off to the side and out of sight.

Who said mimes aren't funny? The kiss

Rodin's *The Kiss* may be a masterpiece of French sculpture, but it doesn't get many laughs. Turn your back to an audience and you can pretty convincingly make it look as if somebody is kissing you.

Simply wrap your arms around your body with your fingertips reaching onto your back and, making appropriate noises if desired, move your hands up and down. Perhaps this is best done in reasonable proximity to your other half, unless you fancy explaining when you get home why the kids saw you kissing somebody in the park.

Who said mimes aren't funny? The strangler

Not all our ideas are cribbed from old TV comedians (see page 66) but it was certainly Eric Morecambe of *Morecambe and Wise* fame who first demonstrated the potential of the phantom strangler to us.

What do you think of it so far?

Baring your arm to the halfway mark, grab your own throat, ensuring that your elbow is hidden behind a wall or curtain from your audience's point of view. Make it look as though you're struggling against the hand's attempts to pull you away, using the other hand to give the impression you're trying to free yourself. Simple, but very effective.

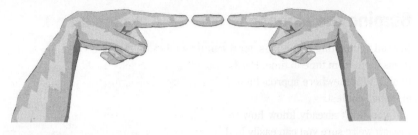

Spectral sausages

With your hands some way apart and roughly nine inches from your eyes, point your index fingers at each other. As you look at something in the distance, gradually bring your fingers towards each other. When they're just a few inches apart, a ghostly 'sausage' should appear in mid air in between your two fingers.

Banging your head on a wall

There are surely times when your offspring make you feel like indulging in a gentle session of headbanging, not to soothing heavy metal music, but against a nearby wall.

You can get all the benefits of this time-honoured method of relieving frustration without any of the usual danger of bruising, lumps or stitches.

As your head comes close, but not quite into contact with the wall, kick your foot into the base to make the corresponding knocking sound. This works particularly well with the resonant bases of kitchen units. If you chose to economize when you had them installed, a gentle tap might be more sensible than a full-blooded Shearer penalty-taker.

Weird handshakes

Shake your child's hand. At the last minute, tuck your middle finger in so it rests against your palm. 'Don't mind the wart,' you say as they squirm.

Other handshake jokes involve shaking in the manner of different professions: say 'I'm a dairy farmer' as you repeatedly squeeze their fingers; 'I'm a train driver' as you pump your arm back and forth like a piston; 'I'm from the electricity company' as you vibrate your middle finger; 'I'm from the Left Handed Society' as you extend your left hand towards their right; 'I'm a submarine captain' as you make to shake their hand, then duck yours beneath at the last moment.

Burping the alphabet

Instead of chanting at the kids, for the umpteenth time, 'Don't do that', try to out-gross them from time to time. Hard to do, it's true, but you should at least be able to sink to somewhere approaching their level by challenging them to a 'burp the alphabet' contest.

If you don't already know how to burp intentionally, it's a bit tricky to learn, though we're sure you can easily find children willing to teach you. There's a sort of tiny swallow involved inside your throat. Connie, our resident young professor of burping, advises that you need to 'burp in, then burp out'.

Once you can do it, you have to sound out a letter as you burp it. Like ventriloquism, certain letters are easier and others harder. The soft ones like 'C', 'J' and 'S' are tricky, the vowels a doddle.

It's possible that other, less enlightened souls, may find a group of kids burping the alphabet, even with a supposed grown-up in attendance, a bit offensive. In that case, you mustn't forget your manners. Everyone should remember to say 'pardon' after each burp.

Thumb wars

This cut-down version of arm wrestling is a great time-occupier if there aren't any handy distractions. Bend your four fingers inwards and interlock your hand with that of your opponent. Both move your thumbs in alternate, opposite directions as you chant, '1–2–3–4, I declare a thumb war'.

Then, hands still locked together, each must try to press down their opponent's thumb with their own and hold it down.

Thumb you win, thumb you don't...

Levitation for beginners

Get this right and, in an amazing feat, four children will lift an adult into the air using only their index fingers. The adult should sit upright on a hard chair, arms folded, while four children (aged eight years up seems to work fine) stand next to it, two ready to lift under the arms and two under the knees.

Under both arms...

... and under the knees

The four should first attempt to lift the adult by clasping their hands and putting their index fingers together. Not surprisingly, they probably won't be able to budge the person at all.

The children should then stretch their right hands in turn above the victim's head followed by their respective left hands. They need to keep their hands there for a short while, counting to 10, or chanting some mumbo-jumbo over and over such as, 'Arise, Sir Whoever' or '2, 4, 6, 8, Who are we to levitate?' or whatever takes their fancy.

After 10 –15 seconds, they drop their hands and immediately lift the person with their joined index fingers. Miraculously, they should be able to raise them several inches from the chair. (Just what we need, kids finding yet another way of getting a rise out of an adult.)

This didn't work *every* time we tried it. Some practitioners claim it works better if the children actually put their hands on the victim's head and press down gently. Others say it's best if the chanting is of a more mystical bent. We find the whole thing somewhat perplexing. It's worth persevering, though, because when it does work, it really is utterly extraordinary.

Bet you can't do this

Everyone knows that it's tricky to rub your stomach and pat your head at the same time. But it's not *that* tricky. Certainly not as tricky as this.

With your arms extended, point your index fingers at each other. With one arm, draw a circle in the air, returning to the same point. Now do it with both arms, but in opposite directions. Your fingers ought to pass each other at the bottom and the top of the circle.

When you've mastered that, try circling your arms at different speeds, in opposite directions, then going the same way. Lastly, and this is the one we still can't quite get right, try moving one hand inside the orbit of the other, again trying both directions.

If you think this is childish, we'd like to point out that it was apparently thought up by Nobel Prize-winning theoretical physicist and inveterate practical joker, Richard Feynman. So there! Incidentally, when Feynman's mum once heard him referred to as the 'smartest man in the world', her response was, 'If that's the world's smartest man, God help us!'

Once your kids master this, you can always bet them that they can't lick their elbow. This is pretty well impossible for most people, though naturally nobody takes this on trust until they've made themselves look mildly ridiculous by trying it out. It is, however, apparently an urban myth that nobody can do it. *Guinness World Records* receives several claims a day from people who can, indeed, lick their own elbows.

Doing the Quofit

We've christened this the 'Quofit' because we've no idea what this method of travelling sideways is really called. It's fun, though, and a good test of coordination.

Start with your heels together and your toes pointing outwards. To travel to the right, pivot your right foot on your toe and your left foot on the heel until the toes

come together. Put your feet down and, in a continuous motion, pivot on your right heel and left toe until the heels are together again. Now keep going – if you can. Then try travelling backwards.

Once you've all mastered it, put on some music and you're doing the Quofit.

And now the news and weather

This is one of our all-time favourites. It's daft in the extreme but invariably has us all in stitches. Best carried out with an audience, one person elects to be the newsreader while another gets behind them and puts their arms through, ready

to do all the actions. It doesn't seem to matter whether the puppeteer can be seen or not.

The newsreader (Dad may want to get the ball rolling) should talk about things that can easily be illustrated visually. As we hear about people being stabbed or strangled, for instance, the hands are showing us just that. When the police are puzzled, the hands can rub the chin or scratch the head. Frankly, when we're in a giggly mood, even an itchy leg being scratched will set us off.

If more children want to be involved, you can simulate a TV interview, with one of them asking questions and another doing the actions. Or you can swap and have a spell at it yourself. You can even adapt it for telling bedtime stories with the help of an older sibling.

The dematerializing knees

From a spectator's point of view, it looks as though your knees are passing through each other and coming out the other side. No *Star Trek* wizardry is involved, however, just a plain simple parlour trick of old.

You'll need a bit of slow-motion practice before you trundle it out. Sitting down, plant your feet firmly on the ground close together. Put your hands on your knees and bring your knees together. Stretch your thumbs and index fingers across and place them on the other knee, one hand in front of the other, and lift off the other fingers. As you pull your knees apart, your hands should now continue their journey on their new knees.

The knees should continue out then back again. As they come together this time, transfer your outer fingers across to the other knee and continue as the hands return to their original position.

As you get up to speed and find that you can do it without thinking, the continuous motion of the hands as they cross and uncross makes it appear that your legs have crossed over. Before long, you should be able to do this standing up as well.

The broken nose trick

Nobody nose how I do this

This is another great way to gross out your kids. Claim that you can dislocate or break your nose whenever you want. With your thumbs in your mouth, place your hands either side of your nose. Quickly bend them (and your nose) to one side, at the same time flicking your thumbnails against your front teeth to make a clicking sound. Then reset it, moving it back to its original position, again flicking your teeth.

Exhaustive research with a tape recorder and headphones (we may be sad, but at least we are *thorough*) reveals that the aperture of the mouth is important, as the interior acts as an amplifier. Don't leave it wide open: instead, hold it in a relaxed position, with just a slight gap between your lower lip and your thumbnails.

Cheeky music

Slapping your cheeks with open palms (preferably your own) makes an elementary sort of music. After a somewhat bruising testing session, it turns out that Simon's mouth has a range of an octave which makes it perfect, for instance, for accompanying nursery rhymes. *Baa Baa Black Sheep* works particularly well.

If your children have refined musical tastes (i.e. if they like the old-fashioned music *you* like), you can always play them *Hot Butter* by Popcorn. We've found ourselves reminiscing about a childhood summer holiday, sitting of an evening at al fresco Italian cafés with this on the jukebox and tables full of kids all gaily slapping their cheeks as the Moog warbled away. Or maybe not. Your call.

Making a noise like a wood pigeon

In the list of animals it would be cool to impersonate, the wood pigeon must come pretty well near the bottom. Unfortunately, we have absolutely no idea how to roar convincingly like a lion, neigh like a horse or warble like a nightingale. So, dull and commonplace though it may be, you'll have to settle for recreating the soft mellifluous cooing of the wood pigeon.

Place the palms of your hands together at 90°, right over left. Curl your fingers around the opposite hand. Open up a gap between your hands but, at the same time, try to avoid any holes in what will be the sounding box.

Keeping them parallel, place the end of your thumbs on your right index finger. Bend the knuckles of your thumbs out a little, placing your mouth either side of them. Now blow softly: oo–*oo*–oo, oo–oo is the proper sequence.

Cooing like a wood pigeon, it turns out, is not quite like riding a bike. Even if you were a demon wood pigeon cooer in your youth, it can take a while in adulthood

to get a sound at all, and even then it may sound like the sort of bird that might have asthma from roosting too near a chemicals factory.

Persevere, though, and with luck your skills will improve. Above all, you must ensure that you're blowing softly. If you really find it difficult, console yourself with the knowledge that while Simon can conjure up a perfect pigeon at the drop of a feather, despite his expert tutelage Steve remains to this day entirely unable to produce a single warble.

The unsupported circle

If you have eight or more people at a loose end, get them to stand up and form themselves into a tight circle, each person facing the back of the next person, only a few inches separating them.

Slowly, everyone should lower themselves until they are sitting on the knees of the person behind. It may take one or two tries but you should be able to create a circle with everyone sitting on somebody else's knees and the entire ring rock solid, even though nothing is actually holding it up.

A capital trick

Bet your kids that you are so brainy that you know every capital in the world. Get them to ask you the capital of any country, anywhere on Earth, or even any American state capital.

They might try to trip you up with a difficult one and demand to know something like the capital of Kyrgyzstan. 'That's easy,' you say. 'It's "K".' 'The capital of Mississippi?' 'M.'

There'll be groans and they'll refuse to shell out on the bet. But you can bet they'll be trying it on their friends in school the next day.

The phantom hand

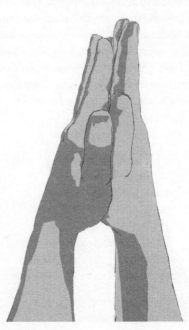

Hold your hand up against your child's, palms flat, thumbs together. Get them to stroke the middle finger and thumb of their *other* hand up and down a pair of fingers – one of yours, and one of theirs.

The effect is rather spooky: to the child doing the stroking, they can feel one of the hands from the 'inside', but not the other one. They know it's there, but it's as if they can't fully sense it. It works particularly well if they also close their eyes.

Jiving fingers

Our parents lived in a wacky age when you couldn't carry music around with you piped directly into your ears. Not only that, if they wanted to listen to music, the chances are that the place wouldn't even have a dance licence. So, law-abiding citizens that they were, they hand-jived instead.

There are still places where a hand-jive is more appropriate than strutting your stuff in full view of others. From your children's point of view, that's no doubt *everywhere* ('No, Dad! Not where people can *see*.'). Ideally suited to rock'n'roll or swing, you need to select four different hand movements from those available. Most are done leading first with the right hand, then the left and repeating both before changing to another 'step'. The four movements are cycled in the same order over and over again. Hand-jiving with a couple of kids is great fun and is relatively unlikely to involve any embarrassing age-related dancing injury on the Dad's part.

Among the movements to pick from are:

- Holding one elbow with the other palm while you draw a circle in the air with your index finger.
- Passing the right hand over the left in a scissor-like motion twice.
- Holding your forearms parallel to each other, then spinning them around each other one way, then the other.
- Hitting your fists together twice, beginning right fist on top.
- Hitting your palms on your legs twice, then clapping twice.
- A hitchhiking motion, starting with thumbs going outwards.

Get the kids to come up with some more. Give them names, then they can 'call' the dance as you go along.

3 The rubber band: a Dad's best friend

SOME WILL TELL YOU that a man's best friend is his dog. But dogs need feeding, walking and, occasionally, neutering. The rubber band requires no such time-consuming attention, but will always help you out. About the only thing it won't do is rescue you from a snowdrift with a barrel of brandy round its neck.

Invented in 1845 by London coachmaker Stephen Perry, the rubber band is useful for all manner of temporary repairs, will hold things together while glue dries, is an essential component of catapults, a power source for small model planes and boats, a primitive musical instrument, a stress reliever and can even, apparently, be used for treating haemorrhoids (although this isn't recommended as a DIY procedure).

It used to be that you could never lay your hands on a rubber band when you needed one. But that was in the days before the Royal Mail decided to distribute them, free, to every household in the land, bound around bundles of junk mail. If you can't find one, just wander down your street. Chances are, the postman will conveniently have left some lying on the pavement for you.

Chopsticks for butterfingers

Few things are more frustrating to the hungry child than a plate of steaming food and a pair of chopsticks they can't use. Out comes your trusty rubber band, which you use to fasten the chopsticks together near the top.

Roll up the wrapper the chopsticks came in and shove it between the chopsticks, just below the top loops of the rubber band. Now the chopsticks will be far easier to use, springing apart between food grabs rather like tweezers. If you're not too nifty with chopsticks yourself, you can also try it, claiming you're doing it so as not to show up your kids.

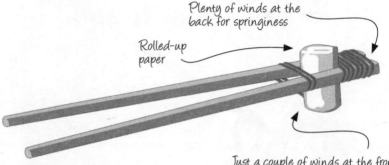

Plenty of winds at the back for springiness

Rolled-up paper

Just a couple of winds at the front to hold the paper in place

The best way to fire a rubber band

Hang a rubber band off the tip of your little finger. Shape your hand as if you're simulating a gun, with the thumb and index finger extended and the other fingers curled. With your other hand, stretch the rubber band around the base of your

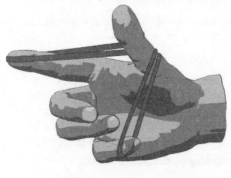

thumb and over the centre of your index finger. To fire the band, simply move your little finger.

As the band slips from your little finger, it will whip around your thumb and rocket off your index finger. Rubber bands fired this way have been clocked at 11 miles an hour and distances of over 20 feet should pose no problem.

The anti-gravity escalator

Snap or cut a rubber band so you have one long piece. You need something to slip over it. A wedding ring will do, but a paperclip is equally fine.

Thread this 'passenger' onto the band, keeping it near your right hand. Holding the backs of your hands towards your audience, hide the better part of the band in the palm of your left hand and stretch the rest of the rubber band between the thumb and forefingers of each hand.

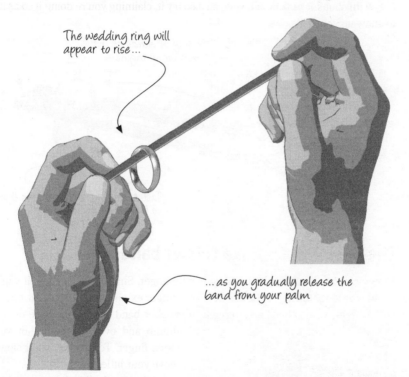

The wedding ring will appear to rise...

...as you gradually release the band from your palm

Raise your right hand until the passenger slides down towards your left hand, showing the effect of gravity. Keep the right hand raised. As you use your powerful, telekinetic eyes to defeat gravity – or whatever voodoo you invoke – let the hidden part of the rubber band gently slip through your left thumb and forefinger. Hey presto! The passenger will appear to be climbing up the rubber band.

The amazing jumping rubber band

With just a little practice, you can make a rubber band jump 'magically' from your first two fingers to your outside two fingers in the blink of an eye.

Put a rubber band over your index finger and middle fingers, positioning it at their base. With the back of your hand to the audience, pull the band to the outside of your hand on the pretext of showing that it's only a bog-standard rubber band. As you're doing it, bend all four fingers down, and put the ends through the band.

Straighten your fingers out quickly and immediately clench them again: the rubber band will appear to jump in an instant to your ring finger and pinky. Stretch the band back the other way, curl your fingers through once more, straighten them, and it has jumped back again.

This trick can be made to look even more impressive. After slipping the rubber band over the two fingers, twist another rubber band around the tops of all four fingers. Pulling the fingers together, this will appear to 'imprison' the first rubber band and make the jump seem that much more miraculous.

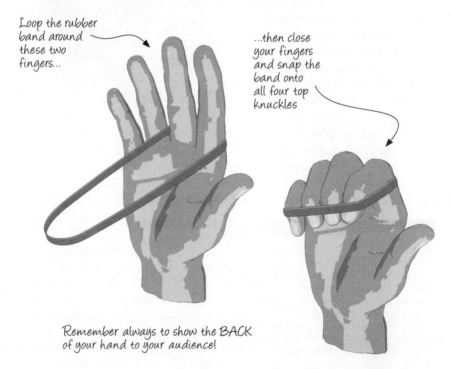

Loop the rubber band around these two fingers...

...then close your fingers and snap the band onto all four top knuckles

Remember always to show the BACK of your hand to your audience!

The rubber band booby trap

Here's a great way to surprise any unsuspecting passer-by. Take two pieces of paper rolled into cylinders (short pencils work just as well) and loop a thick rubber band round their centres. Twist one at least 20 times, propeller-fashion, until the rubber band is good and tight.

Place the entire assembly beneath a large or heavy object – a book, shirt, box of chocolates, for example – so that it's fully concealed. When someone lifts the object off, the rubber band assembly will spring into life with a clattering sound, as if a small but noisy animal has been released.

Making a rubber band ball

A handy way of keeping track of all your rubber bands is to combine them into a rubber band ball. Knot a rubber band until it is as compact as possible. Put another band around it, twisting it as needed to keep it in place. Keep doing this with successive bands until you no longer need to twist them.

Feed me! Feed me!

You can cheat at the start by using a crumpled piece of paper or tin foil as the core. If you fancy a particularly bouncy rubber band ball, put a SuperBall at the centre. Assuming you remember what a SuperBall is, of course.

Although the presence of a rubber band ball in the home means you can always find a rubber band, children (or Dads) with an obsessive or compulsive nature should be discouraged from starting one.

There is stiff competition for the title of the world's largest rubber band ball. The current record holder comprises more than seven hundred thousand bands, is eight feet high and weighs over a ton!

FASCINATING FACT

After five years of making his rubber band ball, the previous record holder, Welshman Tony Evans, became curious to see how high it would bounce. The giant ball was dropped from a cargo plane a mile up over the Mojave Desert. Sadly, it did not bounce at all. Instead, once the 20-feet cloud of dust cleared, it revealed a four-feet wide rubbery crater which survives to this day.

Building a rubber band tank

Before the more militaristically minded kids get too excited at the prospect of making a tank, it should be stressed that this one is more akin to an unsophisticated prototype of a World War One tank than, say, a modern M1A2 Abrams with turbine engine and Chobham armour.

You need a cotton reel, a couple of used matches, a candle stub about half an inch long and, naturally, the ubiquitous rubber band.

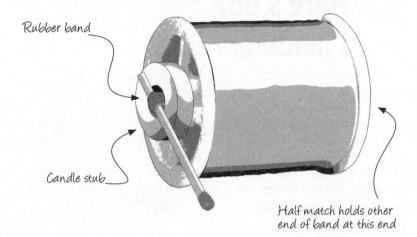

Rubber band

Candle stub

Half match holds other
end of band at this end

Use a skewer or bradawl to carefully make a hole in the candle stub, then push one end of the rubber band through the hole just far enough to push a match through. Pass the other end of the rubber band through the cotton reel. Fix that end of the band in place with a match that's been snapped in half.

The long match is what 'drives' the tank. Position it so that only a tiny part of the match is on one side of the rubber band. Then, using the long end of the match, wind up the rubber band. When it's as tight as it can go without the risk of snapping, place the tank on a smooth surface with the match touching the ground. The tank will begin trundling along as the rubber band begins to unwind itself.

4 Here's one I made earlier

KIDS LOVE MAKING THINGS. From model airplanes to Lego houses, from potato heads to matchstick models, few things generate such a sense of satisfaction as presenting their parents with something they've crafted themselves.

Sometimes they need Dad's help to get started. It's unlikely most kids would realize how to make animated movies on their own, for instance. But, once they're shown how it's done, they can go on to create further masterpieces unaided.

Best of all, though, is the stuff they can make from the most unlikely of raw materials: who would have thought you could make a kite from a dustbin liner? Or a battleground for toy soldiers from a sheet of polystyrene? Or a rocket from an empty film canister and an Alka Seltzer tablet?

This section also has some stuff where Dads will have to do the hard graft – such as the homemade garden swing and longbow – though it will be the kids that get the benefit.

Dioramas for model soldiers

Most boys have at least a hundred model soldiers. (Girls don't tend to play with soldiers until they're old enough to go clubbing in Aldershot.) They'll range from cheap, badly moulded sets bought for £1 for 20 from the local newsagent, to lovingly hand-painted (and hugely expensive) Warhammer models.

But what use are all these soldiers without somewhere to display and play with them? Building a large diorama is fun for both Dad and kids, and is an activity that can be spread over several evenings and weekends. Best of all, the whole thing can be made for less than the cost of a typical Warhammer set.

Begin with a polystyrene sheet for the base. You can buy sheets 60 cm by 120 cm (2 ft by 4 ft) from DIY shops: buy two of them. One will serve as the base: the other is the ground level on top of this, in which you can carve out rivers, potholes, trenches and bomb craters.

Polystyrene is a great modelling material to work with. It can easily be cut with a knife for a hard edge, which is great for making trenches: but scratch away the top layer with your fingers and something marvellous happens. That smooth, flat surface turns into a stony, lumpy piece of waste ground. Cut a chunk of river out, then crumble the edges to make the banks: turn pieces of crumbled-away surface upside down to make rocky outcrops of rough boulders that now have a perfectly smooth underside for fixing onto the ground. Shape pieces to make bridges, houses, and sections of broken wall. You can glue the pieces down with

Crumble away potholes with your fingers

Cut a river from the top sheet

PVA or wallpaper paste, or just pin them in place with small nails. You can also drip polystyrene cement onto the model to melt away potholes.

To make the river bed, lay a piece of tinfoil between the two main sheets of polystyrene before you glue them together. This will give a good reflective appearance. Then paint it blue or grey with felt pens, ink or translucent paints or stains: a couple of coats of PVA on top will build up a good thick shine. Drip PVA into bomb craters to flood them. Use household objects for their texture: corrugated cardboard, with the top layer peeled away, makes a great roofing material; lolly sticks can be turned into fences; coils of wire make convincing barbed wire.

The model should first be painted dark grey or black overall, using a matt water-based household paint. This creates a good base colour and protects the polystyrene from further damage. Then use those little tester pots of paint (the ones with a built-in brush are best) to dab colour onto the walls, masonry and grass. Short, stabbing actions of two different greens make the best grass, and the technique works well for house walls as well.

The best moment of all is when your son's friends come to visit. '*I made that*,' he'll announce proudly, '*with my Dad.*'

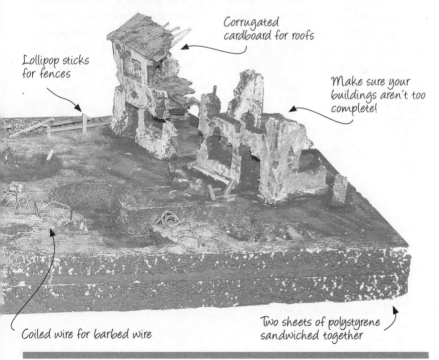

Corrugated cardboard for roofs

Lollipop sticks for fences

Make sure your buildings aren't too complete!

Coiled wire for barbed wire

Two sheets of polystyrene sandwiched together

How to take 3D photographs with any camera

With children reared on a diet of special effects-driven Hollywood blockbusters, it's getting ever harder to impress them with mere photographs.

3D photography could do the trick. Find a scene which has some foreground elements as well as a significant distant feature. Take one shot, preferably using the camera in the portrait position – vertical rather than horizontal.

Try it for yourself. You may find it easier to see if you place a piece of card here

Take a pace to one side and take another shot of the same view, keeping the background feature in roughly the same place in the viewfinder.

To view the images in 3D, place the photos side by side with a piece of card between them (A4 will do). The viewer should bring their face towards the photographs so that their nose is in line with and almost touching the card.

The technique also works if you display the images side by side on a computer screen, holding a bit of card in place. It may be sensible to switch the screen to a higher resolution, making the images smaller so that they melt together more easily. If you don't have any card, the images can also be viewed by deliberately going wall-eyed (the opposite of cross-eyed), but this can take a bit of practice.

Children amazed by this should know that it really is nothing new. It's simply a variation of the Victorian stereoscopes popular 150 years ago.

Möbius and his performing strips

Cut a strip of paper along the long side – an inch or so wide – and twist it once before sticking it together to form a loop. The longer the strip is, the easier the loop will be to play with.

Ask a child to draw a red line down the middle of one side and a blue line down the other. They'll soon realize it can't be done. There is only one side. Mark a spot on the edge with a pencil or a paperclip and they'll discover it also has only one edge.

Cut the strip down the middle all the way around, asking what they think will happen. They'll suspect it will become two loops. In fact, you end up with just one loop, half the width and double the length of the first (and with four twists in it).

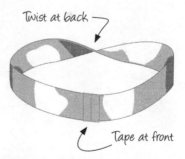

Create another loop, a little wider than before and cut along it a third of the way in. After a while you'll find you're cutting two-thirds of the way across to form one long cut. You end up with one long strip and one shorter one.

This wackiness was discovered in 1858 by two German mathematicians independently, August Ferdinand Möbius and Johann Benedict Listing. Listing got there first, by two months, but the immortality went to Möbius, presumably because everyone thought his name was far cooler.

How to make animated movies

Although we talk of 'movies', what we're really watching is a rapid succession of still images (24 a second in the cinema, 25 on TV and video). Thanks to an effect known as persistence of vision, our brain is fooled into thinking it looks real.

It isn't difficult to make animated movies. The easiest way is to download an app for your phone. You need one that will shoot one frame at a time. You'll also need to hold your phone very steady: if you don't want to buy a tripod mount, support it on Blu-Tack (but make sure it doesn't get into the headphone socket). The phone must be in landscape orientation or you'll have black bars either side when you put it on YouTube.

The principle behind any stop-motion animated movie is the same. Capture one frame, move whatever you're shooting slightly, capture another frame, move your subject a little and so on, over and over again.

A good starting point is to video building blocks. Film nothing first, then put a block in the frame, film it quickly, put another in shot, film again, then bring in

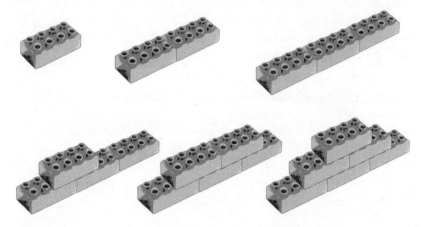

When it's seen building itself, even the simplest model seems magical

another block, shoot it and just keep going until you've completed a wall, tower or life-size model of the Taj Mahal. Make sure the base stays absolutely still!

The effect is extraordinary. You're a sorcerer. You've taken something incredibly familiar to them, something they play with every day, and brought it magically to life. Blocks appear out of thin air, one after another, and a pyramid or whatever is constructed with no visible human intervention.

The next stage is up to you. Start with something already built and have it vanish, brick by brick. Make something from construction bricks and gradually transform it into something else. Paint a diorama for a background and move wheeled models in front of it. Film pliable figures, made from modelling clay, moving them incrementally for each shot. Scenarios can be written, storyboards planned and drawn, costumes and sets made, music added. It may all seem very basic by the standards of Pixar movies, but this is how Wallace and Gromit were born.

The films you make together may get more sophisticated but it's unlikely you'll ever achieve the thrill the children get when their building blocks first come to life on the TV screen.

Making a bow and arrow

Building a bow should be simple: you just take a stick and bend it, right? Wrong. Unless you live by a forest that grows planed, seasoned yew trees, bending sticks won't give you anything like the power and springiness needed.

A far better technique is to make a sandwich of flat strips of wood (you can find these in the dowel section of most DIY shops, or make your own if you have a table saw). Cut the strips into a series of three or four decreasing lengths, and stack

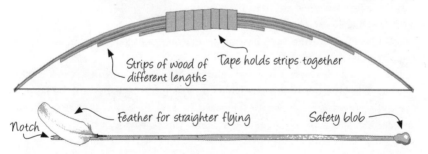

Strips of wood of different lengths

Tape holds strips together

Feather for straighter flying

Notch

Safety blob

them on top of each other: bind the centre together with tape, as in the diagram above. When you now fix a string to each end, bending the bow so the shorter strips are on the inside, you'll have a strong bow that really works.

Arrows can be made from any straight pieces of dowel or bamboo – twigs from your garden won't be straight enough. Cut a notch in the end for the bow string to slot into, and tape a feather or scrap of paper slightly further down for a flight. Fix a blob of Blu-Tack or Plasticine onto the business end: this will provide extra weight to ensure better flight, as well as minimizing damage to windows and corneas.

The indigestion rocket

Would digital photography have taken off so quickly if every Dad knew the fun to be had from those plastic 35mm film containers? With only a drop of water and a fizzing antacid tablet such as Alka Seltzer you can transform one into a rocket. How come our own Dads didn't tell us this?

Hardly anyone shoots on film these days, but these canisters have so many other uses that it's very easy to buy them online – and if there's a shop that process film near you they may well keep the old ones.

Alka Seltzer and water combine...

An al fresco launch site is most sensible. Pop a tablet into the canister then, with the lid ready in your hand, drop in a teaspoon of water. In double quick time, slam the top on, making sure it's sealed, and place the canister upside down on the ground or a table.

...to fire the film can into the air

Retire a few feet and wait. 10 to 20 seconds later the main part of the canister should shoot 10 feet or so into the air with a satisfying pop, leaving behind a partly dissolved tablet and the lid.

This happens because when the tablet begins to dissolve it creates carbon dioxide. The pressure of this gas builds up inside the canister until the lid pops open. The process is similar to that used by real rockets, although their fuel and aerodynamics are rather more efficient. Unlike NASA's craft, however, the aerodynamics of a film canister can be further improved with cardboard fins and a nose cone.

If you don't have antacid tablets to hand, you can try other fuel. Baking powder works pretty well, either mixed with water or lemon juice. You can also try antacid powder instead of tablets. Wrapping it in a thin layer of tissue or toilet paper will delay the reaction by a precious second or two.

Next time somebody tells you how great digital photography is, you ask them if they can shoot a flash card 10 feet in the air with just a tablet and some water. That should shut them up.

The spinning helicopter

We all remember collecting sycamore seedpods, throwing them in the air and watching them spiral to the ground. Here's a more impressive version that's easy to make, requires no advanced knowledge of tree identification (see page 56) and can be produced at any time of year.

Begin with any sheet of scrap paper. Cut it into a rectangle in roughly 2:1 proportions – any size will do – and then trim away two smaller rectangles to form a squared-off Y shape (see diagram). Cut down the middle of the thick part and fold the two 'rotors' 90° in opposite directions.

Attach a small weight to the bottom – a paperclip works best – and drop it from a height, such as a kitchen chair or down the stairwell. The paper will spin appealingly as it flutters to Earth.

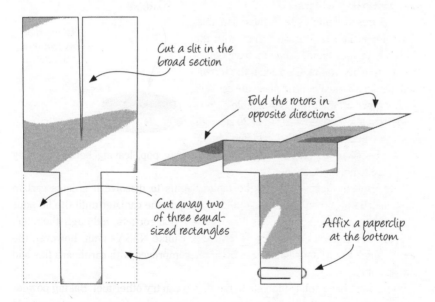

Cut a slit in the broad section

Fold the rotors in opposite directions

Cut away two of three equal-sized rectangles

Affix a paperclip at the bottom

This is a great activity for a group of bored kids on a rainy day: challenge them to vary the size of the paper, length of the rotors and number of paperclips to come up with the 'best' design – the one that stays in the air longest.

Do make sure it *is* scrap paper they're using, and not your tax return, the children's birth certificates or publisher's royalty cheques.

How to make your own kite

While shop-bought kites are certainly fun to use, nothing can compare with the sense of satisfaction you get from making your own out of scrap. This version is made from an ordinary plastic dustbin liner. It's the brainchild of web designer and kite enthusiast Roy Reed, and you can find out more about it and about kite flying on his website, www.reeddesign.co.uk.

First, lay your bin liner out and cut it according to the diagram below. (The darker portion is the section that will become the kite.) The cut-off portion on the left should be cut into 35mm strips, to be used for making the tail.

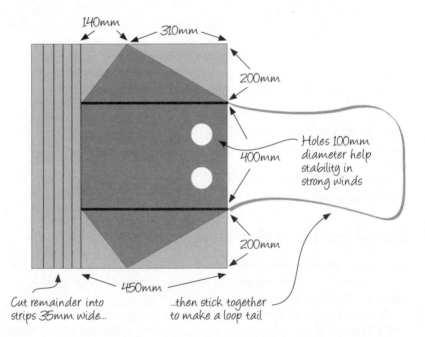

140mm

310mm

200mm

400mm

Holes 100mm diameter help stability in strong winds

200mm

450mm

Cut remainder into strips 35mm wide...

...then stick together to make a loop tail

The two holes in the sail (the rectangular, central part) are optional, but help to stabilize the kite when it's really windy. Once you've cut the kite out, lay sticks or dowels along either side of the rectangular central area and tape them in place, then fold up the two edges at 90° to the main body.

You'll need to reinforce the corners of the wings, where the bridle is attached, or it will simply tear out: tape a scrap piece of bin liner over the corners, doubling

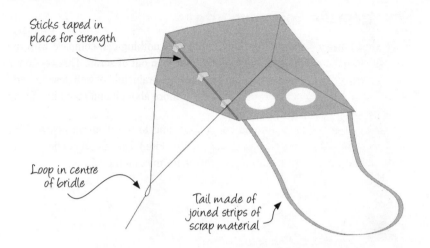

Sticks taped in place for strength

Loop in centre of bridle

Tail made of joined strips of scrap material

its thickness for extra strength. Tie a nylon line for the bridle to both corners, making a loop at exactly the centre point: then tape together all the offcut strips to make the tail (around 900mm long) and fix it in place beneath the main sail. Like the holes in the sail, the tail isn't strictly necessary, but it does help the kite to fly better.

And that's it – your kite is ready. There's plenty more about kite lines and flying techniques on pages 60–62.

Baked bean tin telephones

They don't have to be baked bean tins, of course – any old tins will do (although if they've previously been used for cat food, give them a good wash first or your children will recoil when you kiss them goodnight).

This is such an old staple that it hardly seems worth repeating – until you realize that kids aren't shown how to do this in school any more, and that for any children brought up on a diet of satellite TV, the internet and home computers, the idea that any device can transmit your voice without electricity is truly astounding.

Make a hole in the bottom of each of the two tins and thread a length of string (it can be up to 100 feet or so) between the two. You could also try some of that line you cut off your kite when it got stuck in the tree. Tie a knot in each end so that when you pull the string taut, they don't slip out. Talk into one end, while your child listens in the other: Echo Uniform Romeo Echo Kilo Alpha!

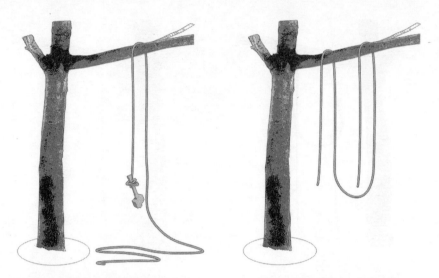

1: Tie a weight to one end of the rope and sling it over the branch

2: Throw the other end over the branch about two feet away

How to hang a garden swing

Swings appeal to kids of all ages, from toddlers who rock gently back and forth to young teenagers who treat them as a cross between an army assault course and a jungle vine.

What puts most Dads off hanging swings is the effort involved: risking life, limb and pride trying to climb the tree, screwing bolts into the branches or trying to recall knots from Boy Scout days. Here's a much better method, that involves neither fixings nor ladders. It can be used to hang a swing from the highest of branches, and can be completed in around ten minutes (depending on your aim).

Make sure you choose a strong, thick branch on a good tree. The branch should be as close to horizontal as you can find, otherwise the swing will veer off to one side. The branch should be in good condition: if it has plenty of leaves at the end, that's fine. If it looks bone dry and sprouts nothing but dead twigs, you may have to rethink.

You need a length of rope roughly three times as long as the height of the branch. A third of this will be cut off later, but you can always find a use for a good piece of rope. Nylon rope is strong, efficient, cheap and ugly; traditional hemp rope looks more attractive but will tend to expand and shrink with the weather. It's

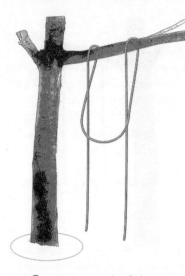

3: Pass the two ends of the rope through the loop on the other side

4: Pull on the rope ends to tug the loop up to the top

your call, and you have to balance aesthetics against practicality. If you do choose nylon rope, make sure it's thick enough for children to get a good grip on without cutting their hands.

Begin by tying a weight to one end of the rope – a wooden mallet with a handle is easy to throw. Sling this over the branch (1). It can take a few attempts to get it in the best place, but it's worth the effort of getting it right. Tie the weight to the other end of the rope and throw this over so there's a gap of around two feet between the two overhangs (2). This gap, which should be at least the width of the swing, is important: again, take the trouble to get it right.

Now take the two ends and pass them through the loop that's hanging over the other side of the branch (3). Pull on the ends, and the loop will raise itself up to the top. When you pull tight, this loop will lock the ropes in position against the branch (4), providing a fixing-free attachment that will be good for years to come.

Swing yourself on each rope in turn to check for strength: if each is strong enough to hold your weight, then the combination of the two should be enough for anything your kids can do to them. Thread the ends through a wooden seat, knot them, and cut off the excess.

The thunderclap

If you're old enough to remember the days (it wasn't *that* long ago) when comics came with free gifts you actually wanted, then you'll experience a nostalgic thrill when you make a thunderclap. It's what we've christened those triangular-shaped toys that make a satisfying bang when you whip them through the air.

The easiest way to make them is to use those 'Please Do Not Bend' A4-sized envelopes, with cardboard on the back and a paper front. You've probably tucked a few used ones away for reuse. If you're like us, the chances are you've had them for years so you may as well use them now.

On the cardboard back of the envelope, mark a triangle the entire bottom width and as tall as it is wide (almost 9 inches in the case of A4). Cut it out, cutting through the entire envelope. Measurements aren't critical so don't beat yourself up if you don't have a perfect isosceles triangle.

Unfold the paper triangle. Fold the double triangle of cardboard and paper along the centre line, using a ruler or a book to score the cardboard. It should be folded so that the paper stuck to the cardboard is on the *inside*. The paper triangle should then be cut down into a smaller triangle. In our experiments, the optimum height was around two-thirds of the height of the cardboard.

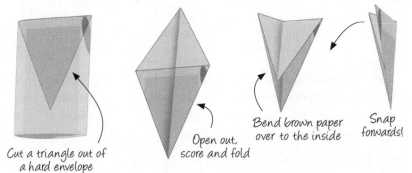

Cut a triangle out of
a hard envelope

Open out,
score and fold

Bend brown paper
over to the inside

Snap
forwards!

Fold the paper triangle inside the cardboard. Hold the pointed end of the cardboard triangle, slightly open, with the paper triangle towards the ground. Bring your arm down sharply and you should hear a satisfying crack.

You can make bangers from sheets of newspaper or brown paper. But although the noise they make is similar, the nostalgic frisson just isn't the same. It is virtually guaranteed, of course, that the moment you cut up your remaining cardboard envelope you'll need to send something that mustn't be bent.

5 Town and country

IT'S A DANGEROUS PLACE, the countryside. Cows glare menacingly over hedges and deposit booby traps on footpaths. Seemingly shallow puddles turn out to be knee-deep potholes. And vultures gather on telephone wires, waiting for the hapless hiker to collapse with exhaustion.

Worst of all, urbane Dads-about-town are supposed to shed decades of metropolitan sophistication and transform themselves into experienced pastoral guides able to identify trees, start a fire with their bare hands, and predict what the weather will be doing a week next Thursday.

Urban excursions can be equally fraught. How do you keep children amused during a lengthy shopping trip? How do you make them wait patiently for their meal to arrive, or for you to finish that well-deserved pint?

This chapter is for Dads venturing far from home comforts, TV and the security of their cars. We can't make The Great Outdoors a safe place to visit, but we can make it more bearable.

How to skim stones

Stone skimming, also known as *Ducks and Drakes*, is an ancient diversion which once saw people trying to bounce oyster shells on water. Now they use stones, which no longer restricts them to those months with an 'R' in them.

Fortunately for those who aren't natural stone skimmers, a team of French researchers, armed with a mechanical catapult and more Euros than sense, has investigated the optimum conditions for getting stones to skim on water.

As you might expect, a stone is more likely to skim if it is spinning than one that isn't: the faster it spins the better. Flicking the stone with your index finger as you

release it will increase the speed of rotation. The speedier the stone, the more likely it is to bounce.

When hunting for stones, the flatter and rounder they are, the likelier they are to skim well. If you still find the stones aren't spinning, the French team's earth-shattering discovery is that the perfect angle for a spinning stone to touch the water is 20° (imagine a right angle, halve it, halve it again, shave a tiny bit off and you're there).

For those who feel ready to take on anyone at *Ducks and Drakes*, the World Stone Skimming Championships are held each year at a disused slate quarry on Easdale Island, the smallest permanently inhabited island of the Inner Hebrides. Although the amateur stone skimmer usually takes pride in the number of 'bounces', the Championships value distance instead. If you can't keep a stone going for at least 100 feet, you haven't an earthly.

The French researchers are even now investigating the most efficient method for grandmothers to suck eggs.

Shaun the sheep

I'd rather not be shorn, thank you

Not many people know that every flock of sheep contains one called 'Shaun'. Your kids might be sceptical but if you yell 'Shaun' out loudly, you are almost certain to be rewarded by at least one sheep turning its head to look at you. That, of course, is Shaun.

Amateur weather forecasting

It's said that townies are now so disconnected from what goes on in the countryside that many kids don't even realize that milk comes from cows. Country folk, on the other hand, are supposed to be so much at one with nature that they can even use it to forecast the weather.

Pine cones, for instance, are said to be an infallible weather indicator. They open out in dry weather and return to their normal shape in wet weather. Amazing. You'd have thought that by the time you've trudged through a couple of sodden fields to find a pine cone, you'd already have a pretty good idea of how wet it is.

If these jolly rustics aren't studying pine cones, then it's cows. When they sense rain, cows will apparently all troop off to one side of the field and lie down together. Does it work? It's Britain. It rains. They're bound to get it right most of the time. But if cows are so good at forecasting weather, how come an enterprising TV channel hasn't signed one up? After all, it would be a lot cheaper than a human forecaster and would almost certainly have better dress sense too.

Whether townie or yokel, if you know somebody who claims they can sense approaching rain through aches in their bones, they might not be talking total rubbish. After all, the weight of the Earth's atmosphere is so great that, at sea level, we all – depending on our size – live with ten to twenty tons of pressure squeezing us from all sides.

Bad weather is preceded by a drop in atmospheric pressure – this is the only time you'll hear frogs croak – so it's bound to affect our bodies as well. And that includes Granny's knees, which now seem just as reliable a weather forecaster as pine cones, or most of the 'professionals' on TV.

Our fathers used to keep highly polished mahogany barometers, which they would rap with their knuckles at regular intervals. They'd peer for long periods at the arcane markings on the crackled enamel dial, before pronouncing with a deafening finality: 'Changeable'.

Barometers may now be electronic and plastic-cased, but if you're ever called upon to make a prediction, 'changeable' is still your safest bet.

Identifying trees by their leaves

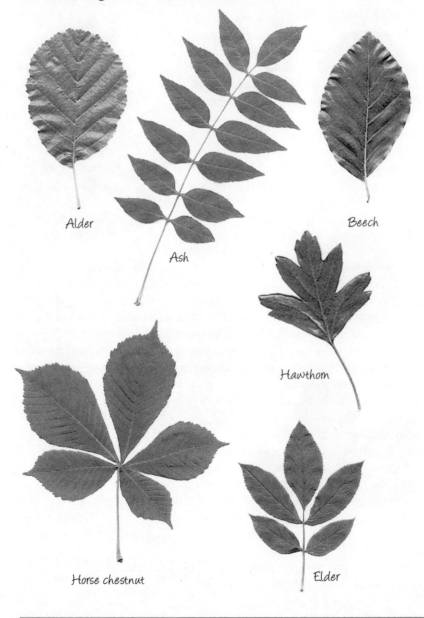

Alder

Ash

Beech

Hawthorn

Horse chestnut

Elder

Hazel

Holly

Oak

Birch

Sycamore

Field maple

Images courtesy of the Woodland Trust.
More free nature stuff for families at
www.naturedetectives.org.uk.

Daisy, daisy...

Encouraging children to make daisy chains – another traditional pastime we rarely seem to see any more – is an excellent way of buying yourself a bit of peace and quiet. When they collect the daisies, they should break off a decent length of stem. The longer they are, the fewer daisies are needed to complete a chain.

Split the stem with a fingernail

Whether you make the chain as you go along or collect a supply of daisies first, the method is the same. Make a hole with the fingernail halfway down the stem, long enough to open up to take another daisy stem but not so long that the stem will split. Push the stem of another daisy through the hole until the flower stops it going any further. Make a hole in the stem of this one, thread another daisy through that, and so on.

You can make necklaces, bracelets, crowns or even garden or table decorations. And if there are no daisies to be found, suggest the children make a dandelion chain instead.

The magic helping hand

When you're out walking, tired kids (or adults) occasionally need a helping hand, particularly when tackling hills. Instead of knocking yourself out by pushing them along or even carrying them, place your hand on what new-agers call the Sacral Triangle. For those whose knowledge of anatomy is less than perfect, this is simply the base of the spine.

You don't need to push, just place your hand there. Without any pressure being applied, it is as if some mysterious force is helping to propel them along.

We know it sounds barmy, rather as if we're extolling the power of pyramids or crystals. But work it does, despite expending no energy. If you don't believe us, go out and try it while we get back to our cold fusion experiments.

How to get out of a maze

There are only four score or so public mazes in the UK. Some are the full monty, with impenetrable walls of hedge, brick or even mirrors. Others are floor patterns made of turf, brick or even water. Kids love mazes and usually charge around them at full pelt.

Dads may prefer to demonstrate their calmness and intellectual superiority. If the maze is of a simple construction, such as at Hampton Court, merely keep one hand next to the wall on that side and turn in that direction at every opportunity. You'll encounter many dead ends but will eventually emerge at the exit.

Unless you're sure of the maze, don't boast to your kids that you can beat them through it. Irritatingly, many modern maze-makers design tricky island mazes with disconnected sections where the one-hand-to-the-wall method dooms you to going in circles. You can trust logic and common sense to get you through or else find a way to mark each failed route. If you're of a classical bent, you could always pay out thread as you go. If you encounter a ferocious man with a bull's head, though, it's probably best to retire gracefully to the pub, to think up some really good excuse about what became of the children.

Just in case you find yourself going there – study this map of Hampton Court maze first!

Take aim... duck!

Feeding the ducks is a great outdoor occupation for smaller children. But it bores the average Dad silly. Surely this innocent pastime can be given a twist?

The solution is to pick one duck from a flock and throw the piece of bread so that only *that* duck gets to eat it. It takes both careful aim and diversionary strategies to get it right, and means you'll be playing for as long as your child wants to.

I've done it! I've done it!
...where's everybody gone?

How to fly a kite

Number two in the hit parade of Dad images, only just behind chasing a bike yelling 'I won't let go', is Dad trying to get a kite aloft by running backwards and falling flat on his arse in the process.

The point of kites is that the wind should do the hard work, not you. Throw a bit of grass or sand up and see which way the wind is blowing. If you're on a hill, a good launching spot is a little way below the peak. Get someone to stand behind the kite and hold it, right way up, facing the wind while you unwind a decent length of line. Take up the tension on the line but don't pull yet.

When the wind picks up, yell to your assistant to let go. Tug the line and the kite should rise into the air. If the only way to stop it fluttering back down to the ground is to run backwards, then there isn't enough wind. If it nosedives into the ground, there's too much. Look at the treetops, ensuring they aren't too close or you can bet that's where your kite will end up. The branches should be moving a little. A wind of five to fifteen mph is suitable for most kites. If you're finding the wind uncomfortable, then so will a standard kite.

As the kite goes up, pull the line to get it to climb to a peak before paying it out again, repeating the process until you're near the end of the line.

Once the kite is safely in the air, you can make it move about the sky by pulling and releasing the line, always being ready to wind the line in gently to keep the kite up if the wind drops. Keep some of the line in reserve. If the kite dives, let the line go slack and it should right itself. If you pull on the line, you'll simply exacerbate the dive.

If the kite doesn't perform properly, try adjusting the angle of the bridle, the bit you attach the line to. Make sure you mark it, though, so you can restore it to the factory-set position if you make a horlicks of things. In higher winds, move the bridle up towards the nose of the kite. In lighter winds, move it down so the kite is at a more perpendicular angle to the wind.

And if your kite does get stuck up a tree, leave it there. Rather than risk limb, if not life, it is easier to buy another one. If the kids are fond of it, get one that looks the same. Much like guinea pigs, really.

The right kite for the job

These days, there are more kites to choose from than there are models of car and with far more exciting colour schemes. It makes sense to buy two or three so you can take advantage of different conditions – kites, that is, not cars.

In light winds, use a light kite or a kite with a large surface area. If the wind is substantial, the kite needs either to be small or vented (with holes in it). Single-line kites can be difficult to fly in heavy winds and might necessitate wearing gloves to avoid burns from the line. It's best to stick to flying in moderate conditions.

The most popular designs for family flying are the diamond (those with a curved horizontal spar tend to fly best) and the triangular deltas. Kites with tails not only look prettier, but are often more stable. Parafoils – like sophisticated windsocks – can be pricier, but fly in a wide variety of conditions.

Different kites may need different strengths of line. Using the wrong weight will harm the kite's performance or could even lose it altogether. Ask for advice from an expert. If you're in a kite (or fishing) store, buy some clips and swivels. The clips go on the end of the flying line and the swivels on the bridle. They will stop the line twisting and save a good deal of time getting the kite ready… and putting it away when the kids get bored.

How to fly a stunt kite

If your children enjoy kites, consider adding a stunt kite to your collection. Controlled by two lines rather than one, these are great Dad toys. Pull on the right control and the kite moves to the right. Pull further and it loops the loop to the right. And vice versa.

Needing dependable winds to fly properly, stunt kites are immense fun, swooping through the sky at your will. Get one with a tail that inflates with air and you can make shapes and letters in the air. Start with a robust and inexpensive model while everyone is still wearing L-plates.

Stunt kites are hard to get into the air without a helper. After you've assembled one, making doubly sure all the bits are in the right place, unwind both lines, lying them on the ground. Flying with the lines fully extended cuts the chance that they will be uneven, sending the kite into an inescapable death spin. This might damage the kite and will almost certainly take an age to untangle.

As with single-line kites, the helper should stand with their back to the wind and the nose of the kite up. Make certain the control in your right hand is attached to the right of the kite and vice versa. As you launch, pull both lines together and the kite should climb.

Only when the kite is at its peak should you, very gently, pull the kite first one way then the other. As you become more confident, you can try looping a loop. Remember to bring your hands level again when the kite becomes vertical after the required number of loops. It makes sense to loop the kite an equal number of times the other way to get the lines free again.

Once you become an accomplished stunter, the cool way to land is to fly the kite to one side and touch it down on the ground gently. If you get really cocky, you can even attach several stunt kites together. It looks fantastic, but you really don't want to find yourself with a train of half a dozen kites ready to be brought down and put away, only to discover that your posse of assistants have become bored and wandered off.

FASCINATING FACT

When they wanted to put a bridge across the Niagara River near the famous falls in the 1840s, they were faced with a serious problem. The water was too dangerous to work in, so how could they span the 800-foot wide gorge?

Somebody suggested kites and a contest was set up. An American boy, Homan Walsh, won the 10-dollar prize when his kite got caught in a tree on the Canadian side. A light line was attached to his kite string and pulled across. A slightly heavier line was fastened to that and so on, until they eventually got a heavy-duty wire cable across.

That kite line was the beginning of what became, in 1854, the world's first suspension railway bridge.

Starting a fire

Every Dad should be able to build a campfire. Or, at least, be able to show how it would be done if only you'd been lucky enough to have assembled the right combination of leaves, sticks, stones and weather.

You'll need to gather some dried grass and leaves, placed around a small hollow in a log or the ground. If it's been raining, forget it. You won't have a chance. You then need a fire stick – any straight stick around a foot and a half long will do. This rests on another piece of wood in the assembly of leaves and twigs: the other end is held in place with a stone that also has a slight hollow in it, deep enough to allow the stick to rotate freely. You'll also need a makeshift bow, made by tying a piece of string between two ends of a bendy stick.

With one hand, hold the stick in place by pressing lightly with the stone on the top end. With the other hand, wrap the bow string around the stick once, and then saw back and forth, spinning the stick in the leaves and grass. This method is far more effective – and far easier – than trying to spin the stick between your hands. With any luck (and you'll certainly need some), after a couple of minutes the friction caused will start a small fire in the dried grass and leaves.

Don't forget to take a box of matches with you, though, so you can whip it out when no one's looking and start a *real* fire.

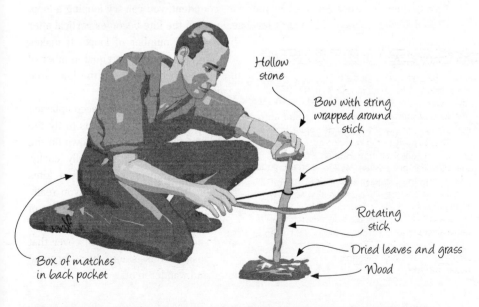

Hollow stone

Bow with string wrapped around stick

Rotating stick

Dried leaves and grass

Wood

Box of matches in back pocket

Pub games

Although pubs, particularly away from the big cities, are generally more welcoming to families than in days gone by, your children may still get bored before their Cokes go flat. You may need to find ways to keep them happily occupied.

If you've come unprepared, ask the staff. The unlikeliest of pubs keep a selection of games behind the bar. Even a pack of cards will suffice.

If not, you may have to resort to that old standby – flipping beermats. This is an essential life skill your children really need to acquire, particularly if they plan on going to university.

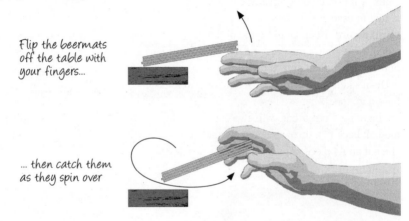

Flip the beermats off the table with your fingers...

... then catch them as they spin over

A pile of beermats is placed on the table sticking out a little way over the edge. Without touching the table, the back of the hand must be brought up smartly to launch the stack of beermats into the air and then catch them cleanly after they have turned through 180°.

How many can you manage? Six? Eight? Perhaps ten? Don't get too smug. While Britain may struggle to make much of a showing at the Olympics, when it comes to pub sports we're in a league of our own. Dean Gould of Felixstowe holds the current record – 208. He can also speed flip: 25 piles of 40 in 45 seconds.

Mr Gould is a prodigious chap. He holds records for pancake tossing, egg holding, brick flipping, CD flipping, stamp licking, currant eating, grape eating (with plastic spoon), rice eating (with chopsticks), sweetcorn eating (with cocktail stick), dry cream-cracker eating, spaghetti eating, meatball eating (both with and without juggling them first) and even winkle-picking (50 from their shells in

1 minute 22 secs, since you ask). He can also recall the first 1,000 digits of pi from memory in just over eight minutes.

If you encounter him in a pub, buy him a drink by all means. Just don't make a bet with him.

Flippin' heck

With your arm bent back, place a 10p coin on your elbow. Bring your hand forward and, palm down, snatch it. Got the hang of that? Now see if you can manage two coins or more. If you drop any, count only those successfully caught.

Just in case you or your brood feel inclined to have a pop at the coin-snatching world record, Dean Gould (yes, him again) holds the current title, for snatching – and this is not a misprint – *328* 10p coins in one grab. It's probably not worth bothering trying to snatch dominoes, either. Dean's been there already.

Dean's kids, presumably so fed up of Dad breaking so many records, decided to have a go too. When we first wrote *Dad Stuff*, Amy, 8, and Adam, 11, held records for hanging from a bar with two hands, while Adam was top dog at heading a football back to a thrower and Amy had no equal at paper-cutting. In ten minutes, she cut an A4 piece of paper into 1,171 pieces.

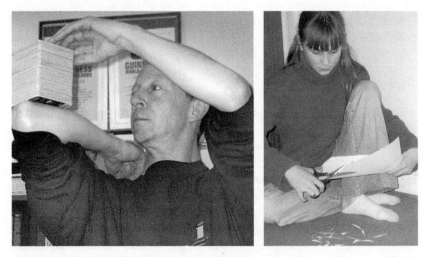

Record-breaker Dean Gould demonstrates his beermat snatching technique, while his daughter Amy shows how to cut a piece of paper into 1,171 pieces

The 'Harry Worth'

Back in the 1960s, one of the most popular comedians was amiable bumbler Harry Worth. He was best known for the opening of his TV show, imitated at the time by almost every child in the land.

Stopping by a glass-fronted shop, Harry stood sideways in the doorway. Pressing his nose against the glass with only half his body showing, he lifted one arm and leg: the reflection gave the appearance of raising both sets of limbs at the same time.

The gag deserves reviving.

In the 1960s, this is what passed for cutting-edge comedy

It's an excellent way of lifting spirits when you're trudging through town or waiting in shoe and clothes shops. It's amazing how eager assistants become to speed you on your way when you and the kids are using the store's full-length mirrors for such shenanigans.

Resist the temptation to do 'The Full Harry'. Donning a drab suit, thick glasses and a trilby could mean your kids refuse ever to be seen in public with you again.

Put a knot in it

You're sitting at the table in a restaurant waiting for the food to arrive. The kids are getting fractious. If the place is posh enough to provide proper serviettes, try challenging your brood to see if they can tie a knot in theirs.

The catch is that they must grasp it at opposite corners and make the knot without letting go. As they twist and contort themselves, trying to do the impossible, your table may well become the object of attention of other diners. Fine. The challenge works even better with an audience.

When the others finally give up and tell you it can't be done, fold your arms with one hand in front of an arm and the other behind. Pick up your serviette at each end with your hands in this position and then pull your arms apart. The serviette will have a knot in it.

6

Are we there yet?

PLANES, TRAINS AND AUTOMOBILES all test a Dad's ingenuity and entertainment skills to destruction. You may be the best juggler in the neighbourhood. You may be the best piggy-back mount west of the Urals. But neither will be a jot of use when you're on the move. You're on your own, with only your wits to help you.

Keeping children occupied on long journeys takes more than iPods, in-car movies and packets of crisps. Eventually even the most seasoned adolescent traveller will utter the four words that make every Dad raise his eyes in despair: 'Are we there yet?' It isn't the words themselves that are so chilling, but the implication behind them: that the child is now so bored that they are looking to you for entertainment – and woe betide you (and your fellow travellers) if you fail in the task.

In this chapter you'll find car games, train games and even plane games to keep young minds amused and active as the miles tick away. From a multitude of diversions which can be used to occupy children, we've chosen those that, in our experience, give the maximum entertainment value for the effort expended.

Number plate games

There are any number of games you can play making up phrases or sentences from the letters in the number plates of passing cars (chosen, of course, by Dad). Our favourite is *Pub Signs*. You must make up a plausible pub name based on the three letters at the end of the registration. So DDA might be the Duke of Devonshire's Arms ('little' words are allowed to sneak in), while TBT might be The Butcher's Trousers, and so on.

Dads can greatly help the game by astutely picking appropriate number plates. Look for those with a middle A (for 'and'), as well as those ending in A, H, T ('Arms', 'Hotel' and 'Tavern'). There are no winners; or, a better way of looking at it, no losers.

Alphabet search

This is a good game to play in towns or on country roads rather than motorways. Look for something you pass beginning with the letter A (such as an airplane, Audi, or even 'A' road). After they've seen an A, move on to B, and so on, right through the alphabet.

It must be something you pass. While E is indeed for elephant and O is for ostrich, unless you're driving through Whipsnade Zoo you can assume they haven't quite grasped the rules of the game.

A couple of additional pointers. Q can be for 'quarterlight', that triangular section at the rear of passenger windows that usually won't open. If you're stumped by X it can stand for 'crossing', unless you find yourself driving down Chung Cheng Road in Hsin-Tien City, Taiwan, where there's a xylophone factory. (Thanks, Google.)

The game can be played in two teams if you're feeling competitive, but it works just as well as a collaborative effort. Consider banning words you've had before, otherwise C for 'car' and R for 'road' may become a touch repetitive.

Are we there yet?

Car cricket

Each player takes it in turns to 'bat'. They score one run for each car that you pass, or that passes you in the opposite direction. Motorbikes score two; vans four; anything larger, such as a lorry or a bus, scores six.

If it's a red car, though, they're out, and play passes to the next player. This keeps going until someone reaches an arbitrary score decided in advance, everyone gets bored or you do finally get there.

You may want to vary scoring methods, depending on whether you're on a busy motorway or a quiet country road. To save later argument, it's worth establishing a few ground rules that can be enforced when the time comes (and believe us, the time will come). No, you don't score a century if you pass a car park full of lorries. Yes, if a car overtakes you, you can score it. Yes, if it's a red car, you're still out. No, if you've stopped at traffic lights, you can't count all the cars that cross your path. And no, I won't break the speed limit to overtake that transporter loaded with shiny new cars.

The yes/no game

How hard is it to avoid saying 'Yes' or 'No'? Harder than you might think. This great game is perfect for cars and is suitable for all ages, a great bonus being that adults have no real advantage over kids.

The rules are simple: whoever is 'It' has to answer all questions – either randomly or on particular topics – without saying 'Yes' or 'No'. If either word pops out, they lose. It isn't easy when there are so many ways of tripping people up, such as saying, 'You said "Yes" just now' – to which the inevitable response is, 'No I didn't!' If they get good at it, you might consider introducing the additional rule that they're not allowed to use improbable, unwieldy answer constructions, such as 'I reply in the negative'.

Think of something...

If you drive a people carrier, or any large car, you'll often find yourself having to entertain a group of children of widely differing ages, whose only common factor is that they're seatbelted directly behind you. *Think of Something* is a game which has served us well, and is as much fun for kids of 4 and 14.

Each child, in turn, is asked to think of an object with a particular characteristic. The game's success depends on Dad varying the question to suit the ability of the child. So young children might be asked to think of something furry, or green, or made of wood; those a little older might be asked to come up with something magnetic, or Japanese, or soluble; teenagers might be asked for something Elizabethan, or contradictory, or made of aluminium.

The older children can answer all the questions in their heads, of course, and it's a great learning tool as younger children aspire to the knowledge of their elders.

Car-colour bingo

A short, easy game for younger children. Each picks a colour, and scores a point for each car of that colour you pass. The winner is the first to reach, say, twenty.

If you're the type of Dad who can't bear losing, pick silver. Few children ever do, and it's a sure-fire winner in these drab, dreary days of automotive anonymity.

Animal, vegetable, mineral

The all-time classic car game – also known as *Twenty Questions*, although we don't really see the point in stopping at twenty. Just keep going.

One player thinks of an object, and then defines it as animal (leather, bone, wool and so on as well as real animals), vegetable (anything that's grown, such as wood and cotton) or mineral (just about everything else). It can be a combination of these: so a bottle of milk, for example, might be described as 'mineral and

Are we there yet?

vegetable, with animal connections' – on the basis that it's made of glass, the contents are made (ultimately) of grass, but with significant animal intervention.

Plastic is tricky, being petroleum-based, as many scientists argue that oil is not a fossil fuel but formed from the remains of plants and animals. Just so long as your children aren't secret subscribers to *New Scientist* magazine, we suggest simply opting for mineral.

The other players then take it in turns to ask suitable questions to try to work out what the object is. Here are a few of the things that might be asked:

Is it man-made?
Is it decorative or functional?
Have we got one?
Is it used inside or outside the house?
Would it fit in a matchbox?
Is it bigger than my head? (A much better question than '*Is it big?*')
Have I ever seen one?
Can you eat it?
Is it solid?
Is there just one of them, or lots?
Is it heavier than a car?

Questions like 'Does is start with the letter "T"?' should be discouraged.

The answerer should only reply 'Yes', 'No' or, in some cases, 'I don't know'. If you're being kind, you might add a 'Usually' or 'Sometimes' if asked whether mud is found in the house. Again, kindness suggests you'd answer 'Yes, but not only children' if you're asked whether children use CDs. Adults asking imprecise questions should be shown no such mercy.

Whoever gets the answer right gets to pose the next puzzle. With practice, children can come up with some really tricky posers. We struggled for ages with Joe's mineral, bigger than our house, not a building or a mountain, before we discovered it was a cloud.

5-4-3-2-1

Players take it in turns to spot an interesting object, such as a cow, barn or church steeple, out of the window of the car. They then say 'Cow!* 5…4…3…2…1' and the other players have to locate, point to and say the name of the object before the countdown has reached 1. Whoever identifies the object first is the next spotter.

If you're feeling competitive, you can add to your score the number the questioner reached when the spotter interrupted the countdown. It's a great inclusive game for the whole family, and has the great advantage of encouraging kids to put down their damn iPads and actually look out of the window for a change.

* Unless the object isn't a cow, of course.

Pub cricket

This is an old game, and one that's more suited to pottering around quiet country roads than chasing down motorways. But it's also a great game to play when driving through towns, where the density of pubs is much higher.

It's similar to *Car Cricket*, mentioned earlier, except that players score 'runs' by counting the number of legs on the pub signs they pass. So The Green Man will score two, The Red Lion scores four, and if they're lucky enough to spot a Coach and Horses they'll be able to rack their score up by sixteen or more. When you pass a pub sign with no legs, they're out and play moves to the next child.

Arguments are inevitable, of course. How many legs does The King's Head have, for example? In these cases, we feel that common sense should prevail. So the number of legs connected to it should be counted as two, unless the king in question is Charles I. Such issues can themselves lead to a lively debate that will take up yet more road-time.

Sometimes you need to look closely at the pub sign itself, rather than just the name of the establishment. We recently thought Joe's unbroken score of 48

runs was about to come to an end when we passed The Olde Oak – but, on close examination, the sign depicted a woman walking a dog beneath the tree. Another six runs. The next pub was the Queen's Arms, and there we thought we'd got him: except that this particular Queen's Arms sign featured a lion and a unicorn – which scored another eight runs.

Pub Cricket is the sort of game you can be playing continually, interspersed with other activities. It's become a constant game for us, with scores being topped up each time a pub is passed.

Dad, I feel sick

Are there any words more calculated to jab an icicle of horror into the heart of a motorway-driving Dad who has just passed the last service station for 45 miles? Suddenly, that phrase from babyhood you thought you'd never hear again – projectile vomiting – returns to haunt you.

The old standby of opening the window does actually help. Even on a freezing day, it's better than the alternative. Also helpful, apparently, is deep, slow breathing. Researchers in the Psychology Department at Pennsylvania State University threw 46 men and women around in a 'rotating optokinetic drum', the sort of torture device for which kids happily queue for hours at a theme park. Those guinea pigs who did slow, deep breathing before a second session in the drum were much less likely to chunder than those who didn't. So the earlier you can get sickness-prone kids to breathe deeply, the better. Make them desist from reading and get them to look at distant objects out of the window instead.

And if it doesn't work... well, that's what plastic bags were invented for.

On planes and boats, you might want to supplement the breathing with medication given long before it becomes necessary. Just as with adults, the very act of taking something may alleviate the problem.

Are we there yet?

Faster! It's gaining on us!

Car snooker

Each player takes it in turn to be at the snooker table. Their turn begins when you pass a red car, equivalent to a red ball in snooker: they score one point. They then have to look out for the next snooker colour you pass, and score the value of that colour as if they'd potted that ball in snooker:

Yellow	2 points	Blue	5 points
Green	3 points	Pink	6 points
Brown	4 points	Black	7 points

After spotting the colour, they then have to (s)pot another red car, then a colour again, and so on – just like snooker. If the first car you pass after a red car isn't one of the snooker colours, then it's the end of their break, and the next player gets to have a go.

To bring an added level of excitement into the game, you can introduce the idea of penalty points. If you pass a white car after the player's first red has been spotted, then this counts as potting the white ball; all the other players are awarded four points each, and the turn ends.

If you're the kind of Dad who likes to play strictly by the rules, then keep a tally of the number of red cars potted: once you've reached 15 (the number of red balls on a snooker table), then players have to pot each of the colours in turn. You'll be lucky to spot a pink car, though, unless Lady Penelope is driving past.

This is a game which works equally well on busy main roads and on motorways. If there's a lot of traffic, you can vary the rules to suit the circumstances: count only the cars that pass you in the opposite direction, for instance, or only the cars that you overtake.

Name that tune

Each player takes it in turn to hum the theme tune to a well-known film or TV show: whoever guesses it correctly has the next go.

This is a game that's harder for parents than it is for kids, as we'll constantly have to remember *not* to sing *Dallas*, or *The A-Team*, or any of those programmes our kids have never heard of but which are still rattling around in our heads decades after the damn shows stopped being broadcast.

Character counting

An excellent game, which we invented purely by chance. We were driving along, talking about what a great TV show *The Simpsons* is, and wondered how many regular characters there were. Thirty? Forty? We counted 130 in total – and that's just the characters who appeared enough times to be recognisable.

And so a game was born. Each player takes it in turn to name a character, with others helping out if they get stuck. The great thing is that this is a collaborative game, where you're all working together, rather than one in which you're pitched against each other. Leave it to the younger kids to come up with the obvious Marge, Homer, Mr Burns and so on, while more adept players nominate lesser-known characters such as Professor Frink and Principal Skinner's mother.

It doesn't have to be just *The Simpsons*, of course – choose the show that matches your family's viewing habits. Here's a suggestion of some character searches that should get you thinking:

Harry Potter (all books and movies)	*Toy Story*
Star Trek	*Musicals*
Star Wars movies	*Lord of the Rings*
Pantomimes	
EastEnders	As well as…
Coronation Street	*Politicians*
The Beano	*Planets, stars and constellations*
Premier League footballers	*Artists and composers*
James Bond movies	*TV presenters*
Fairy stories	*Actors and actresses*
Nursery rhymes	*Kings and queens*
Disney animations	*Cartoon animals*

Countries of the world

The first player names a country beginning with A, such as Afghanistan. The next then has to think of a country that begins with the *last* letter of the country just named – Norway, for instance. And so the game continues, until no more countries can be thought of.

To make it easier, you can allow kids to think of cities as well; you may even choose to allow country names in their own language – Deutschland, España, and so on. And, of course, former names such as Ceylon and Rhodesia are allowed.

The number plate place game

Since the year 2001, all new cars have been issued with number plates that follow a standard format for displaying their place and date of origin.

AB52 CDE

The first letter shows the licence issuing centre, the second is a subcategory within that area. The next two numbers show the year of registration, with 50 added for the half year: 12 is March to August 2012, and 62 is August 2012 to February 2013. The final three letters are randomly chosen, and identify individual cars.

A East Anglia
B Birmingham
C Cymru (Wales)
D Deeside
E Essex & Herts
F Forest & Fens

G Garden of England
H Hants & Dorset
K Luton & Northants
L London
M Manchester & Mersey
N Newcastle & North

P Preston & Pennines
R Reading
S Scotland
V Vale of Severn
W West Country

The map shows the location of origin of all the current car plates. So a number plate that begins with A will have been sold in East Anglia, for instance. Most of the letters of the alphabet are used, with a few exceptions: I, J and Z are not used at all, and Q is used only for cars whose age cannot be verified (it may be an import or a kit car, for instance).

Simply spotting where the cars come from is entertaining in itself. But you can make a game of it by trying to get from one location to another – say from Cornwall to Scotland (that's W to S on the chart), only moving to the next location when you see a plate that's registered there. Follow the lines shown on the map on the left to move from region to region.

This is the kind of game that can be played on busy motorways, and is a great ongoing game for long journeys: it's particularly satisfying if you happen to be driving from Cornwall to Scotland!

Alphabet shopping

The first player begins, 'I went to the supermarket and I bought an apple.' The next player has to think of something you can buy in a supermarket beginning with B, such as bananas; the next player has to think of something beginning with C, and so on. (You'll be surprised how many people end up buying xylophones.)

Vary the game by visiting other kinds of shops – bookshops, record shops, and so on.

An alternative is for Dad to begin by saying, 'I went to a supermarket and bought something beginning with D.' All the kids then have to think of as many things you can buy in a supermarket that begin with that letter as they can. The advantage of this version is that Dad can choose easy or difficult letters, depending on the age of the children.

The name game

The first player says the name of a well-known figure, including a description of what they're well known for – such as 'Gordon Brown, former Prime Minister'. The next player has to name someone who shares the same first or second name: 'James Brown, singer'. And so it continues: 'Jesse James, outlaw'; 'Jesse Owens, athlete'; 'Owen Wilson, actor', and so on (you can take a few liberties with the names if you like). By specifying the characters' occupations, you're helping the kids to learn a little history – and proving that the person you've named is real.

A good variation is to miss out every other character, so that your kids have to work out the missing link. So if you go from 'Robbie Williams, singer' straight to 'Venus de Milo, statue', they have to figure out that the missing link is 'Venus Williams, tennis player'.

Celebrity challenge

This game is similar to *Animal, Vegetable, Mineral*, in that players have to ask questions to arrive at the solution. The difference is that in this game, you think of a well-known figure: your kids have to ask questions about their lives and accomplishments in order to work out who the person is.

Good questions include 'Male or Female', 'Living or Dead', 'Real or Imaginary' – since you can include cartoon and fictional characters as well. Liven things up by asking silly questions: 'Does he like mashed potato?', 'Has she got a hair dryer?', and so on. It's a game that makes kids think harder about celebrities, especially when it's their turn to think of someone: it's fun to see them struggling with such philosophical problems as whether or not King Arthur owned a DVD player!

The noises game

This is a good game for younger players. Every time you pass something that makes a recognisable noise – a fire engine, a police car, a telephone box, a cow, a train, and so on – they have to make the noise of the object, and everyone else has to spot the thing they're emulating, and make the same noise when they see it.

Recommended only for Dads with strong nerves, particularly if they happen to be driving.

Uncle Bobby

Uncle Bobby reads books, but not magazines. He's a good accountant, although he can add, but he can't subtract. He eats noodles, but not pasta. He likes the colour green, but not blue or red.

Uncle Bobby, of course, only likes things that have double letters in them – and the clue is in his name. Once each player has worked out the rules, they can continue to take part by saying additional things that Uncle Bobby likes and dislikes.

The game can be adapted to incorporate other rules, just so long as they aren't too complicated to be guessed. So Mr Browning might only like things that contain 'ing' (skiing, but not football; sprinting, but not the high jump; swimming, but not golf; singers, but not musicians). You might include Aunt Jemima, who only likes things ending in a vowel; or Policeman Plod, who only likes two-word phrases in which both words begin with the same letter.

What has an eye but no nose?

Whoever's got it – give it back now

The answer, of course, is a needle. And it's a game that can be extended endlessly with little mental effort: you'd be surprised how many body parts are used figuratively in everyday speech.

It doesn't have to be just body parts, of course: you could use pairs of objects associated with cars, for instance.

Here are some examples to get you started:

What has a tongue but no teeth?.................................... a shoe
What has teeth but no lips? ....a comb
What has legs but no arms?.................................... a table
What has arms but no hands? ....a coat (or a chair)
What has hands but no fingers? ....a clock
What has fingers but no knuckles?.................................. fish!
What has a neck but no head?................................ a wine bottle
What has ears but no cheeks?.....................................corn
What has calves but no shins?................................... a cow
What has brows but no lashes? ....a hill
What has shoulders but no arms?...........................a motorway
What has a face but no hair? .... a watch
What has a beard but no moustache?..............................a goat
What has palms but no wrists? ....a desert
What has feet but no knees? .... a tripod
What has skin but no fur?...........................custard (or a drum)
What has canines but no molars? .... a dog's home
What has a heart but no liver?...................................a lettuce
What has veins but no arteries? .... a leaf
What has a heel but no toes?.................................. a shoe
What has a chest but no shoulders? .... a pirate ship
What has three feet but no ankles?................................. a yard
What has wings but no claws?.....................................a plane
What has feathers but no beak? .... a pillow
What has a horn but no teeth?...................................a car
What has scales but no gills?..............................a greengrocer

Scavenger hunt

Prepare a list of items to look out for on the journey, and print one out for each child. They cross each item off the list when they spot it. This is the kind of game that can be played, on and off, throughout a long trip.

If it's a route you know well, you can customise the list by adding things that you know you're going to pass on the way, but which may otherwise be rare. Here's a sample checklist you can photocopy:

☐ Church	☐ Tesco supermarket	☐ Ambulance
☐ Dog walker	☐ Phone box	☐ Tractor
☐ Statue	☐ Caravan	☐ Grain silo
☐ Roadworks	☐ Bus	☐ Electricity pylon
☐ Police car	☐ Taxi	☐ Plane overhead
☐ Boat	☐ Crane	☐ Post office
☐ Bridge	☐ Pig	☐ Foreign number plate
☐ School	☐ Vintage car	☐ 'School' sign
☐ Zebra crossing	☐ Shell petrol station	☐ 'Danger' sign
☐ Postbox	☐ Man in uniform	☐ 'Old people' sign
☐ McDonald's	☐ Bus stop	☐ Horse box
☐ Little Chef	☐ GB sticker on car	☐ Flower seller
☐ Cow	☐ Train	☐ Traffic warden

If you don't mind your kids staring at other cars, you can also add a list of things they might have with them, be wearing or be doing:

☐ Bluetooth headset	☐ Beard and glasses	☐ Picking their nose
☐ Moustache	☐ Tattoo on arm	☐ Talking on phone
☐ Three children	☐ Green jumper	☐ Sleeping passenger
☐ Dog in the car	☐ Sat nav	☐ Elderly couple
☐ Suit on hanger	☐ Eating	☐ Kids watching TV

Of course, the very best thing your kids can do while you're driving is to look out for speed cameras. Make sure they don't spot them out of the rear window, though. It'll be too late by then.

Car songs

Nothing helps revitalise sagging spirits on a long journey than a family singsong. The most useful are those that continue for some time, either with variations of the words or with extensions to every verse.

Here are our favourite musical masterpieces. We've provided the music, too, just in case you happen to have a piano in your car.

On Top of Spaghetti

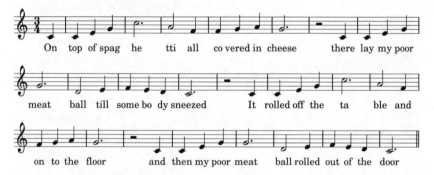

On top of spaghetti all covered in cheese.
There lay my poor meatball till somebody sneezed.

It rolled off the table, and onto the floor,
And then my poor meatball rolled out of the door.

It rolled in the garden and under a bush,
And then my poor meatball was nothing but mush.

The mush was as tasty as tasty could be,
And early next year it grew into a tree.

The tree was all covered with beautiful moss.
It grew great big meatballs and tomato sauce.

So if you eat spaghetti all covered with cheese,
Hold on to your meatball and don't ever sneeze.

Johnny Was a Paratrooper

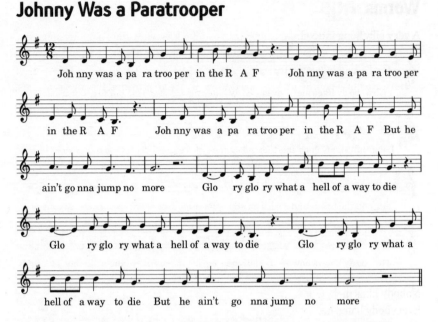

Johnny was a paratrooper in the RAF, Johnny was a paratrooper in the RAF Johnny was a paratrooper in the RAF, But he ain't gonna jump no more.

Glory, glory, what a hell of a way to die, Glory, glory, what a hell of a way to die Glory, Glory, what a hell of a way to die, But he ain't gonna jump no more.

He jumped without a parachute from 40,000 feet…

They scraped him off the tarmac like a blob of raspberry jam…

They put him in an envelope and sent him home to mum…

She put him on the mantelpiece for everyone to see…

She put him on the table when the vicar came to tea…

The vicar spread him on his toast and said, 'What lovely jam'…

Worms

A very silly song indeed.

No bo dy likes me ev ery bo dy hates me I'm go ing out to eat worms

Long thin sli my ones short fat jui cy ones goo ey goo ey goo ey goo ey worms You

bite off the heads and suck out the juice and throw the skins a way

No bo dy knows how I sur vive on a thou sand worms a day

Nobody likes me
Everybody hates me
I'm going out to eat worms
Long thin slimy ones,
Short fat juicy ones
Gooey, gooey, gooey, gooey worms.

You bite off the heads,
And suck out the juice,
And throw the skins away
Nobody knows how I survive
On a thousand worms a day!

Long thin skinny ones
Slip down easily,
Big fat juicy ones stick.
Hold your head back
Squeeze their tail
And their juice just goes drip, drip.

Have you any idea where I've been?

You'll Never Get to Heaven

The trouble with many songs is remembering the lyrics. This one gets around the problem by getting Dad to say the lines first, which are then repeated by everyone else.

Oh, you'll never get to heaven in a baked bean tin
Cause a baked bean tin's got baked beans in.

I ain't gonna grieve my Lord, I ain't gonna grieve my Lord
I ain't gonna grieve my Lord no more
I ain't gonna grieve my Lord. I ain't gonna grieve my Lord
I ain't gonna grieve my Lord no more

...On a furry mat, cause the Lord will think you killed his cat

...On a jumbo jet, cause the Lord ain't built no runways yet

...In a bottle of gin, cause the Lord won't let no spirits in

...On rollerskates, cause you'll roll right past those pearly gates

...On a boy scout's knee, cause a boy scout's knee is knobbly

...In an old Ford car, cause an old Ford car won't get that far

...In a ping pong ball, cause a ping pong ball is much too small

...In a limousine, cause the Lord ain't got no gasoline

...In a rocking chair, cause the Lord don't want no rockers there

...In your girlfriend's bra, cause your girlfriend's bra don't stretch that far.

An alternative chorus is to substitute the following for the third and fourth lines of the chorus at a faster speed: 'I ain't gonna drink, I ain't gonna swear, I ain't gonna...Ooh, I wouldn't dare', and then on to the last line as before.

B-i-n-g-o

Each time the song is sung, it changes slightly: first one and then successively more of the letters of the name are clapped instead of sung. The second time around, for example, the spelling part would be 'clap-I-N-G-O'; the third time, it's 'clap-clap-N-G-O'. The sixth and final time the song is sung, all five letters are clapped.

There was a far mer had a dog and Bin go was his name o   B   I   N G O

B   I   N G O   B   I   N G O and Bin go was his name o

There was a farmer had a dog
and Bingo was his name-o
B-I-N-G-O, B-I-N-G-O, B-I-N-G-O,
and Bingo was his name-o.

If you're driving, perhaps you shouldn't take both hands off the steering wheel to clap, particularly if you're driving past a police car at the time.

Games to play on planes

When travelling by plane, the most interesting things are all happening outside, so let the kids grab the window seat. Not only will the view keep them quieter, but you'll be able to see over their heads anyway.

If you can't pre-book decent seats, get to the airport early. Make sure you ask for places that aren't over the wing (obscuring your view) or too close to the toilet (obscuring your nostrils). Windows on planes rarely line up precisely with the seats. If you are allowed to pick your own seats, try to get them slightly behind the window rather than slightly in front. If you don't get a good position, make a note of the best row numbers on the outward journey so you can ask for them on the way back – remembering, of course, that the interesting sights will be on the other side of the plane.

If you're usually subjected to incessant questions as to where you are, what speed you're doing and what height you are, try to fly on one of those airlines that have video screens showing a map and information on the progress of the flight. It's the perfect 'Are we there yet?' tool.

If you're truly obsessed with getting the best seats possible, a short visit to www.seatguru.com will give you all the information you need. And when we say all, we mean *all*.

Angles of flight

Cars go forwards and backwards. Trains usually go forwards, even if it doesn't always feel like it. But planes also go up and down and bank from side to side. This means there's a whole game to be played in estimating the plane's angle, and there are several methods of doing this.

The simplest is to half fill a glass or transparent plastic cup with water. For take-off, you can make a simple gauge with suspended paperclips (assuming taking paperclips on planes isn't regarded as an act of terrorism by the time you read this). If it is, some thread with something to weigh it down will do.

Are we there yet?

Find the word

Even the most diligent Dad can sometimes find himself on a plane, surrounded by children, with no obvious means of entertaining them.

The one thing you're always sure of finding is an ample supply of in-flight magazines. A fair amount of time can be whiled away with simple word searches – from the more obvious 'novelty' and 'keyring' to harder-to-find words such as 'cheap' and 'nasty'.

Good words for Hangman

Hangman is a great game for planes, since you're all sitting in a row facing the same way. (It's harder on trains, where some of you will be looking at the paper upside down.)

Everyone plays *Hangman* at some point. It's a common misconception that long words are harder to guess. Of course, it's the other way around: the longer the word, the more chance randomly chosen letters will appear in it, and the more structure will become apparent to let you guess the word.

Short words are much harder, especially if they don't contain any standard vowels. Our favourite is Lynx, but words like Ply, Jinx, Rhythm, Twelfths and Fjord will certainly keep them guessing.

Do establish right at the outset an agreed construction of gibbet and victim so that everyone will get the same number of guesses.

Games to play on boats

Boats – of the ferry variety – are like giant, metal nannies with plenty of room to run around, cinemas, playrooms and shops.

Our favourite game is *Hide and Seek*. Off they scamper as you cover your eyes and count to fifty. Then, it's 'Coming, ready or not', and you can peacefully spend the rest of the voyage in the bar.

Are we there yet?

Games to play on trains

In a car, you're all strapped into place and facing forwards, so there's not much chance of eye contact or more physical activities. If you're on a train, and are lucky enough to have secured a set of seats across a table, there are many more possibilities for whiling away the journey.

Buffet bingo

Each player chooses either Man, Woman or Child, and scores a point for each one that passes on the way to or from the buffet. For added variation, you could choose people wearing black or brown shoes, or overcoats, or glasses.

An interesting extension of this game is to examine the people who are passing and try to guess what sort of food and drink they're buying. There are no right or wrong answers (unless you pursue your quarry back to their seats), but as an exercise in speculative psychology it can be entertaining, and it is a good way to encourage your children's imagination.

You can try to guess people's names and their occupations, and even make up their life stories.

Your children should appreciate that it is rude to stare at, and comment on, your fellow passengers. Naturally, this only applies to those within earshot. Those on their way to or from the buffet car are fair game: back in their seat, they'll no doubt be playing *Buffet Bingo* too.

I Spy...

You really don't have to play this game. It is tedious in the extreme and, on a train journey, becomes downright annoying as whatever was chosen vanishes from view long before there's any chance of guessing it.

It will make even the shortest of journeys seem like the Trans Siberian Express. Never teach it to your children and, if they know it, ban them from playing it in your presence. If every Dad does the same, we can kill it off in a generation.

Counting down the miles

'How fast is the train going, Dad?' Pity the child foolish enough to ask this one. For, alongside every mile of train track in Britain* are positioned white mileposts. Sometimes there are even quarter-mileposts (marked with 'I', 'II' and 'III'). Watch at the ready, you ask them to count the number of mileposts the train passes in, say, five minutes.

'How many five minutes are there in an hour?' you ask, hoping to get the answer, 'Twelve.' Multiply the number of mileposts by 12 and you get the train's speed in miles per hour.

If you immerse yourself in a book or paper for the five minutes and emerge only to be told that the number of mileposts counted in that time is 'One', then the train is stationary. You can then teach them a grown-ups' game, trying to guess what lame excuse will eventually be given to 'customers' for the 'non-motion' of their train.

If you find stretches of track without mileposts, please complain to Network Rail rather than us. They assured us every bit of track has mileposts.

What am I drawing?

A pen and pad of paper are invaluable on train journeys. As well as being pressed into service for *Noughts and Crosses* and *Hangman*, there's a good collaborative game to be played. Each player takes it in turn to draw an everyday object – a house, a bicycle, a spider, and so on. The other players have to try to guess what they're drawing.

It's a surprisingly even-handed game: older children will try to conceal the finished object by drawing the key elements last (such as the wheels on a bicycle), while younger children may have more trouble simply representing their object, which means it won't become apparent until they've added a lot of detail.

Are we there yet?

Going dotty

The *Dot Game* is a splendid time-filler for journeys. Dads may fancy they have the intellectual advantage, but they are just as likely to make daft mistakes, particularly if they're trying to play *Buffet Bingo* at the same time.

Simply draw a rectangle made up of dots. A square of eight dots by eight is a sensible size. Each player takes turns to connect two dots, the aim being to complete one or more boxes by filling in the last line. That player's initial then goes in the box to be tallied for the final total. Games between Steve and Simon are particularly satisfying, since we both end up believing we've won.

After a player has completed a box, they must then draw another line somewhere. This often leads to strings of boxes being completed in one go, but can then mean the other player also gets a string of boxes to fill in: it's a question of counting the linked boxes to see which offers the best advantage.

We'll be there before you can say...

'...sixteen slimy serpents slithered surreptitiously on the silver sand as they sped silently southwards.' Or 'On Monday morning I made a model of a magical mouse with many mandibles, and mailed it to a man in Manchester.'

It takes a few moments' thought on Dad's part to come up with such sentences. It helps if it's alliterative, like the examples above.

Each time your child gets the phrase wrong, you should repeat it (and you should do your best to remember it exactly, as they're certain to pick *you* up on any mistakes). It's then down to personal ruthlessness: you shouldn't let the children get away with even the tiniest slip as they try to say the exact phrase back to you. But don't point out their mistake: just say they've got it wrong, and repeat the phrase once more for them. If you can.

7 What where who why how?

CURIOSITY MAY HAVE KILLED the cat, but for children it seems to be an energy source. Whatever their first word is, their second will probably be 'Why?' And it's usually to Dad that they turn to satisfy this boundless thirst for knowledge. Among their many other necessary skills, Dads have to be walking encyclopaedias.

What a cruel trick of nature, therefore, that the arrival of children so often coincides with the atrophying of brain cells in fathers. Nuggets of trivia you've had at your fingertips for years suddenly vanish from your memory and you must suffer the ignominy of having to tell your child that you have no idea what causes tides or how big the Universe is.

Fret no longer. Help is at hand. This chapter will answer only a small fraction of the barrage of questions you will be bombarded with. However, with an expert swerve, you should be able to divert their inquiry into an area in which you can now be an expert. You may not know everything, but you can give the impression you do. Your performance on pub quiz nights should improve too.

Why is the sky blue?

To get to grips with this, two things need to be understood; that white light is actually made up of lots of other colours, and that the sky is not empty.

Gaze upwards and you are looking into the Earth's atmosphere, without which life would be impossible. It provides air, water and warmth, while protecting us from meteorites and dangerous radiation. Although it goes on for 300 miles or more, compared to the Earth's size, it is no thicker than the skin on an apple.

The important bit to us is the first ten miles or so. That seemingly empty sky is actually full of water, dust and a combination of gases (78% nitrogen, 21% oxygen and lots of also-rans). Gases, like everything, are full of particles – molecules and atoms. There are 10^{19} of them in just one cubic centimetre of air (around a quarter of a teaspoon).

Sunlight – so-called 'white light' – is actually made up of a combination of colours. To prove this to doubting minds, divide a cardboard circle into seven equal segments and colour them the colours of the spectrum: red, orange, yellow, green, blue, indigo and violet. Push a pencil through the centre and spin it as quickly as you can between your palms. The colours all merge into white.

When sunlight passes through the atmosphere it smashes into all those particles. Light at the redder, long-wavelength gets through almost unscathed. But at the shorter, bluer, end, it's a different story. Affected 16 times as strongly as red, the atmosphere's particles bat blue light around the sky like a crazy game of celestial ping-pong. As a result, wherever we look there's blue light.

A level teaspoon of air contains 25,000,000,000,000,000,000 molecules. Careful not to spill them!

This scattering not only turns the sky blue, but also makes the Sun appear yellow. Out in space, with nothing to scatter light, the Sun appears white.

Why are sunsets red?

The sky isn't always blue or we wouldn't have quaint country sayings like, 'Red sky at night, the barn's alight'.

As the Sun sets, the light has to pass through much more of the particle-filled atmosphere. The blue light now gets scattered so much it is absorbed by the atmosphere and we hardly see it at all, while the redder colours are scattered more than before, in the way blue normally is, and so predominate.

Why are clouds white?

The water (and often ice) molecules in clouds are so large that all light colours are scattered equally. Thrown together again the colours recombine and, as we've seen, all the colours together produce white.

If clouds are grey, it could either be because higher clouds are casting shadows on them, or because they are so thick that the sunlight is absorbed higher up, creating a shadow within the cloud.

What does a cloud weigh?

I seldom forget a face

We're glad you asked. Scientist Peggy LeMone of the National Center for Atmospheric Research in Boulder, Colorado, USA, took to wondering about the weight of clouds, presumably after being asked by an inquisitive child.

She worked out that the water vapour in an average-sized cumulus cloud – that's one of the pretty white fluffy ones – weighs 550 tons. If you have trouble envisaging that, she suggests thinking in terms of elephants. As an elephant weighs around six tons, that means the water inside a typical cloud weighs the same as 100 elephants.

The obvious next question is: 'How does it stay up there?' If clouds were made of elephants, they wouldn't. Those 100 elephants would plummet to Earth wearing very surprised expressions and make a sizeable mess when they hit the ground. Fortunately for them – and us – the water is in the form of minute particles that are light enough to float on the warmer air rising below the cloud.

Surprising herself with the figures, LeMone carried on and figured out that the weight of a big storm cloud, one which was 10 times bigger in all dimensions than the cumulus cloud, was a whopping 200,000 elephants.

That still wasn't enough for her. She calculated that the water vapour in a hurricane the size of the state of Missouri (a little bigger than England and Wales combined) would weigh the same as 40 million elephants.

Why is sea water blue?

Water actually *is* blue. It might look colourless and clear when it's in a glass, but that's because it's only very, very, slightly blue. Put a lot of it together and its true colour becomes evident, particularly if the water is deep and clear. Look into a swimming pool, for instance, and the water will probably look a little blue (even if the swimming pool tiles aren't).

If your tap water *does* look blue when it's in a glass, it might be a good idea to check the water cistern to see whether anybody has dropped a loo-freshening tablet into it.

Is every seventh wave a big one?

It's often said that every seventh wave is a whopper, with every *seventh* seventh wave a monster. Although it can be fun to count them as you wave-watch, that's not quite how things work.

Waves are caused by the effect of wind on the surface of the water. The stronger the wind, the higher the waves. Waves don't actually travel towards the shore. That's an optical illusion. In fact, the water simply goes up and down. You can show how waves behave by blowing across the surface of a container of water with something floating on it. This will show that the water doesn't travel horizontally. Flicking a rope will also demonstrate the principle: a wave appears to travel down the rope, but in fact the rope only moves up and down.

In the sea, waves do come in packets of a few smaller waves followed by a few larger ones. The largest of all tend to occur somewhere between the fifth and eighth wave: hence, presumably, the widespread belief that it's every seventh wave that's the biggest.

As you flick the rope, you will see waves apparently travelling down it

What causes tides?

The Moon. As the Earth and the Moon dance around each other in the sky, the interaction of their two gravitational fields causes tides – regular rises and falls in the level of the Earth's seas. The Moon's gravity attracts the water nearest to it, while the water on the other side of the Earth also bulges out since it isn't receiving any gravitational pull at all from the Moon.

There are two cycles of high and low tides each day. During beach holidays, when you have a little more time to contemplate nature in all its beauty and perplexity, you may have wondered why the tides aren't at the same time each day. A little too complicated to go into here (no, we do understand it, really), it's to do with tides being regulated by the Moon while our days are determined by the Sun (we think). Suffice it to say that the corresponding high (or low) tide the following day will be roughly 45 minutes later.

The strongest tides are spring tides. These have nothing to do with the season but occur when Earth, Sun and Moon are in a line, when the Sun's gravity assists the Moon's. These happen during the full moon and the new moon.

During quarter moons, the Moon and Sun are perpendicular to each other, so we get weaker – or neap – tides.

How far away is the horizon?

Depends how tall you are. Seriously. It does. The horizon is simply the physical manifestation of the curvature of the Earth. That's why ships seen disappearing over the horizon vanish bit by bit. So the higher up you are, the further you'll be able to see.

Someone with eyes 120 cm from the ground will be able to see 4.2 kilometres. A typical adult with eyes 170 cm off the ground will be able to see just over 5 kilometres. Stand on a cliff so your eyes are 20 metres up and the horizon will be 17 kilometres away.

There's a way to work it out, since you asked. Multiply the height of the eyes (in centimetres) by 0.15. The square root of this will give you the distance to the horizon in kilometres.

Incidentally, it's an interesting fact that the horizon is always, always, *always* at the same level as your eyes: you stare horizontally to look at it. It doesn't matter if you're standing up, sitting down or looking out of a high window. It's a key rule in perspective drawing, but it's very surprising until you try it out!

How many colours are there in a rainbow?

Did you say 'Seven'? Go to the back of the class. Even if you have a physics textbook that says that it's seven, we don't care – it's wrong.

There's an indeterminate number of colours, just as in the spectrum. Red doesn't suddenly become orange, nor yellow turn green at some precise point. On the contrary, the colours blend gradually into one another. Try looking at the business side of a CD in sunshine or under bright light, or reflect it onto paper: you'll see plenty of colourful 'rainbows' as the light hits the disc's ridges.

FASCINATING FACT

People will often talk about rainbows as if they contain every colour there is. This is nonsense, of course. Try looking for brown, white, black, grey, or such colours as silver and gold. They're simply not there.

It's all Sir Isaac Newton's fault. He knew that there were, effectively, an infinite number of colours in the rainbow, but for the sake of convenience he split them into seven. Through everybody else's sloth, idleness and sloppy thinking, this has since become the norm. Nature is a source of infinite wonder. It would be depressing beyond belief if there really were fewer colours in the rainbow than there are in bathroom suite catalogues.

What causes rainbows?

As we've seen, sunlight actually consists of lots of colours. A rainbow is nature's prism, turning white light back into its constituent parts. For a rainbow to appear, the Sun needs to be behind the observer and low in the sky, which is why they usually occur in late afternoon. The bow will be opposite the Sun when it is raining or has just rained. The mist of water droplets in a waterfall is another possible source of rainbow sightings.

As sunlight enters the raindrops it is bent, then reflected from the back of the raindrop and bent again as it re-emerges from the front. But each colour is bent to a slightly different degree: red is bent at a 42° angle and violet at 40°, with all the intermediate colours sandwiched in between.

If you see a double rainbow, it simply means that those droplets have reflected the light inside twice.

A rainbow is really a circle, but the horizon cuts off the bottom half. Complete circular rainbows are, however, occasionally visible from the air.

You can only see rainbows from one side. This is simply demonstrated on a sunny day by making your own rainbow with a garden hose set to produce a fine spray. With the Sun behind you, the rainbow will be visible to you but not to someone the other side of the water, facing the Sun.

A good way of showing how water can split up light is to fill a glass or jar with water and place it on an outside table on a sunny day so that almost half of it is off the table. Place a sheet of paper on the ground so the Sun shines through the glass and creates a rainbow on the paper.

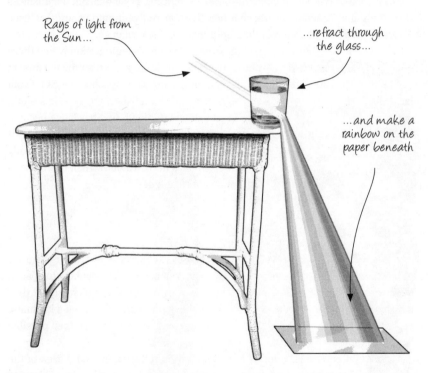

Rays of light from the Sun...

...refract through the glass...

...and make a rainbow on the paper beneath

Despite the legends, there really is no pot of gold at the end of the rainbow. If you move towards a rainbow, it will simply move ahead of you. It's not that we've looked for the gold or anything daft like that. That would be an utterly ridiculous waste of an afternoon, involving such pathetically stupid things as driving a family car through grotesquely wet fields, getting stuck in the mud, arguing with an irate farmer and having to pay him a small fortune to pull us out with a tractor. That's why we'd never be so stupid as to go looking for the pot of gold in the first place. It doesn't exist. Believe us. It really doesn't.

How does a flying buttress work?

Flying buttresses – those pillars of masonry that suddenly lurch over at the top to rest against the outside walls of cathedrals – are almost unique among the arcana of ecclesiastical architecture: not only can we remember their name but they inspire giggles among younger fans of *The Simpsons*. But what do they do?

For a great practical demonstration, make your child stand with his arms leaning forward at a 45° angle. Explain that he's the wall of the cathedral, and his arms are the roof. Then go on to say that, because of all the lead in church roofs, there's a tremendous weight pressing down from above: at the same time, push on his outstretched arms. He'll naturally move one leg back to steady himself, which is exactly what you want to happen: point to the leg, and tell him: *'That's* a flying buttress.'

Your child's body is the wall of the cathedral and his arms are the roof

As you press down on the roof, he puts his leg back to steady himself – and that's what a flying buttress does

Where do babies come from?

Er… ask your mother.

She said I should ask you.

I'm busy right now, ask me tomorrow.

No, really, where do babies come from?

Sooner or later, you may have to tackle this one head-on. The standard technique is to fold your newspaper, take a deep breath, and wonder where to start. What you should be doing is wondering where to stop.

Too often, parents can overwhelm their children with information they didn't ask for, aren't ready for, and can't cope with all in one go. Explaining obstetrics in full gynaecological detail is as bad as trying to fob them off with drivel about birds, bees and storks. The entire truth is too startling and too downright implausible for a single conversation.

A better approach is to give just enough information to answer the immediate question and no more. Don't try to fill their heads with details they're too young to assimilate. Let them come back to you, in their own time, with follow-up questions once they've processed what you've already told them.

A typical question-and-answer session, which may be spaced over several weeks, might go like this:

Where do babies come from?
They come from inside Mummy's tummy.
How do they get out?
The baby pushes itself out when it's grown big enough.
Where do they come out?
There's a special opening that expands to let the baby out. It's sometimes quite difficult, which is why Mummy needs a doctor to help the baby be born.
How do they get in there?
A tiny seed from Daddy is planted inside Mummy's tummy. It starts off really tiny, so small you can't see it. In nine months it grows into a baby, just like a plant grows from a seed.
How does the seed get in there?
Er… ask your mother.

How do planes fly?

They're big. They're heavy. Their wings don't flap. Just how do those metal monsters stay up there? The usual explanation invokes the Bernoulli Effect. This says that air will flow more quickly over the upper, curved section of a wing than the flat underside. A faster flow of air reduces the pressure, giving the wing lift.

What will happen when your child blows between the ping pong balls?

There are some great experiments to illustrate this. Cut a 5 centimetre strip lengthways from a piece of paper. Hold it on your lower lip and blow straight ahead. The sheet of paper will rise to the horizontal, even with a paperclip attached.

Suspend a couple of ping pong balls or balloons from lengths of cotton or string, so that they are level and a short distance apart. Ask a child what they'd expect to happen if they blew between the gap. They'll usually expect the balls or balloons to move apart. But in fact they come together, the faster airflow resulting in a reduction in pressure.

Hold a funnel upside down – the cut-off top of a water bottle will do. Blow into the narrow end while holding a ping pong ball inside it. As long as you keep blowing, the ball won't fall out because the faster-flowing air – where the pressure is lower – is above it. Hold the ball in the palm of your hand, blow hard, and, amazingly, the ball will be sucked up into the funnel.

FASCINATING FACT

The very first flight, in 1903, by the Wright brothers, lasted only 12 seconds, the plane travelling 36 metres. The Wright Flyer could have made the entire trip within the length of a modern jumbo jet.

Cut a straw in half and hold it in a glass of water. Blow air hard through a straw held horizontally at the top of the vertical straw. After a little trial and error, the decrease in air pressure at the junction of the two straws should create a spray of atomized water.

Point a hairdryer upwards and place a ping pong ball in the stream of air. It will bounce round in the airstream. You can even point the dryer away from the vertical and the ball will stay trapped in the faster air current. Try it with a balloon. Try it with both. If the kids somehow think it's because of the hot air rising, turn the heating element off. You can do the same experiment with one of those bendy straws, the short bit pointing upwards, and a ping pong ball.

The standard explanation of how a jumbo jet, weighing nearly 400 tons, flies is that it accelerates to over 150mph on the runway, at which point the air flowing over the wings is travelling so much faster than the air below the wing that sufficient lift is generated to suck the plane off the ground and keep it there. This is, in fact, complete nonsense.

You can keep a balloon aloft and steer it around, using an ordinary hairdryer

So how do planes really fly, then?

The Bernoulli Effect is the standard way of explaining how powered flight is possible. It's used in schools, colleges and textbooks. It's great fun to demonstrate. It's also wrong, massively so, when people claim that the air going the longer route over the curved upper wing has to rush to 'catch up' with the air beneath it.

It's tosh. Ask yourself – or prepare to be asked by an alert child – how the Wright brothers could fly when the wings of the Wright Flyer were flat, not curved, just like a paper dart? How does that fly? And how can a plane fly upside-down, when the curved side is towards the ground?

Newton is the key. His Third Law of Motion tells us that for each action, there's an equal and opposite reaction. Wings are tilted backwards or have a tilted trailing edge. As a plane is propelled forwards, the wing forces the air beneath it downwards. In reaction, the air pushes the wing upwards, providing lift. This effect is most obvious with a helicopter. Its rotors are thin, quickly revolving 'wings'.

Hold a piece of paper down on a table and blow on one of the shorter edges. It will flap about. Crease it a third of the way down and bend that edge up. Now hold it and blow again. The leading edge will rise up. That's how planes can fly. They are effectively 'surfing' through the sky. Bernoulli does contribute, because the curvature of the wing improves the lift efficiency. But it's not the whole story.

How do birds fly?

A bird's grace and agility makes all our high-tech planes look positively elephantine. It doesn't need a long runway – not when it can land on a target as tiny as a telephone wire.

When gliding, a bird's outstretched wings are angled slightly downwards, increasing air pressure below the wings and reducing it above. This gives the bird lift as it moves through the air. If there are warm air currents around, called thermals, it can seek them out and use them to soar to higher levels, just as glider pilots do.

When a bird flaps its wings, on the downstroke it deflects air backwards to give it forward thrust. On the upstroke, it partially folds its wings to reduce drag, much in the way that somebody swimming breaststroke does while they're preparing for their next scoop.

I've caught a fish!

Whoops

Birds are incredibly efficient flying machines. To change direction, they can flap their wings at different rates, as well as tilting and changing the shape of their wings and tail, thus simulating the complexities of the flaps, ailerons, rudders and elevators on planes.

A bird's bones are hollow. If they weren't, it would be too heavy to fly. This is the case with penguins, whose ancestors did fly. But their bones, which are now solid, make it easier for them to swim and dive underwater for fish.

Why is the sea salty?

Although river water tastes fresh (assuming you're high enough up in the hills so that no chemicals or other pollutants have yet washed into it), the water you're drinking actually contains small quantities of mineral salts from rocks and soil which it carries into the sea.

As sea water evaporates, the salt remains behind. Over the years and millennia, sea water gets saltier and saltier. One cubic foot of sea water contains, on average, one kilogram of salt. 97% of all the water on Earth is salty, with only 3% fresh (and two-thirds of that is frozen in ice sheets and glaciers).

The saltiest water is in the Red Sea and the Persian Gulf, where there's little fresh water input but high evaporation because of the high temperatures. The Dead Sea in Israel is saltier, at 33%, but it's a lake, not a real sea. At 400 metres below sea level, it's also the lowest spot on the surface of the Earth.

Interestingly, when ice forms from sea water, the salt is forced out and sinks. Eskimos and explorers can get drinking water just from melting the ice.

Is it worth runnin' in the rain?

If it's raining, will you get more or less wet if you run through it? Scientists with too much time on their hands have debated this periodically (i.e. in learned periodicals) over the years. But it wasn't until 1997 that we got a definitive answer when two meteorologists, Dr Thomas Peterson and Dr Trevor Wallis, decided that there was only way to know for sure.

Marking out a 100-metre track behind their office, they dressed in identical sweatshirts, hats and trousers and sat down to wait for rain. Being meteorologists at the United States National Climatic Data Center in North Carolina, presumably they had a pretty good idea how long they'd have to wait.

When the rain came, out they went. Dr Wallis ran down the track at 9 mph and Dr Peterson ambled along at 3 mph. While Dr Wallis's clothes weighed 130 grams more, the slower Dr Peterson's clothes gained 217 grams. In other words, if you dawdle in the rain you'll get almost twice as wet.

Further research found the difference to be most marked in heavy rain in windy weather. In light rain it matters much less whether you walk or run.

As for knowing whether it's going to rain or not, the learned Professor Sod, whose Law holds true in so many walks of life, found that it usually happens when you don't have your umbrella or mac with you.

What causes thunder and lightning?

Much like sparks resulting from static electricity (see page 12), lightning is caused when the electrical charges in a cloud separate, with negative charges forming at the bottom of the cloud. These repel the negative charges on the ground, resulting in an overall positive charge at the surface.

As air is a bad conductor of electricity, these opposite charges keep building up until the resistance of the air is suddenly overcome, a circuit is completed and the negative charge finds a way to the ground. A single lightning strike may carry a charge of 100 million volts or more, compared to the 240 volts of our electrical appliances. The temperature in a lightning bolt is over 27,000°C – five times as hot as the surface of the Sun. Thunder is caused by lightning instantaneously heating the air which expands explosively. If you blow up a paper bag and burst it, you get an idea how this happens.

The forked lightning that so impresses us actually travels *up*, not down. It happens too quickly for us to see, but there are actually two strikes for each fork of lightning. The leader coming down from the cloud is like a feeler: a short way from the ground, it attracts a return charge, suddenly connecting ground and cloud.

How far away is a thunderstorm?

In movies, thunder is heard the instant lightning flashes. If this happened in a real storm, we'd be in danger of being struck by lightning.

Although the flash of lightning reaches our eyes more or less instantly, sound takes longer to get to us. The speed of sound is about 760 miles an hour, or a fifth of a mile in a second. Start counting the seconds from the flash to the roll of thunder. Saying 'Mississippi one, Mississippi two' pretty much ensures you're counting in seconds, even if you're not sure how to spell Mississippi. Divide the number of seconds by five and that's how many miles away the storm is.

You've probably been taught that one second equals one mile. It's a lie! That lightning is much closer than you thought!

What should you do in a thunderstorm?

Stay indoors. It's the safest place.

If you are caught outside, remember that lightning takes the easiest path to ground. That's why tall buildings are struck more often than short ones. Get off

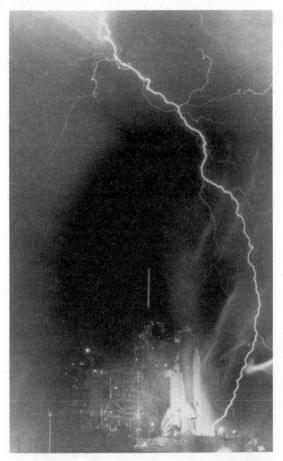

Try to stay away from tall objects, especially tall metal objects filled with rocket fuel

PHOTO: NASA

high ground and keep as low as you can, crouching or kneeling if you can't find any hollows.

Get rid of anything metal and don't stand under or near trees, lampposts or telephone poles. Don't shelter in a cave, stay clear of water and keep your distance from other people.

It's a myth that rubber-soled shoes or rubber tyres provide protection. They don't, so don't ride a bike. A car is a pretty safe place as its metal shell will conduct electricity better than you, but keep the windows up and don't touch any metal parts. Commercial airliners are not in much danger in a storm. While it may seem frightening – and bumpy – if you experience it first-hand, most planes are struck once or twice a year. The metal in the fuselage conducts the current around it and away, much like in a car.

Indoors, don't use electrical equipment, particularly those old-fashioned phones that plug into the wall. Avoid water as it's a great conductor of electricity. So no baths or showers. Don't wash your hands or do the dishes, and stay off the toilet. Even kings can die on the throne.

Despite the saying, lightning *can* strike twice in the same place. The Empire State Building gets 100 lightning strikes every year.

Why is it colder the further north you go from the equator?

The wrong answer is that, because it's a globe, the Earth's northern latitudes are further away from the Sun. The difference in distance is insignificant.

Instead, it's to do with the angle of the Sun's rays. The further north you go, the more obliquely they strike the Earth. The sunlight is spread over a greater area, leading to lower temperatures. You can demonstrate this most easily by shining a torch onto a piece of paper. It's easy to see that if the angle is slanted then the light (and heat) are being distributed over a bigger area than if the torch shines directly onto the paper.

Seasons are also unconnected with the Earth's distance from the Sun. Oddly enough for those of us in the northern hemisphere, the Earth is closest to the Sun at the beginning of January, the middle of winter. Seasons occur because the axis around which the Earth rotates every day is tilted. As the Earth takes its annual tour around the Sun, if the northern part of the globe is tilted towards the Sun then it's summer; the Sun's rays strike more directly and the days are longer. The opposite applies in winter, and in the southern hemisphere.

Thickness of atmosphere travelled through in northern hemisphere

Thickness of atmosphere travelled through at the equator

Light from Sun

Why do we have leap years?

Although we think of the Earth going around the Sun once a year, in fact it takes 365 days, 5 hours, 48 minutes and 46 seconds. If nothing was done about that extra quarter of a day each year, our calendars would soon get out of kilter with the solar calendar, which determines our seasons. Then Christmas really would get earlier every year.

So a day is added to our calendars every four years, giving February 29 days rather than 28. If we did nothing, within a few centuries Christmas would be in the middle of summer.

But this isn't quite enough. If we left it at that, we'd gain another day every 128 years. By 1582, when Pope Gregory put things right, we were 10 days adrift. The new, Gregorian, calendar not only leapt ahead those 10 days; it also avoided future minor drifting by skipping leap years in three out of every four century years. So 1700, 1800 and 1900 weren't leap years, though 2000 was.

How much does the Earth weigh?

Nothing. Seriously. Weight depends on gravity and there is none in outer space.

However, the Earth's *mass*, which doesn't depend on gravity, is 6 sextillion metric tons; that's 6×10^{21} metric tons (6,000,000,000,000,000,000,000 metric tons).

What's more, the Earth is gaining weight, at the rate of 40,000 metric tons each year. It's the result of tons of dust and micrometeorites entering the atmosphere every day.

Is it possible to dig right through the Earth?

No. Sorry, but there it is. So you might as well put your spade back in the shed and eat your packed lunch now. You'll never get there.

The deepest hole ever dug is around 7.5 miles deep. It's called Kola SG-3, and was drilled by geophysicists in northern Russia between 1970 and 1989. That's certainly a deep hole, but the distance from the surface to the centre of the Earth is nearly 4,000 miles – so even after nineteen years of digging, Kola barely scratches the surface.

If the Kola hole were the thickness of one page of this book, you'd have to drill through the equivalent of six copies to get all the way through. (Feel free to buy another five copies to try this.)

How many moons does the Earth have?

Calling that thing we can see in the night sky 'The Moon' could turn out to be something of a misnomer.

In 1986, a second moon was discovered. It's only 3 miles across and, strictly speaking, it's a 'co-orbital Near-Earth Asteroid'. Just like the Earth and the Moon, it takes a year to go around the Sun, although its path is hugely eccentric from the Earth's point of view, resembling the outline of a horseshoe. Its orbit passes Venus, almost gets to Mercury and then turns back and nearly gets to Mars before heading back again. It's called 3753 Cruithne (pronounced 'Croo-EEN-ya'), named after the Celtic tribe better known as Picts.

The closest it gets to us is 10 million miles, 40 times the main Moon's distance. But Cruithne does share Earth's orbit around the Sun. It might not be what you or I would call a moon of ours, but lots of astronomers do.

In September 2002, there was much excitement when an amateur astronomer from Arizona found a small object in a perfect 50-day orbit around the Earth. Thought to be a third moon, it was named J002E2. Then, to everyone's embarrassment, they realized it was *Apollo 12*'s abandoned 3rd-stage booster. Oops!

Some argue that a subsequently discovered Near-Earth Asteroid called 2002AA29 is a third moon. This one's only 330 feet across and visits the Earth just once every 95 years, the last time in January 2003. So it's really a part-time moon or quasi-satellite.

Perhaps that's just as well for the poets. They might be able to find a rhyme for Cruithne, but they'd have a heck of a job with 2002AA29.

Is the Moon made of green cheese?

In 1546 English dramatist John Heywood jotted down umpteen 'proverbes' for posterity, including one that 'the moon is made of a greene cheese'.

Fortunately for those who don't care for four-and-a-half-billion-year-old cheese, it was Moon rocks, rather than cheese, that the astronauts brought back from the Moon. The idea still persists though.

Oddly, though, Moon rocks are only about a quarter as dense as the rocks of Earth. Their density is far closer to... *cheese!* By transmitting shock waves through Moon rocks and assorted Earthly cheeses, scientists found that while Basalt 100017 from the Moon has a seismic velocity of 1.84 km/sec, Vermont Cheddar has a seismic velocity of 1.72 km/sec.

What are the phases of the Moon?

The Moon is unusual in that its rotational and orbital speeds are identical – which is why it always presents the same face towards us. The Moon turns both around its axis and around the Earth once every 27.32166 days.

New   Crescent waxing   Half moon waxing   Gibbous waxing

Full   Gibbous waning   Half moon waning   Crescent waning

Is there a man in the Moon?

When the Moon is relatively full, it's easy to imagine that you can see a man's face up there, mouth gaping wide with astonishment.

The eyes are in fact two lunar 'seas', Mare Imbrium and Mare Serenitatis, and the mouth is Mare Nubium. Though named as seas by ancient astronomers, these are actually just large dark plains of volcanic rock.

The ancients were keen on trying to find recognizable shapes up in the heavens. But different people saw different things. Other cultures, for instance, didn't see a man in the Moon at all, but things as varied as a hare, a buffalo, a woman and even a kissing couple.

Twelve real men have stood on the Moon. Neil Armstrong of *Apollo 11* was the first on 20 July 1969 and Gene Cernan of *Apollo 17* the last on 14 December 1972.

Spot the difference

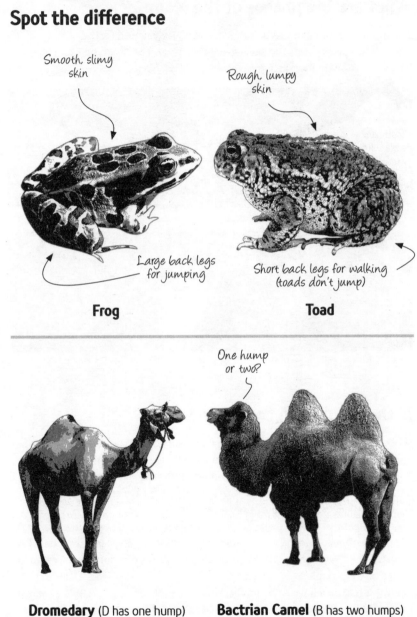

Smooth, slimy skin

Rough, lumpy skin

Large back legs for jumping

Short back legs for walking (toads don't jump)

Frog

Toad

One hump or two?

Dromedary (D has one hump)

Bactrian Camel (B has two humps)

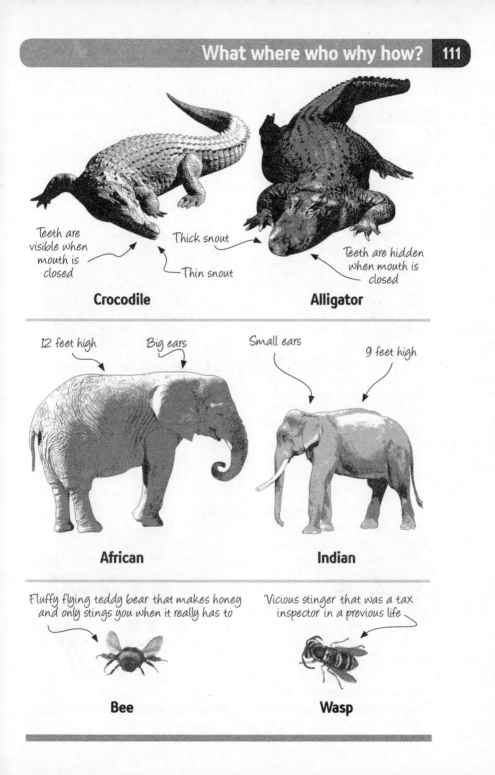

Teeth are visible when mouth is closed

Thick snout

Thin snout

Teeth are hidden when mouth is closed

Crocodile

Alligator

12 feet high

Big ears

Small ears

9 feet high

African

Indian

Fluffy flying teddy bear that makes honey and only stings you when it really has to

Vicious stinger that was a tax inspector in a previous life

Bee

Wasp

3·5 billion years ago:
land begins to form

550 million years ago:
life starts on Earth

The bog-standard history of the Earth

Although the Earth is 4.5 billion years old, human beings in a halfway recognizable form have only been around for, at the most, about 200,000 years. It's pretty hard to get kids' minds (or even adults) to grasp just how minuscule a proportion this is. Unless, that is, you unwind an entire loo roll.

You may not be as sweet as that mischievous puppy on the adverts, but you can bet that you'll have your kids' attention when you begin rolling out the paper. It's unlikely you'll have enough room to keep going in a straight line. It doesn't matter. Go in and out of rooms, and up and down the stairs. Let the kids dictate where it goes. Try to arrange it so the last few feet run straight and true. (Keep the tube for The Hole in the Hand, see page 15.)

Grab a tape measure and check the length of the loo roll on the pack. If yours is 30 metres long, as our well-known brand was, then each foot (30 centimetres) will represent 1% of Earth's history, or 45 million years. (You may have to make adjustments if you're using an inferior brand.) Find a way to mark the paper, either directly or on something you can attach to it. Explain that the beginning of the roll is when the Earth was formed, along with the Sun and the rest of the Solar System, around 4,500 million years ago.

Assuming your pace is roughly one metre, follow the loo roll for seven strides. Make a mark and explain that at this point, 3.5 billion years ago, land began to form and the first, very primitive life appeared in Earth's oceans.

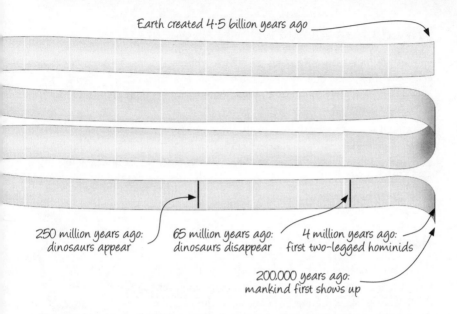

Earth created 4·5 billion years ago

250 million years ago: dinosaurs appear

65 million years ago: dinosaurs disappear

4 million years ago: first two-legged hominids

200,000 years ago: mankind first shows up

You need to go another 22 paces before you can stop and make another mark. Here, 550 million years ago, life really got going in earnest, with an abundance of plant and animal species. The earliest fossils found date from this time. No sign of mankind yet, though.

March on until you near the end of the loo roll. 170 centimetres before it runs out, you should mark the point where, 250 million years ago, the first dinosaurs appeared on Earth.

Half a metre from the end, you can show where, 65 million years ago, a giant asteroid wiped out 70% of all living things on the planet, including the dinosaurs. (Probably – the scientists are still arguing over that one.)

The first two-legged hominids, where we began to become distinct from our ape ancestors, didn't make their appearance until around 4 million years ago. This, your audience should be amazed to discover, occurred on the very last two centimetres of the loo roll.

Homo sapiens, the species that we now call mankind, first appeared 200,000 years ago. That's just over a millimetre away from the end of the loo roll, too minute a gap to mark, except with a line across the very end bit of the paper. You'd need a magnifying glass to see the start of recorded history 10,000 years ago, and even an incredibly powerful microscope wouldn't find the spot that marks when you or your kids were born.

Why do fingers get wrinkly in water?

Stay in the bath or a swimming pool for a while and you'll notice your fingers getting wrinkly. This happens because our skin is lubricated and protected by an oil called sebum produced by our bodies. It's why water runs off when we wash or get caught in the rain.

Stay in water for a long time, though, and the sebum gets washed away, allowing water to penetrate and waterlog our skin. Our hands and feet have the thickest skin and so absorb most water, getting wrinkly, much like the pages of a book dropped in the bath. Elsewhere, our skin is thinner and too tightly stretched to make much difference.

How do fireworks work?

There are two ways of getting fireworks into the air. A rocket has a lower chamber that contains gunpowder, also known as black powder. As it burns, it produces hot gases that escape through a small hole, propelling the firework skywards. Other aerial fireworks are launched from a mortar tube where the explosion of a lift charge fires the firework up to 1,000 feet into the air.

Controlled by a time-delay fuse, the business end of the firework is designed to go off when the firework reaches its maximum height. Pellets of chemicals packed into the firework burn in an enclosed space. The pressure builds until the firework blows up, producing a bang which ignites and scatters the so-called stars, which work much like coloured sparklers.

The colour of the stars is determined by the metals used. Barium nitrate produces a green effect, strontium is red, sodium sulphate is yellow, magnesium and aluminium are white, carbon is orange, and copper sulphate is blue.

FASCINATING FACT

Many fireworks are still made by hand – *very* carefully. They're so dangerous that even a sharp knock can detonate a star. The danger of sparks from static electricity is such that firework makers are compelled to wear cotton, right down to their underwear.

8 Number crunching

ALL KIDS LOVE NUMBERS. Oh, all right then, all *boys* love numbers. Ever since the first caveboy learned to tot up the number of mammoth bones in his primordial soup, they've been counting everything in sight. Comparing, cataloguing and enumerating physical objects has been a favourite pastime for millennia.

This can be a problem for the unprepared Dad. Which *is* taller, the Statue of Liberty or the largest of the Pyramids? Does your car weigh more than an elephant? How big is the Earth? How many hairs are there on your head?

Even in a book of this size (total page area: 12 square metres) we (combined height of authors: 3.58 metres) can't hope to include every fact your child might demand of you. But there should still be enough facts here to keep them going from Time Immemorial (1189, a legal term meaning 'dating from before the reign of Richard I') to the end of the world (December 23rd 2012, according to the ancient Mayan calendar – but it seems they were proved wrong).

How much was Falstaff's chicken?

In Shakespeare's *Henry IV Part 1*, Prince Hal finds a tavern bill in Falstaff's pocket showing that he spent two shillings and sixpence on a capon with sauce. That's equivalent to 12.5p in today's money. Or is it? You couldn't even buy a KFC bucket for that little today. So how much did it really cost?

We've compiled the table opposite from data supplied to us by the Bank of England. To use it, simply multiply the figure shown for each year (or decade, before 1900) to get the value of any sum today.

If we date Falstaff's chicken to 1600 – Shakespeare clearly used Elizabethan prices – we get a figure of 140. Multiplying this by our 12.5 pence gives us 1750 pence, or £17.50 in today's money. Clearly, Falstaff favoured expensive restaurants.

So next time your kids' great grandmother tells them that she earned £4 a week at her first typing job in 1948, a glance at the table (and a multiplication of 24.7 by that £4) will give an equivalent wage of a fraction under £100 today – not too shabby for a 17-year-old girl's first earned income, especially when you think that her bus ride to work only cost tuppence. Oh, hang on a minute…

Useful dates in British history

1314	Bannockburn (Scots 1, Eng 0)	1805	Trafalgar (Eng 1, France 0)
1348	Black Death	1815	Waterloo (Eng 1, France 0)
1381	Peasants' Revolt	1837	Queen Victoria (to 1901)
1415	Agincourt (Eng 1, France 0)	1854	Crimean War (Eng 1, Russia 0)
1513	Flodden (Eng 1, Scotland 0)	1861	American Civil War (to 1865)
1536	Dissolution of monasteries	1876	Invention of telephone
1558	Elizabeth I (to 1603)	1903	First powered flight
1588	Armada (Eng 1, Spain 0)	1914	World War I (to 1918)
1605	Gunpowder Plot	1917	Russian Revolution
1620	Pilgrim Fathers set sail	1929	Wall Street Crash
1642	English Civil War (to 1649)	1936	Spanish Civil War
1649	Charles I beheaded	1937	Invention of jet engine
1666	Great Fire of London	1939	World War II (to 1945)
1776	Independence (USA 1, Eng 0)	1952	Elizabeth II
1788	First British colony in Australia	1965	Vietnam War (to 1975)
1789	French Revolution	1966	World Cup (Eng 4, Germany 2)

Multiply any historical amount of money by the figure listed next to that year in the table to calculate how much it's worth now (see facing page).

2014.......1.00	1978.......5.22	1942.......36.2	1906.......87.2	**1600**........187
2013.......1.03	1977.......5.62	1941.......36.2	1905.......81.7	1590........218
2012.......1.06	1976.......6.55	**1940**.......39.6	1904.......81.7	1580........261
2011.......1.10	1975.......7.62	1939.......45.9	1903.......81.7	1570........238
2010.......1.16	1974.......9.49	1938.......46.7	1902.......81.7	1560........290
2009.......1.20	1973.......11.0	1937.......46.7	1901.......84.4	1550........436
2008.......1.20	1972.......12.0	1936.......49.3	**1900**.......84.4	1540........436
2007.......1.25	1971.......12.8	1935.......50.3	1890.......81.7	1530........523
2006.......1.31	**1970**.......14.2	1934.......51.2	1880.......68.7	1520........654
2005.......1.34	1969.......15.0	1933.......52.3	1870.......65.4	1510........654
2004.......1.38	1968.......15.8	1932.......50.3	1860.......67.0	**1500**........654
2003.......1.42	1967.......16.6	1931.......49.3	1850.......74.6	1490........654
2002.......1.46	1966.......17.0	**1930**.......45.9	1840.......56.8	1480........654
2001.......1.48	1965.......17.7	1929.......44.3	1830.......63.8	1470........654
2000.......1.52	1964.......18.6	1928.......43.6	1820.......53.4	1460........654
1999.......1.55	1963.......19.1	1927.......42.8	1810.......43.6	1450........654
1998.......1.59	1962.......19.5	1926.......42.1	**1800**.......45.9	1440........654
1997.......1.64	1961.......20.3	1925.......40.8	1790.......81.7	1430........654
1996.......1.70	**1960**.......21.1	1924.......41.5	1780.......90.1	1420........654
1995.......1.77	1959.......21.3	1923.......41.5	1770.......90.1	1410........654
1994.......1.81	1958.......21.4	1922.......39.6	1760........109	**1400**........654
1993.......1.86	1957.......21.9	1921.......31.8	1750........124	1390........654
1992.......1.89	1956.......22.7	**1920**.......29.0	1740........124	1380........654
1991.......1.97	1955.......23.9	1919.......33.6	1730........124	1370........523
1990.......2.06	1954.......24.9	1918.......33.6	1720........119	1360........523
1989.......2.27	1953.......25.4	1917.......40.8	1710........109	1350........654
1988.......2.41	1952.......26.1	1916.......49.3	**1700**........114	1340........871
1987.......2.54	1951.......28.8	1915.......58.0	1690........124	1330........654
1986.......2.67	**1950**.......31.2	1914.......72.6	1680........119	1320........523
1985.......2.81	1949.......32.2	1913.......72.6	1670........119	1310........654
1984.......2.94	1948.......33.0	1912.......72.6	1660........109	**1300**........654
1983.......3.08	1947.......50.5	1911.......74.6	1650........109	1290........871
1982.......3.21	1946.......35.3	**1910**.......76.9	1640........124	1280........654
1981.......3.48	1945.......35.8	1909.......76.9	1630........131	1270........654
1980.......3.88	1944.......36.1	1908.......76.9	1620........138	
1979.......4.55	1943.......36.2	1907.......79.2	1610........138	

Animal speeds

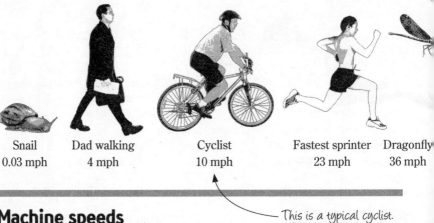

Snail	Dad walking	Cyclist	Fastest sprinter	Dragonfly
0.03 mph	4 mph	10 mph	23 mph	36 mph

Machine speeds

This is a typical cyclist. The fastest ever was 132 mph, achieved by cycling down a glacier

Stephenson's Rocket ...... 30 mph
Fastest steam train .... 126 mph (Mallard)
Fastest ever UK train ...... 208 mph
Fastest production car ..... 240 mph (McLaren F1)
Fastest boat .... 317.6 mph (Spirit of Australia, 1978)
Fastest train .... 321.8 mph (French TGV)
Jumbo jet .... 565 mph
Thrust SSC .... 763 mph (land speed record, 1997)
Concorde .... 1,336 mph
Fastest plane .... 2,193 mph (SR-71 Blackbird, 1976)
Space shuttle .... 18,000 mph
Fastest man-made object ... 153,800 mph (Helios 2 probe, 1976)

FASCINATING FACT

The fastest man in the world is not, as you might think, the 100-metre sprinter, but the 200-metre. The 100-metre man's average speed is cut by the time it takes him to get up to speed, a smaller factor over 200 metres.

Animal longevity, typical (years)

Tapeworm	2	Lobster, lion, rhino	15
Mouse	3	Polar bear, gorilla, horse	20
Rabbit	5	Grizzly bear	25
Kangaroo, red fox	7	Asian elephant	40
Squirrel, pig, giraffe	10	Killer whale, sturgeon	50
Cat, dog, camel	12	Box turtle	100

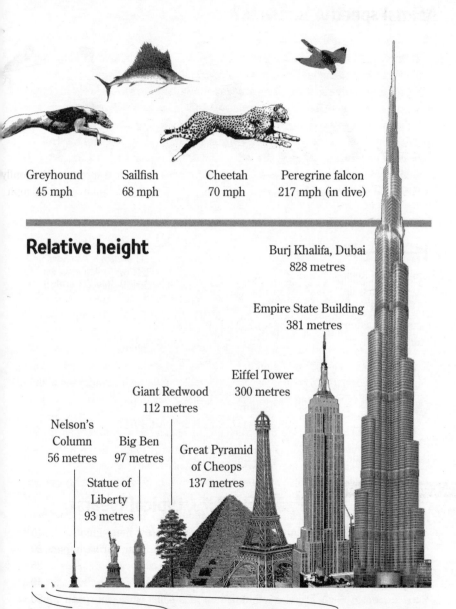

Greyhound	Sailfish	Cheetah	Peregrine falcon
45 mph	68 mph	70 mph	217 mph (in dive)

Relative height

Burj Khalifa, Dubai
828 metres

Empire State Building
381 metres

Eiffel Tower
300 metres

Giant Redwood
112 metres

Nelson's
Column
56 metres

Big Ben
97 metres

Great Pyramid
of Cheops
137 metres

Statue of
Liberty
93 metres

Average Dad: 1.8 metres; double decker bus: 4.35 metres; giraffe: 5.8 metres

How big is the Universe?

Very, very, very, very, very, very big.

If the Sun was shrunk to the size of a basketball, our own Solar System would still be a mile across and the nearest star 5,000 miles away.

According to astronomers, to get an idea of how many stars there are, you should try to imagine the total number of grains of sand on every beach in the world. Got it? Well, there are said to be a million stars for every one of those grains.

There are 400 billion stars in our own Galaxy, the Milky Way, and the Hubble telescope has shown that there are 200 billion or more galaxies in the Universe. If the Milky Way is an average-sized Galaxy, that means there must be some 80,000 billion, billion stars in the Universe.

We said it was big.

The Earth

The third planet from the Sun, the Earth is 4.5 billion years old, like the rest of our Solar System. This is reasonably young in comparison to the Universe, currently estimated to be almost 14 billion years old. The planet travels through space at 67,000 miles an hour as it orbits the Sun once a year.

The Earth rotates on its own axis every 23 hours 56 minutes and 4.1 seconds. It takes almost another four minutes until noon becomes noon again. This is because, in a day, the Earth has travelled 1.6 million miles in its annual 584 million mile elliptical orbit around the Sun, so each day it has to turn a bit further than 360° before the same spot faces the Sun.

The Earth's radius at the equator is 3,964 miles, and its circumference 24,901 miles. If you could walk right around the planet, doing 10 miles a day, it would take you almost seven years to arrive back where you started from.

Imagine a string of people standing on the equator holding hands. Assuming each person with outstretched arms took up 1.5 metres, you'd need 26 million people to complete the chain. With a population of 6.5 billion people, the chain could loop the Earth 250 times. As 200,000 more people are born than die every day, by 2050 the population will have grown so that the chain will loop round 350 times.

If you cut the Earth in half, it would look like a peculiar hard-boiled egg. The Earth's crust (the shell) is very thin and only 20 miles or so thick. The Earth's mantle (the white bit) is 1,800 miles thick. Inside that is the core (the yolk).

There's no way we can journey to the centre of the Earth. In fact, the deepest that geologists have drilled is under 8 miles, not even halfway to the mantle. The core is reckoned to be made mostly of iron. It is incredibly hot, over 3,800°C, the outer part of it being molten.

The Sun

The Sun is 93 million miles away. If we could drive a car to the Sun at 70 mph it would take 150 years to reach it. It's 860,000 miles across, 109 times the 7,900-mile diameter of the Earth. A million Earths could fit inside it.

The Sun is a ball of gas, three-quarters hydrogen and a quarter helium, with a core temperature of over 11,000,000°C, while the surface is over 5,000°C.

Like all stars, the Sun is a massive nuclear reactor, turning 600 million tons of hydrogen into helium every second through nuclear fusion, releasing energy in the form of heat and light.

The Sun has used up half its lifetime's supply of hydrogen. In a mere 5 billion years or so, it will run out of fuel and become an unstable red giant, expanding outwards and vaporizing all life on Earth.

Relative sizes of the Sun and the Earth (right). If the Sun were the size shown here, the Earth would be 58 pages away

Moon facts and figures

It is 2,160 miles across compared to Earth's 7,900, and the Moon's distance from Earth varies between 222,000 and 252,000 miles. The average is about 238,000 miles, roughly 30 times the diameter of the Earth.

Full moons occur when the side of the Moon illuminated by the Sun directly faces the Earth. The time between full moons is actually 29.53 days. During the 27.32 days the Moon takes to revolve around us, the Earth has moved in relation to the Sun. It's another two days and more before the Moon catches up to the same position relative to the Earth again. The time between new moons – when we can't see the Moon at all at night – is the same. This occurs when the Moon is between the Sun and the Earth, the Sun illuminating the side we can't see.

The Moon has no air, indeed no atmosphere at all, so there is no rain nor weather of any kind. Its temperature varies wildly, from 100°C (hot enough to boil water) to minus 147°C.

Gravity is a sixth of that on Earth, from which the Moon moves an inch and a half further away every year.

Relative sizes of the Earth (left) and the Moon (right). If the Earth were the size shown here, the Moon would be 15 pages away

Relative weights

Averages are just that. You may weigh more or less than the average Dad, although it's unlikely you know your weight in tons. And the average car is a Ford Fiesta, since you asked.

Average Dad	Average car	African elephant	Blue whale	Jumbo jet
0.077 tons	1.2 tons	6 tons	125 tons	400 tons

Not included here is the world's largest vehicle – the Jahre Viking supertanker, which weighs in at an astonishing 555,000 tons.

Wacky number trivia

● You can write every number from 1 to 99 in words without using the letter 'a'.

● 111,111,111 × 111,111,111 = 12,345,678,987,654,321.

● Every time a fictional phone number is given in an American film or TV programme, it includes the area code 555.

● Celtic shepherds counted their sheep thus: Yan, tan, tethera, pethera, pimp, sethera, lethera, hovera, dovera, dic, yan-a-dic, tan-a-dic, tethera-dic. After every 13 sheep (the number chosen to confuse the gods) they'd make a mark on a stick and start again. A great way of counting children you're trying to herd!

● The 100 Years' War lasted 116 years. (The shortest war, when Zanzibar surrendered to Britain in 1896, lasted just 38 minutes.)

● The international dialling code for Russia is 007.

● There are 170,000,000,000,000,000,000,000,000 different ways of playing the first 10 moves in a game of chess.

● If all the Lego in the world were divided up evenly, we'd get 30 pieces each.

How to count up to 1,023 on your fingers

How high can you count on the fingers of both hands? Ten? Not very practical when you're totting up the number of white cars you pass on the motorway or the number of fries in the average McDonald's portion.

There is a better way. It turns out that a digital calculator is one of the accessories included with the human body.

Your fingers are, you may be surprised to know, numbered in powers of two, binary fashion. On your right hand, the thumb is 1, the index finger is 2, the next is 4, the next 8, and the last 16. On your left hand, from thumb outwards, the numbers go 32, 64, 128, 256 and 512. If you have trouble remembering these numbers, get your kids to write them on your fingers.

Hold your hands, palm down, above a flat surface. Touch your thumb to the surface: that's 1. Raise your thumb and touch the index finger down: that's 2. Add

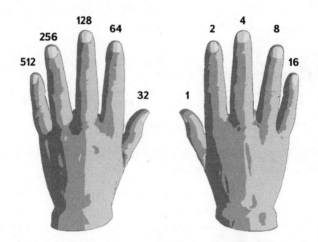

the thumb again, and that's 1+2=3. The chart opposite shows how to make the numbers from 1 to 31; when you add the left hand, you can get all the way up to 1,023 (it's one less than 1,024, which is 2 to the power of 10). It takes a bit of practice but soon becomes second nature. Indeed, practising the finger sequence is a great way of nodding off at night. Don't actually count. Just do the movements.

When you've finished tapping out your fingers, add up the value of those fingers that are pressed down to get the grand total. Of course, if you're equally dextrous with your toes, you'd be able to count up to 1,048,575…

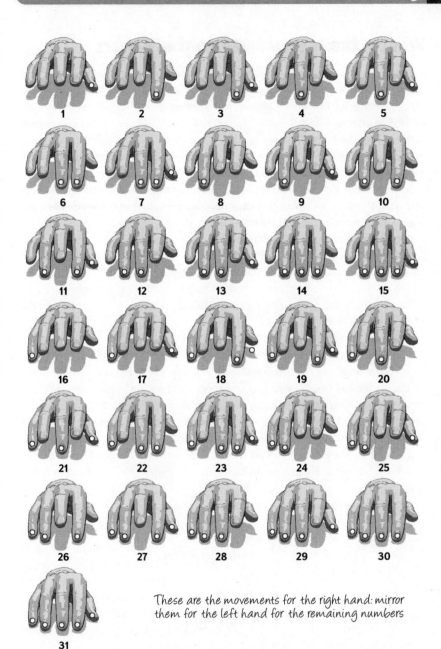

These are the movements for the right hand: mirror them for the left hand for the remaining numbers

What is the biggest number of all?

It's hard to envisage even a million of something.* A million pound coins, for instance, would form a stack 2 miles high. A million seconds is about 11.5 days. If you counted at the rate of one number a second with no breaks, it would take you 12 days to get to a million.

At the same rate, it would take 32 years to count to a billion. In Britain and some other places a billion used to be a million million, but these days pretty much everybody accepts a billion as 1,000 million (1 with 9 noughts).

A trillion is a thousand billion, i.e. 1 with 12 noughts. You can continue on upwards, if you're so inclined, with quadrillions, quintillions and so on – see page 128 for some more of this stuff. But it's all a bit unwieldy, so scientists and mathematicians prefer to work in powers.

In the 1940s, mathematician Edward Kasner asked his nine-year-old nephew what he should call 1 with 100 noughts. The boy said 'Googol', and the name has stuck. It's a big number, greater even than the number of atoms in the entire Universe. It's so big it has lent its name, slightly adapted, to the most popular internet search engine.

Even bigger still is the googolplex, 1 followed by a googol of noughts, a number so mind-bogglingly enormous you can't even write it down in full. (One of the many throw-away gags in *The Simpsons* has the family going into a multi-screen cinema called the Googolplex. Just one more fact you can annoy your kids with while they're trying to watch the cartoon.) A googolplex has more *digits* than there are atoms in the Universe. True, mathematicians have played around with larger numbers still, but they're just showing off.

It's hard to know where, in all this, a zillion comes. Bigger than a trillion, obviously, but not as big as a gazillion, which itself can surely be only a fraction of a squillion.

But let's try anyway. To help you visualize a million, the page opposite has 2,500 dots on it. If every page in this book were printed just like this one, the book would contain a million dots. But our publishers insisted on words as well.

Look at the page of dots for one minute. Can you see a face in it?

No? We couldn't either.

How long is a piece of string?

Don't be silly.

Number names

How many zeroes in a billion? Why do we talk about *kilo*grammes, but *milli*metres? Why aren't there 1000 bytes in a kilobyte? All can be revealed...

Name	Prefix	Symbol	Power	Number
septillion	yotta	Y	10^{24}	1 000 000 000 000 000 000 000 000
sextillion	zetta	Z	10^{21}	1 000 000 000 000 000 000 000
quintillion	exa	E	10^{18}	1 000 000 000 000 000 000
quadrillion	peta	P	10^{15}	1 000 000 000 000 000
trillion	tera	T	10^{12}	1 000 000 000 000
billion	giga	G	10^{9}	1 000 000 000
million	mega	M	10^{6}	1 000 000
thousand	kilo	k	10^{3}	1 000
hundred	hecto	h	10^{2}	100
ten	deca	da	10^{1}	10
one			10^{0}	1
tenth	deci	d	10^{-1}	0.1
hundredth	centi	c	10^{-2}	0.01
thousandth	milli	m	10^{-3}	0.001
millionth	micro	μ	10^{-6}	0.000 001
billionth	nano	n	10^{-9}	0.000 000 001
trillionth	pico	p	10^{-12}	0.000 000 000 001
this is	femto	f	10^{-15}	0.000 000 000 000 001
starting to	atto	a	10^{-18}	0.000 000 000 000 000 001
get really	zepto	z	10^{-21}	0.000 000 000 000 000 000 001
silly now	yocto	y	10^{-24}	0.000 000 000 000 000 000 000 001

Although computers use the same prefixes – kilo, mega, giga, tera – the numbers aren't exactly the same. This is because computers use 10th powers of 2, rather than powers of 10: and 2^{10} is 1024, not 1000.

In 1998 the International Electrotechnical Commission moved to rename these prefixes to kibi, mebi, gibi and tibi, for 'kilobinary', 'megabinary' and so on. Yeah, right. Like that's *really* going to make it less confusing.

kilobyte	2^{10}	1 024
megabyte	2^{20}	1 048 576
gigabyte	2^{30}	1 073 741 824
terabyte	2^{40}	1 099 511 627 776

Bits and bytes

Computer storage is measured in 'Mb', which is short for megabytes. So why does your 'superfast' 20Mb broadband connection sometimes seem so slow?

The answer is that '20Mb' stands, confusingly, for 20 mega*bits* per second, not 20 mega*bytes*. A 'bit' is a single piece of binary information: a 1 or a 0. There are eight bits in a byte, so a 20Mb connection, running at 20 mega*bits* per second, will therefore transmit data at just 2.5 mega*bytes* per second.

Except the cheating doesn't stop there. For every 8 bits that a cable modem streams down the wire, it automatically adds in two extra 'framing' bits, one at the beginning and one at the end, so the receiving computer can tell where each byte starts and stops. In other words, for each byte of data, the modem has to send 10 bits in all. So in fact, a 20Mb connection actually delivers a paltry 2 megabytes per second. What a swindle!

Roman numerals

Before the Western world adopted the Arabic system of numbering we use today, the Romans used systems of letters to stand for numbers. They are:

I=1   V=5   X=10   L=50   C=100   D=500   M=1000

It's difficult enough when writing dates – the year 1897, for instance, would be written MDCCCXCVII – but almost impossible for doing maths. Try multiplying LXXV by VIII in your head and see how long it takes you, compared with the simple 75 × 8.

If you add the first six Roman numerals together – DCLXVI – you get 666, a figure referred to in the Bible as the Number of the Beast. Spooky? Or just coincidence?

The figure 4 is always written as IV, except on clock faces, where it's almost always written as IIII. This is a hangover from medieval Latin: the earliest surviving clock face is in Wells Cathedral, dating from before 1392, and shows four o'clock in this fashion.

One of the very few exceptions is the clock face on the Palace of Westminster, better known as Big Ben, which shows the figure four as IV.

World facts and figures

Biggest wave: A wave 1,720ft high swept over Lituya Bay, Alaska, in 1958

Richest: The USA has 442 billionaires, not all of whom work for Google

Highest waterfall: Water at Angel Falls, Venezuela, drops 3,281 feet

Highest (1): Mt Mauna Loa, in Hawaii, rises 2.5 miles above sea level – but there's another 3.7 miles of it underwater

Wettest: Mt Waialeale in Hawaii has an annual rainfall of 472 inches

Driest: The Pacific coast of Chile, between Antofagasta and Arica, records just 0.004 inches of rain a year. It hasn't rained in the Atacama Desert for 400 years

Greatest river: The Amazon pours 4.2 million cubic feet *per second* into the Atlantic Ocean

Hottest: El Aziza reached 136°F (57.8°C) in 1922

Least populated: Mongolia has an average population of under 4.5 people per square mile

Most populated: Monaco has a population of 42,650 per square mile

Largest city: Shanghai, China, has a population of over 23 million

Deepest ocean: Challenger Deep is 6.7 miles below the sea surface

Highest (2): Mt Everest is 5.5 miles high

Lowest: The Dead Sea is 1300 feet below sea level

Biggest volcano: Taupo, New Zealand, erupted 33 billion tons of lava in AD 190

Coldest: The East Antarctic ice sheet is 3 miles thick. Lowest recorded temperature was -129°F (-89.4°C)

The speed of light

Light zips along at 186,000 miles a second. That's 700 million miles an hour, getting on for a million times faster than the speed of sound. In the time it takes a ball dropped from 6 feet to reach the ground, light could bounce all the way around the Earth five times.

Unless it's directed through a fibre optic cable, however, light travels in straight lines. Its speed may seem instant but it isn't. It takes light 1.28 seconds to reach us from the Moon and eight minutes from the Sun, 93 million miles away.

Our nearest star other than the Sun, Proxima Centauri, is 25 trillion miles away. As light travels 5.9 trillion miles in a year, it takes 4.2 years for its light to reach us (that is, 4.2 light years). When we look at the stars, we are looking at the past. It is 30,000 light years from the centre of our own galaxy, for instance, while the nearest galaxy to ours, Andromeda, is 2.2 million light years away.

The most distant objects astronomers have been able to see are about 13 billion light years away. That means that the light we see now left there 13 billion years ago, just 700 million years after the Universe was born.

How to calculate the speed of light

Yes, it can be done, with no more exotic equipment than a microwave and a plate of grated cheese. For microwaves, like radio waves, move at the speed of light.

Take the turntable out of the microwave, spread the cheese evenly on the plate, and cook for around 20 seconds (until the cheese starts to melt). You'll see some

hot spots of melted cheese among the raw stuff: measure the distance between these, in centimetres. You'll find a predominant distance, probably between 6 and 12 cm, depending on your model. This corresponds to half the wavelength of the microwave. If you multiply the full wavelength by the number of times it travels that distance in a second, known as the frequency, you get the speed of light.

But how do you know the frequency? Fortunately, microwave

manufacturers provide this information for you. Turn the microwave around and look at the back. You'll find a label specifying the frequency of the microwave: it's generally around 2450 MHz.

All you have to do now is multiply the distance (in metres, so divide your centimetres by 100) by the wavelength, and that's the speed of light.

Our microwave produced an average distance of 6 cm, which means a wavelength of 12 cm (0.12 metres). Multiplying that by 2450 MHz gives a figure of 294. The 'M' in MHz stands for a million (see page 128): so the speed of light comes out at 294,000,000 metres per second.

In fact, the real speed of light is 299,800,000 metres per second, so our calculations are pretty close!

Are we there yet?

How fast can rockets travel?

Although light travels at 700 million miles an hour, our chemically powered spaceships are somewhat slower. The International Space Station orbits the Earth at a mere 17,000 miles an hour. The *Voyager* space probe, launched in 1977, was the first man-made spacecraft to leave the Solar System and is still out there, travelling at 38,000 miles an hour. At that speed it would take 76,000 years to reach the nearest star, Proxima Centauri, and 500 million years to the centre of our own Galaxy.

Scientists tell us that no matter how fast spaceships go, they will never be able to travel faster than light. 'Warp speed' and interstellar travel are therefore likely, for some time to come at least, to be nothing more than science fiction.

But science fiction often becomes science fact, like the solar-powered ion engine which propelled the experimental probe *Deep Space One*. Sending out a stream of high-speed particles, it could only accelerate at 15 mph per day, the thrust of its engine being no more powerful than a piece of paper would feel resting in your hand. But that thrust – 10 times as efficient as conventional rockets – was constant and eventually got *Deep Space One* up to a speed of 35,000 miles an hour. All that from a propulsion system not unlike the exchange of electrons that gives you a shock when you touch metal after walking on a thick carpet (see page 12).

Human facts: hair...

There are thought to be over 100,000 hairs on the average human head, growing at the rate of 15 centimetres a year.

A German scientist once went to the trouble of counting the hair on women's heads (at least, that was his excuse at the time). He discovered that blonde women have more hairs (140,000 strands) than brown (110,000), black (108,000) or redheads (90,000).

Sadly, many Dads will find the number of hairs on their own heads declining as the years advance. Whether hair loss is directly related to parenthood has yet to be scientifically proven.

...bones...

You start off with over 300 bones, but they fuse together as you grow. As an adult, you have 206 bones in your body, more than half of them in your hands and feet. Oddly, humans and giraffes have the same number of bones in their necks. The giraffe's are just that bit longer.

...sneezes...

A sneeze travels at around 100 mph, faster than a hurricane. It's also impossible to sneeze with your eyes open.

...blood...

Your heart beats around 40 million times a year. If you live 70 years, that will mean almost 3 billion beats. Every day, it pumps the equivalent of 2,000 gallons of blood around your body.

If all the blood vessels in the body were joined end to end, they would stretch 100,000 miles for an adult (60,000 for a child). That's enough to go around the Earth four times.

...and guts

If it were removed from the body, the small intestine would stretch to a length of over 6.5 metres.

9 Puzzles, tricks and jokes

SETTING YOUR CHILDREN PUZZLES is a great way to help expand their minds and hone their skills in logic and deduction. We've included both quickfire questions and mind-numbingly tricky teasers, which are guaranteed to test their brainpower and their tenacity.

Fun though it is to watch kids' brains working, they need to be entertained as well as educated. So here's a selection of riddles and jokes that will make them laugh, groan or – in some cases – merely gaze at you in bafflement. But don't be surprised if you hear an outbreak of giggling from their bedroom later that night, when they finally get the point of one of your more obscure gags.

Magic always fascinates children. They want to believe in it. And you want them to believe, because magic keeps your mortal status hidden for a few more years. So we've got tricks ranging from the truly astounding to the downright dumb. We've also included a couple of great mind-reading routines in which they, not you, can be the stars of the show.

Urban legends

Once bedtime fairy stories become a little passé, move on to urban legends. Most kids love these frequently spooky tales, particularly as they aren't about some woodcutter's daughter who lived once upon a time in a far-off land. They're usually about real places, real people and real lives; and while some say urban legends aren't real, we say there aren't that many houses made of gingerbread.

The key to urban myth telling is embellishment: the more you can do to make them relevant to your children's experience, the better. Rather than repeat these shaggy dog stories in full, we're listing the key moments to keep you on track. How local and scary you make them is up to you.

The choking Doberman

- A dark, stormy night (it usually is).
- Woman alone. Thinks she hears a noise.
- It's her Doberman (could be your own breed, but usually a Doberman). It's having trouble breathing.
- She rushes him to the vet. He tells her there will have to be an emergency operation. She should go home and wait for his call.
- Home, she gets ready for bed. She feels unnerved without the dog there.
- Phone rings. It's the vet, telling her to get out of the house immediately.
- As she emerges, the police arrive, sirens blazing.
- They rush inside and drag out a burglar hiding under the bed, who's clutching his bloody hand. The vet found the obstruction in the dog's throat: it was two bloody, severed fingers.

The breakdown in the woods

- A dark night, possibly even a little stormy.
- A couple driving through woods. On the radio, they hear of an escaped murderer.
- The car breaks down in a remote location. (Nobody had mobile phones when the story first appeared – they'd find that difficult to believe! – so you'll have to explain that it's an area with no reception.)
- The boyfriend says he'll go for help, telling her to lock the doors.
- He's gone a very long time, and she gets frightened. Then she hears a tapping

noise on the roof of the car. Whenever the wind blows, there it is again... tap, tap, tap.

- She is terrified. Daren't get out to look. Finally falls asleep. Woken in morning by a policeman knocking on her window. Tells her to get out of the car and, whatever she does, she mustn't look back.
- As she's getting into the police car, she can't help herself, and turns. Hanging from the tree is her boyfriend, dead, his dangling feet knocking on the roof of the car... tap, tap, tap.

The dead diver

- Massive forest fire, despite the darkness and storminess of the night.
- Police puzzled to find a corpse dressed in scuba gear, tanks, wet suit, flippers, face mask – the lot.
- Post-mortem reveals that he didn't die from heat or flames, but from massive internal injuries.
- Corpse identified from dental records. Been reported missing while out diving off the coast six miles away (distance doesn't matter, but sounds more realistic if you give precise figures).
- Discovered that a fire-fighting helicopter scooping up water had inadvertently picked him up too. The chopper pilot didn't hear his screams and dumped him on the flames.

The mangled rabbit

- Man goes into his garden and finds his dog with a piece of mangled fur in its mouth. It's stormy, and also dark, so he has difficulty identifying it.
- Turns out to be dead rabbit from next door.
- Man is horrified, thinks his dog has killed it.
- Spends an hour washing and drying the rabbit to make it look like it died of natural causes.
- Places rabbit back in neighbour's cage and sneaks back indoors.
- Neighbour comes home from work, finds rabbit in cage. General commotion, grief-stricken wailing, etc.
- Man looks over fence, commiserates with neighbour over the death of the pet.
- 'I can't understand it,' explains the neighbour. 'The rabbit died last night, and I buried it this morning.'

Puzzle 1: The three children

This simple puzzle still catches most kids out the first time because, even though you entreat them to listen carefully, they don't:

John's mother has three children. The eldest is called April, the middle child is called May. What's the youngest called?

Nearly all kids – and a surprising number of adults – barely pause before replying 'June'. The correct answer, of course, is John.

Puzzle 2: Which switch?

Some puzzles can be solved immediately; others necessitate rather more brain wracking. This deliciously fiendish, but hugely satisfying, puzzle falls into the latter category. Most children, and adults, will need a helping hand to get the answer.

How many Dads does it take to change me?

Inside a room is a light bulb. Outside are three switches in the off position. There is no way to see into the room without opening the door. How do you work out which switch turns on the light? You can fiddle with the switches as much as you like, but you're only allowed to open the door to the room once.

You will invariably have to fend off all manner of intriguing and ridiculous suggestions. No, you can't slide mirrors under the door. Nor can you pack ice around the bulb or install CCTV cameras in the room.

Explain that everything needed for the solution is in the question and encourage them to think about the physics of light bulbs. When you turn on a bulb, apart from it lighting up, what else happens? When they figure out that the bulb also gets hot, they're nearly there.

The solution is now straightforward. Turn on the first switch, wait a minute, then turn it off. Turn on the second switch and enter the room. If the bulb is on, the second switch is the one that did the job; if the bulb is off but warm, it's the first switch; if the bulb is off but cold, it must be the third switch that operates it.

Puzzle 3: The camel race

It always helps to listen to the precise wording of the question. This is particularly true in this puzzle.

> *Two princes are desperate to marry the Sultan's daughter. The Sultan invites them to attend him in a tent in the desert. He explains that the contest will be decided by a race: whichever prince's camel reaches the palace last shall marry his daughter. After just a moment's thought, the princes rush out and race to the palace, certain that the first to get there will win the Sultan's daughter's hand. What was their solution?*

One hump or two?

The first approach is usually to suggest that the princes ride as slowly as possible. But this is clearly no solution at all. The answer, of course, lies in the Sultan's exact phrasing: the winner is the prince whose camel is last.

The simple, kick-yourself-afterwards solution is that the princes jump onto each other's camels. If they win the race, their *camel* will not.

Puzzle 4: The hardware store

This is one of those really neat, compact puzzles that will have even mathematical geniuses scratching their heads in anguish, before – or if – they make that leap of imagination and get the answer right.

> *A man goes into a hardware store to buy some items for his house.*
> *'How much is one?' he asks, and is told '£3.'*
> *'How much for twelve?'*
> *'£6,' says the assistant.*
> *'And how much for two hundred?'*
> *'£9,' comes the reply.*
> *There are no bulk discounts involved. What is he buying?*

It's one of those duh! answers. He's buying house numbers.

Puzzle 5: Pick up the olive

...or the peanut, or cherry tomato, or even a ping pong ball. Any object that's more or less spherical, and small enough to fit inside a brandy glass, will do for this puzzle.

Place the olive on the table, and stand a brandy glass next to it. The glass has to be of the bowl variety, with an opening that's much narrower than the middle. The task is to get the olive into the glass without blowing it, tilting the table, or allowing it to be touched by any object other than the glass.

The solution, when everyone's given up, is splendid. Turn the brandy glass upside down over the olive, and move it rapidly in small circles, spinning the olive with it. The olive will run around the edge of the glass and, due to centrifugal force, rise up to the widest part: still spinning, you can now lift the glass off the table, with the olive still going around inside it, and turn it the right way up. Brilliant!

Puzzle 6: The logical explorers

Four logical explorers are captured by, as luck would have it, a tribe of logical cannibals. The cannibals tell them that they'll eat the explorers unless they solve a puzzle. And this is the puzzle.

The explorers are buried up to their necks in sand, three facing one way and one facing the other. There's a brick wall between explorer A and the other three.

You can't eat me,
I'm a vegetarian

A   B   C   D

The cannibals explain that four hats, two red and two blue, will be placed on the explorers at random. Each day the hats will be swapped around, and unless one of the explorers can tell the cannibals what colour hat he's wearing, that night's menu will feature explorer casserole.

The explorers can't see their own hats, nor can they turn their heads. They're not allowed to communicate with each other, and only one word can be spoken by the whole group. And yet, remarkably, each day one of them manages to shout out the colour of his hat. How?

Let's say explorers B and C both have blue hats. Then explorer D, knowing there are only two blue hats, knows his must be red – and shouts out that colour accordingly. But what if explorers B and C have different coloured hats? Explorer D can't then know the colour of his own hat.

And that's the clever part. Explorer C waits to hear what explorer D does. If he says nothing, then explorer C knows that he and explorer B must have different colour hats. He can see the colour of explorer B's hat, and so shouts out the opposite colour. Explorers A and B, in the meantime, say and do nothing. But beneath the sand you can be sure they're crossing their fingers.

Puzzle 7: Walking the dog

Some puzzles appear to be more complex than they really are. Often, it's simply a matter of thinking around the problem.

A man takes his dog for a walk in the park. He walks around a circular pond, which takes him exactly an hour. (It's a very big pond.) He has a stick which he throws for the dog, which the dog retrieves and brings back to him without breaking its run (it's a very well-trained dog). The dog runs at 10 miles an hour. If the man wants the dog to get the maximum amount of exercise, should he throw the stick in front of him, behind him, or across the other side of the pond?

They'll hate the answer: it doesn't make any difference.

The dog keeps running for as long as the man keeps walking. The man walks for an hour, in which time the dog runs 10 miles – no matter in which direction the man throws the stick.

Quickfire puzzles

Some of these simply require thinking through: with others, you'll need to allow your children to ask questions so you can guide them towards the correct solution. Feel free to give as many clues as you like!

● *A man stopped his car opposite a hotel and immediately knew that he was bankrupt. How?*
He was playing Monopoly.

● *Dad has 20 socks in his drawer, 10 black and 10 grey. If he dresses in the dark, how many does he have to take out to ensure that he has a pair?*
Three.

● *Which triangle is bigger, one that has sides of 2, 3 and 4 inches or one with sides of 3, 4 and 7 inches?*
The first. The second is a straight line.

● *Before Mount Everest was discovered, what was the highest mountain on Earth?*
Mount Everest.

● *A mountaineer climbed a mountain with a guide. But traversing a deep crevasse, the guide fell and disappeared from sight. Undaunted, the mountaineer carried on, and gave no thought to getting help. Why?*
The guide was a book.

● *A man buys several loaves of bread at £1 a loaf, and sells them at 20p a loaf. He does it again and again.*

Entirely as a result of this, he becomes a millionaire. How?
He started off as a billionaire, who decided to help the poor.

● *What five-letter word becomes shorter when you add two letters?*
Short.

● *Removing tonsils is a tonsillectomy. Removing an appendix is an appendectomy. What do you call it when a growth is removed from your head?*
A haircut.

● *You're in a race. Almost at the tape, you overtake the person who's second. What position do you finish?*
Second.

● *If two's company and three's a crowd, then what's four and five?*
Nine.

● *A man travels to work in London. His train to work travels at 100 miles an hour and the journey takes one hour 20 minutes. In the other direction, going at the same speed, the trip takes 80 minutes. Why?*
One hour 20 minutes and 80 minutes are the same amount of time.

If post is spelt POST and most is spelt MOST, how do you spell the word for what you put in a toaster?
Bread.

What invention lets you see through walls?
A window.

How much earth in cubic feet is there in a hole 1 foot by 1 foot by 1 foot?
None. It's a hole.

A farmer has four fields. In one, there are 8 haystacks, in the next 7, in the third 9 and in the last he has 11. If he puts them all together, how many haystacks will he have?
One. But it's a big one.

A greengrocer is 6 feet tall, has a 40-inch chest and wears size 13 shoes. What do you think he weighs?
Fruit and vegetables.

It's cold and you're hungry. You have only one match. In a room in your cabin is an oil lamp, a wood-burning stove and a candle. What do you light first?
The match.

Which is greater, six dozen dozen or half a dozen dozen?
Six dozen dozen is 12 times greater.

Which two numbers multiplied together give you 17?
One and 17.

A yacht is moored in the harbour. Over its side hangs a rope ladder, with its end just touching the water. Rungs of the ladder are one foot apart. If the tide rises at the rate of one foot an hour, how many of the rungs will be covered after six hours?
None. The ladder's fixed to the boat and rises with the tide.

There are five apples in a basket and five people in the room. How can you give an apple to each one and have one apple remain in the basket?
You give the basket with one apple in to the last person.

If three cats can kill three rats in three minutes, how long will it take 100 cats to kill 100 rats?
Three minutes.

A bus got lost and tried to drive under a low bridge. Unfortunately, it got stuck and couldn't move forwards or backwards. It was a schoolgirl on the bus who told the bus driver how they could free the vehicle. What was her solution?
Letting some air out of the tyres to lower the bus slightly.

What do you call a deer with no eyes?
No idea.

What do you call a deer with no eyes that's not moving?
Still no idea.

Knock knock

Children adore knock-knock jokes but, unless you can retaliate with a few well-chosen ones of your own, you may find yourself becoming reluctant to open the door. Here are just a handful of what we suspect are tens of thousands of knock-knock jokes, most of which your children will at some point try to tell you.

Danielle. *Danielle who?* (No answer). *DANIELLE WHO?* Danielle so loud, I heard you the first time.

Wendy. *Wendy who?* When de wind blows, de cradle will rock.

Lemon juice. *Lemon juice who?* Lemon introduce myself.

Mikey. *Mikey who?* Mikey has broken off in the lock.

Sam and Janet. *Sam and Janet who?* Sam and Janet evening, you may see a stranger…

Jess. *Jess who?* Jess checking you're in.

Stopwatch. *Stopwatch who?* Stop watcha doing and let me in.

Irish stew. *Irish stew who?* Irish stew in the name of the law.

Matthew. *Matthew who?* Matthew laces are undone.

Sarah. *Sarah who?* Sarah doctor in the house?

Ash. *Ash who?* Bless you.

Spell. *Spell who?* OK, w…h…o.

Wurlitzer. *Wurlitzer who?* Wurlitzer one for the money, two for the show…

Scott. *Scott who?* Scotta be some better jokes than this.

Dee. *Dee who?* Dee-sappear and stop telling me knock-knock jokes.

Dad. *Dad who?* Da doo ron ron ron, da doo ron ron. What d'you mean you don't understand it? It's a famous song, from the 60s. I'll sing you a bit of it… where's everybody gone?

When you've had enough knock-knock jokes to last you a lifetime and have to put an end to them or risk losing your sanity, there's an easy way to kill them off. If anyone says 'Knock knock', simply answer 'Come in'.

The personal knock–knock joke

Instead of opening the door to a vast number of people you don't know – and frankly don't wish to know – why not personalize the knock-knock joke, tailoring it to your child's own name?

Using our own children as an example, Freddy's very own knock-knock joke would be, *'Freddy who?'*, '"fraid he can't come, so he sent me instead.' Joe equals 'D'you...', Izzy translates as 'Is he...', Joseph becomes, 'Just have...' and Connie's joke uses 'Can he...'.

Any suggestion that we chose those names for our children because they were particularly suited to being used in knock-knock jokes is, of course, wholly without foundation.

The wrong answer

Almost everyone (child and adult) gets this seemingly simple maths problem, which must be done in the head, wrong.

Start with 1,000 and add 40. Now add another 1,000. Now add 30. Then another 1,000. Now add 20. Then another 1,000. Lastly, add 10.

What is the total? Most people end up with 5,000 but the answer is actually 4,100. Without a calculator or pen and paper, people tend to round it up wrongly.

The lateral–thinking dentist

A woman had just moved to a new town and needed a dentist. There were only two dentists to choose from. One had a beautiful new surgery, he was a charming man, and his teeth were white and regular. The other surgery was desperately in need of paint, the dentist was grumpy, to a large extent because his crooked teeth hurt him. She chose to go to the second dentist. Why?

It's one of those puzzles that looks like there has to be a trick, but really there isn't. It may take some guidance to help your child work out that each dentist treats the other one's teeth – so it's the one with bad teeth who's the better dentist.

Puzzling pachyderms

Tell your child to pick a number from 1 to 10. Multiply it by 9 and then subtract 5. Add the digits, to end up with a one-digit number.

With numbers corresponding to letters of the alphabet (i.e. A=1, B=2), tell them to find the right letter of the alphabet for their number and to think of a country that begins with that letter. Then think of an animal that begins with the *second* letter of that country. Then think of a colour associated with that animal.

Look at your child quizzically, and say: 'But there *are* no grey elephants in Denmark.' This is almost always the combination people end up with (unless they've played before and are deliberately trying to trip you up) and the sense of wonder is priceless.

The black hole

Black holes can swallow things up – in this instance, a pencil. When you do this trick, your child's mouth should open wide with astonishment.

With one or two kids seated to your left (or your right if you're left-handed), get out a sheet of paper and draw several concentric circles, perhaps a few arrows, all leading to the magic black hole in the middle. Explain that anything touching a black hole will be swallowed up. Warn them that, no matter what they do, they mustn't touch it. They should even take care if they stare at it.

Prepare your arm movement...   *...take a practice swing...*

Without taking your own eyes off it, silently roll up your shirt sleeves, pick up the pencil and study the black hole intently. Perhaps alter a mark or two on the paper. Build up the anticipation of what you're about to do.

Lean over the black hole and, with your finger and thumb, hold the pencil just above it, point upwards. As you go through the count, your hand should go up and down as if you're readying a darts throw. In fact, you're actually preparing to lodge the pencil in that handy nook at the top of your ear (sorry, it isn't a real black hole).

Say '*One*', then bring the pencil up and onto the top of your ear. You are range-finding the spot. On '*Two*', bring it down to hover over the black hole, then back up, slide into a secure position. You can take your time here; attention is most focussed on the counts, not what's happening in between. It will only increase the tension. On '*Three*', bring your (empty) hand down fast to the same position above the circle.

Freeze for a moment or two then, slowly, examine your own hand – and the other one – as if you're trying to figure out what's happened. You might even turn the paper over and examine where the hole in the table ought to be.

Hunt for the pencil with the kids. Look under the table so you're out of sight, and retrieve the pencil from its hiding place, perhaps even producing it out from the underside of the black hole. If there are others in the room, chances are that – only half paying attention – they will have caught the count and the pencil's disappearance, reinforcing the 'magic' of what you've done.

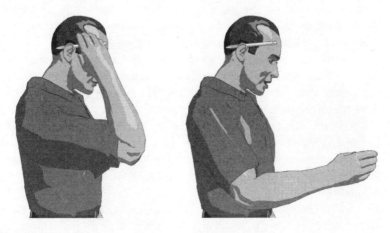

..tuck the pencil behind your ear...   *...and slam down on the table*

Mind-reading for beginners

Despite being incredibly simple to carry off, this really is an impressive mind-reading trick. It can easily be performed by you and a child although, once they've got the hang of it, you risk being dropped from the act if your pupil decides they'd prefer to perform with another stooge. It's a tough game, showbiz.

The mind-reader is either blindfolded, or else turns so that they can't see their partner. In full view of the audience, the assistant (Dad) holds up a number of fingers from one to ten and asks the mind-reader to say how many. Time and again, the mind-reader will announce the correct number.

The key to the trick is the way the question is put to the mind-reader: it should have the same number of *words* as there are fingers being held up. If there are seven fingers, then the question should be, 'How many fingers am I holding up?' If there are three, you can ask 'How many now?'

Clearly, the routine will only work once a child is familiar with the difference between syllables and words. Ensure that the mind-reader has their hands concealed. If they repeat the question while ticking off the words on their fingers, you're going to astound nobody but an elderly relative who is particularly slow on the uptake.

As with all such tricks, leave your audience wanting more. Doing it more than four or five times (fewer with adults) will greatly increase the risk of them guessing the secret.

Advanced mind-reading

With the mind-reader out of the room, the audience collectively decides upon an object. Returning, the mind-reader concentrates as his assistant (Dad) calls out various objects, seemingly at random. After saying 'no' to all the red herrings, the mind-reader will quite confidently say 'yes' when the assistant names the object agreed upon.

After doing this a couple of times, some of the audience will be convinced they know how it's done. The act gets more impressive still as you adapt it to take account of their suggestions. If they think the assistant is giving hand signals to the magician, have the assistant keep their hands behind their back. If they think it's somehow related to the object being chosen, let them pick somebody's shoes. The mind-reader will still choose the right pair.

How is it done? Alarmingly simple. The magician merely says 'yes' to the first thing named *after a black object*. Yup, that's all it is. But don't tell. With luck, you can keep this mind-reading act going for years, a bond of complicity between you and your child against the rest of the world.

The coin's fantastic voyage

Get a coin to travel from one foot to the other – inside your body.

Before anybody's looking, slip a coin under your left foot. If you decide to do the trick with bare feet, then removing your shoes and socks could be a good cover for this. Take a similar coin, visibly place it under your right foot and explain that you will make it work its way up your right leg and down the other one.

As you simulate this happening, twitch and twist as if something is passing through your body, going up one leg and down the other. When you've given the impression that it has reached your left foot, have it travel all the way back again until, pretending you expect wild applause, you lift your right foot and show that it has arrived back where it started.

The children will no doubt protest that this is no trick at all. The coin hasn't moved. With mock indignation, you start again, showing it travelling up your right leg and down your left. Pause for effect, then lift your left foot to show that the coin really has arrived there.

The only thing left to make your triumph complete is ensure that you spirit away the coin that's still under your right foot. A piece of Blu-Tack attached to the coin at the last moment will achieve this perfectly.

What do you call a fish with no eye?

All kids love telling jokes. If they're particularly keen, being on the receiving end is like attending a stand-up comedy venue on a wide-open mike night. You must be able to retaliate. But if the only joke you can recall is the one you heard in the pub about the priest, the hooker and the pineapple, the chances are that it will prove unsuitable.

Here's a selection, sometimes truncated for brevity, that will help you retaliate while still keeping your PG rating. We know some are old chestnuts. Heck, some of these jokes were old when *we* were children. But old to us is very often new to our kids.

- What do you call a girl with two toilets on her head? Lulu. (Be warned that this could spark off a series of 'What do you call...?' jokes.)

- What's grey and has a trunk? A mouse going on holiday.

- What's brown and has a trunk? A mouse coming back from holiday.

- What's large, grey and doesn't matter? An irrelephant.

- What was Beethoven doing when they opened his coffin? Decomposing.

- A man rushes into a doctor's office.
  'Doctor, you've got to help me. I think I'm turning into a moth.'
  'You need a psychiatrist. Why did you come to me?'
  'I couldn't help myself. Your light was on.'

  Ouch!

- What's green and sings? Elvis Parsley.

- What is orange and sounds like a parrot? A carrot.

- What's red and stupid? A blood clot.

- What's red and smells of paint? Red paint.

- What do you call a boomerang that won't come back? A stick.

- Two fish in a tank. One turns to the other and says,
  'Do you know how to drive this thing?'

- Why do ducks have webbed feet? To stamp out fires.

- Why do elephants have flat feet? To stamp out burning ducks.

- A woodworm goes into a pub and says 'Is the bartender here?' (You'll get this one eventually.)

- A Frenchman goes into a bar with a duck on his head. The barman says, 'Blimey, where did you get that?' The duck says, 'Paris – they've got millions of them.'

- A doctor tells his patient, 'I've got some good news and some bad news.'
'What's the good news?'
'You've only got 24 hours to live.'
'That's the *good news*? That's terrible! What's the bad news?'
'I should have told you yesterday.'

- What do Mack the Knife, Winnie the Pooh and Attila the Hun have in common? The same middle name.

- I've got a step ladder. It's nice, but I'm sad I don't know my real ladder.

- Man goes to the doctor with a strawberry growing out of the top of his head. Doctor says, 'Let me give you some cream for that.'

- What do you call a fish with no eye?
'Fsh'.

I see no chips

- Roses are red,
Violets are green;
Not only am I colour blind,
I'm a really bad poet as well.

- A little girl walks into a pet shop and asks in a sweet lisp, 'Excuthe me, mithter. Do you keep wittle wabbits?' The shopkeeper smiles at her, and asks, 'Do you want a wittle white wabby or a soft, fuwwy black wabby or maybe that cute wittle brown wabby over there?' She examines the rabbits, then says to him, 'To be honest, I don't fink my pyfon's all that picky.'

- Why did Robin Hood steal from the rich? Because the poor didn't have any money.

- Why can't you starve in a desert? Because of all the sand which is there.

- What nationality is Santa Claus? North Polish.

- What do you call a snowman with a sun tan? A puddle.

Maths and magic

This maths-based trick requires a little preparation, but it's a real humdinger. The way the trick works is that *any* three-figure number can be juggled to create just one answer, 1089.

First, choose any thick book. Flip through it and, as you do so, pause on page 108 and make a note of the ninth word on the page. It should be the ninth word of the main text, ignoring any headings or page numbers. So, for example, the ninth word on page 108 of *Ultimate Dad Stuff* is 'night'.

Write down the word on a piece of paper, and seal it in an envelope. Give this to an audience member to look after.

Start off with some guff about your supernatural powers, and then ask for a three digit number with all the digits different. Get one of your audience to write this down both forwards and backwards. You need to subtract the smaller from the larger. Although you can do it yourself, if the kids are old enough, it's better to get them to do it. You will now have a number with 2 or 3 digits, with a 9 in the tens column.

Now write this number down backwards. If it only has two digits, add a zero at the end. Add this to the result of the first calculation and, miraculously, you will get an answer of 1089. If not, somebody's maths needs a little work!

Here's an example: if your audience chooses 237, then reverse that to get 732. Subtracting the smaller from the larger results in 495. Reversing this gives you 594: add these two together to get 1089.

Tell a member of your audience to pick up the book, turn to page 108 and read out the ninth word on the page, telling them to exclude any headings or page numbers, just as you did. Make sure they get the right word!

You can now tell them to open the envelope, and they should be gobsmacked when they find that word written inside.

Pop-up popcorn

Here's one to try on the kids in the cinema. It works particularly well during scary scenes. As they'll no doubt expect you to go off and get the drinks and popcorn, you'll have plenty of time to tear a hole in the bottom of the popcorn carton.

Once some of the popcorn has been devoured and the children are absorbed in a particularly tense moment, work your hand up through the hole. When the next mitt delves in for popcorn, grab it. No doubt they'll scream their heads off but you can bet that the next time they go to the movies with their mates, they'll be trying it for themselves.

A vegetable kids do love

Answer these questions as quickly as possible.

What's 3 + 7?
What's 4 + 6?
What's 8 + 2?
Name a vegetable.

Did you answer 'carrot'? Almost everyone does. If you write it down first, your kids will be even more impressed that you could read their minds.

The glass of water trick

Place a glass of water on the table, and lay a hat down over it. Tell your child you can drink the water without touching the glass. Then crawl beneath the table and make slurping sounds. Come back up, wiping your mouth as if you've drunk the water.

When your child lifts the hat to check whether you really have achieved the impossible, pick up the glass of water and drink it. There you go – you've drunk all the water without touching the hat. And in the process, you've probably ensured your child will grow up always making certain they read the small print.

String escapology

Cut lengths of string into pairs four or five feet long. Sort the challengers into twos. One should have the ends of a piece of string tied to both wrists. The other should tie a piece to one wrist, then pass the string over their partner's string before tying the other end to their free wrist so that they are roped together. Then tie yourself to your partner in the same way, ensuring there is just enough slack in the loops on their wrists to pass string through.

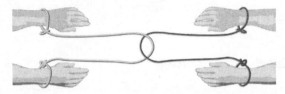

Tell the others that all they have to do is unlink their string from their partner's. They will go through some wonderfully entertaining contortions, turning back to back, stepping through the string, writhing this way and that.

When they've finally had enough and realize it isn't so simple after all, show them how it's done. Take the centre of your string, and pass it through the loop on your partner's wrist and over their hand. With one bound, you'll be free.

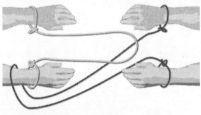

1. Hang string over partner's wrist

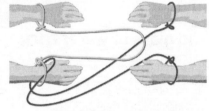

2. Push through partner's loop

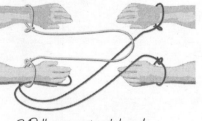

3. Pull over partner's hand

4. Your string will come loose

Keeping an idiot amused

On one side of a sheet of paper, write, 'How do you keep an idiot amused for hours?', adding 'P.T.O.' (Please Turn Over) at the bottom of the paper.

Write exactly the same thing on the other side then wait for someone to pick it up. Chances are that they will turn it over, then over again then, with luck, a couple more times before they realize that they are the idiot being kept amused!

The severed finger

Under one end of a large-sized matchbox, make a finger-sized hole. Then dust your index finger with talcum powder to give it a white, lifeless look, and poke it through the hole where it should nestle on a bed of cotton wool. If you want to go the whole hog, red food colouring can be added to the 'torn' base of the finger.

Close the box as well as you can (you can always cut a notch out of the outer shell) and then, with a suitably gory tale about how you found the severed digit, show your victim the finger. Having the finger on its side keeps your hand in a reasonably natural position, particularly if you disguise your digitally impaired state with your other hand.

As your victim stares, have the finger quiver and then rise to life.

To make blood more convincing, you should experiment with adding a brown tinge through the addition of a little green colouring.

If you're after truly realistic blood for plays or Halloween, mix up corn flour and water then add some golden syrup. Add the red and green colouring to the mixture and, if it isn't going anywhere near young mouths, a little washing-up liquid too. Take care with food colouring, though. It can stain clothing, and your reputation as a responsible Dad.

Is it a bird?

This is a great practical joke to play with your kids rather than on them. When out in an area with lots of people, all stare upwards at something that seems to fascinate you, occasionally pointing. Almost invariably, others will try to see what you're all looking at. They may even stop to get a better look.

If you manage to attract a few people, that's your cue to vamoose, leaving a group behind, none of whom wants to admit that they can't see what the others are so obviously looking at.

The mysterious pendulum

Kids usually like spooky stuff. So why not introduce them to a magic pendulum? It doesn't need to be anything more sophisticated than a weight on the end of six inches or so of string, or a necklace with a charm on it. Something pointy and not too heavy is best.

If you want to go the whole mystical hog, you can use ancient golden thread (picture wire) and a supernatural crystal (bits of an old chandelier you never got round to throwing away would be ideal). Turn down the lights and strew a few candles around to enhance the mood.

With their elbow resting on the table, the subject should hold the pendulum in one hand with the bob dangling just above the surface.

Get them to keep their hand still and concentrate hard on the bob. They should see if they can control it using only the hidden powers of their mind. If it begins moving, suggest they try to make it swing back and forward. Then sideways. How about in a circle? Now the other way. Now make it stop on command.

The weird thing is that, however hard you try not to move your hand, it does somehow make the pendulum do what your brain wants it to.

Once the pendulum can be controlled, things can get stranger still. Draw a circle with 'yes' at the top and bottom and 'no' at either side and ask the power of the pendulum to answer some questions.

Think of a number up to 10, then suspend your pendulum in a glass. Think about the number and the pendulum will swing until it clinks out the number and then mysteriously stop. (Well, it did when we tried it!)

You can make up various games to invoke the power of the pendulum, such as hiding an object under one of several cups and seeing if the pendulum can find it. Sadly, it's not much use when you've lost the car keys or the TV remote.

10 Fun and games

AT SOME POINT, even the most indoor-loving Dad is going to have to step outside. It may involve taking the kids to the park, or the beach, or just mucking about in the garden: but there comes a time when the telly has to go off, and the Great Outdoors has to be faced in all its glory.

Don't worry. If you're one of those Dads for whom an exciting game of football involves a beer, a TV and an armchair, don't panic. Many of the games in this chapter entail little or no physical exercise on your part, although with luck, the little darlings will tire themselves out. As well as some that might be unfamiliar, we've also got some old favourites, injecting a spark of new life into them with some novel twists.

We've also included a set of indoor games that will turn a wet afternoon on its head. The emphasis here is on group and team activities, so there's plenty to choose from to keep your child's next birthday party bubbling along happily.

Tag

This must be one of the oldest and simplest of kids' games. The person who is 'It' chases the others. If they catch anyone, they yell out 'You're It' and that person then becomes 'It'.

There are, however, plenty of variations on the theme, each with different names depending on where they were learned. In *Freeze Tag*, whoever is touched does not become 'It', but freezes in place and can be unfrozen again if one of the free players touches them. Along similar lines, a player who is tagged must stand with their legs apart and can only be freed if a player crawls through their legs. In some quarters, this is known as *Dirty Nappy Tag* or *Stuck in the Mud*.

Your turn to crawl through next!

Hospital Tag requires a tagged player to hold the spot where they were touched with one hand. They are now 'It', but must keep their hand there while they try to tag other players. *Copycat Tag* requires every player to adopt the same posture, no matter how ridiculous, as 'It'. On sunny days, you can even play *Shadow Tag* where 'It' has to step on the shadows of the players in order to hand over the baton.

One variant, fondly remembered from our playground days, has players claiming sanctuary if they can get off the ground by standing or climbing on something. There is usually a set time limit, however, after which they can be tagged. Or the person who is 'It' might shout out a substance which will make players safe, such as 'Metal' or 'Plastic'. Anyone touching something of that material, though only one player per item, is safe.

In *Snake Tag*, for which you need a minimum of six players, each player holds the player in front around the waist. The head must try to tag the tail, a game that is as much fun to watch as it is to play.

French cricket

'French' and 'cricket'. Not two words you usually expect to find in close proximity. Yet *French cricket* is a great game, particularly suited to the beach. Unlike cricket proper, it's easy to pick up, doesn't require the players to be dressed in white and, best of all, it doesn't matter if people get bored and wander off or new ones turn up desperate to play.

Having gathered four players or more, all you need is a tennis ball and a cricket bat, preferably a small one, though you could use a tennis racquet or even a bit of driftwood at a pinch. The batsman, circled by the other players, holds the bat vertically, turning on the spot to face whichever fielder has the ball. That player should bowl underarm in an attempt either to hit the batsman's legs below the knee (they are the wicket) or to get them to hit the ball up for a catch.

Get the batsman out and you take over. As long as the ball is bowled underarm, it's perfectly acceptable to fake throws, hoping the batsman will leave their legs undefended for the real throw. Some people insist that the batsman cannot move their feet at all, making deliveries from the rear somewhat tricky to defend.

If you're playing on sand, a circle can be drawn out to mark a boundary. Get the ball over this and you score six if it doesn't touch the ground; four if it does. There are various ways to score runs. You can mark a spot that must be run to or, alternatively, the batsman must pass the bat around their body as many times as he can before a fielder grabs the ball. One version allows fielders to pass the ball to anyone to bowl but, if this is combined with a ban on the batsman turning, the chances are somebody could end up in traction.

Blow football

It's all too easy to forget just how great some simple games can be. You've got straws, you've got a ping pong ball, you've got a table. You've got yourself a blow football stadium. Set up something at each end of the table for the goals, boxes on their side or books masquerading as goalposts, and start blowing.

Conkering all

Is the game of conkers dying out? It's certainly a great deal less visible these days, particularly as many schools have banned it on spurious safety grounds. The game goes back a long way. Didn't Julius Caesar say, 'I came, I saw, I conkered?' Isn't the proper translation of William I's nickname, 'William the Conkeror'?

You might splutter 'pish' or 'tosh' and point out that the horse chestnut tree didn't exist in the UK until the 16th century. But historians of the great game say earlier players used cobnuts or even snail shells.

Unlike so many modern sports, the entry cost is low. No special equipment is needed, just a deep brown shiny conker on the end of a piece of string or shoelace. Dad may want to help with the hole, using a nail or skewer. (A cordless drill takes the romance out of coring a conker.) Make sure the knot is solid and not so small it might work its way up into the hole.

Now all your potential conker champion needs is an opponent. One holds their conker up while the other attempts to hit and damage it with theirs, steadying the string if need be. Moving a conker out of the way gives the opponent a free shot. If there should be a miss, it's the other player's turn. Play continues until one of the conkers is eviscerated, leaving behind just a sad, lonely piece of string.

Arcane local rules involving 'tipsies', 'snags', 'stamps', 'strings' and so on are far too complicated to go into here.

Each conker is known by the sum of its victories and the victories of those it has defeated. A 'sevenser', for instance, that beats a 'threeser' becomes an 'elevenser' – it gets one for the victory, as well as the three of its vanquished foe.

Collecting conkers is a great activity in itself: pick those that have either just fallen or are just about to fall, helped along by a stick thrown up into the branches. Some people put their collected conkers in water, rejecting those that float and stringing only the denser ones that sink.

FASCINATING FACT

In 2001, Norwich City Council decided that conkers were so dangerous it earmarked several high-risk horse chestnut trees for the chop. You only need to change one letter to turn 'conkers' into 'bonkers'.

In our day every schoolboy (girls, for some reason, seem less fascinated by conkers) sought the elusive secret formula that would harden a conker into a concrete monster. Some took over their mother's airing cupboard. Others baked them in the oven overnight, surely the original spur to the invention of the Aga. Others soaked them in vinegar, applied hairspray or nail varnish or stored them in the fridge. The more patient left them alone to harden naturally. Modern methods apparently include soaking in vodka and injecting with Botox!

While it is certainly sensible to leave a drilled conker for a time before stringing it (and conkers of the previous year's vintage are indeed tough nuts), there is a limit to ageing a conker. Anyone daft enough to store their childhood conkers in a tin box for 30 years in the hope of making his son and heir a conker champion of all England, may find himself disappointed. One knock with a virgin conker just off the tree and these precious relics of Simon's boyhood crumbled to dust.

The World Conker Championships, held the second Sunday of October in Ashton, in Northamptonshire, allow no such 'cheating'. They provide contestants, who come from as many as 40 countries around the world, with fresh conkers.

British Bulldog

A great game to play when you have a mass of kids needing to work off some energy is *British Bulldog*. It can get a little boisterous so is best played under supervision and on soft ground like sand or grass. With two safe areas established opposite each other, one person is appointed 'Bulldog' and stands in the middle. When they yell out 'British Bulldog', all the players have to try to run to the other safe area, avoiding the Bulldog.

Originally, the Bulldog acquired additional Bulldogs by physically lifting a player up or holding them on the ground while saying, '1... 2... 3... British Bulldog.' These days, it's more commonly played as a variant of Tag. Anyone touched by a Bulldog becomes one themselves, and they all hold hands to form a writhing Bulldog chain until just one player remains.

The game is extraordinary for the adrenalin, noise and sheer excitement it generates among the players.

Kubb: the best outdoor game of all

Since we discovered the Swedish game of *Kubb*, we haven't been able to stop playing it. Luckily, everyone we've forced to try it likes it as much as we do, making it a mystery why it isn't more popular than football by now.

Unless you fancy popping round to our place for a game, you'll need a Kubb set. The chances are you won't have one lying at the back of your hall cupboard among all those unused tennis rackets, but it's pretty simple to make a set out of bits of wood: you need ten Kubbs, six throwing batons and one King. But if you flunked woodwork at school, a quick web search should reveal one you can order.

A Viking game that the Swedes claim was once played with the bones of those they defeated, the playing area should be about 5 paces wide by 8 long, though it's easier for children if it's slightly smaller. With the King set up in the centre, each team (up to six people) stands behind their baseline, along which are evenly spread five Kubbs.

One player from each team throws a baton towards the King. The nearest to the King without touching starts, remembering that anyone knocking the King over too early immediately loses that game.

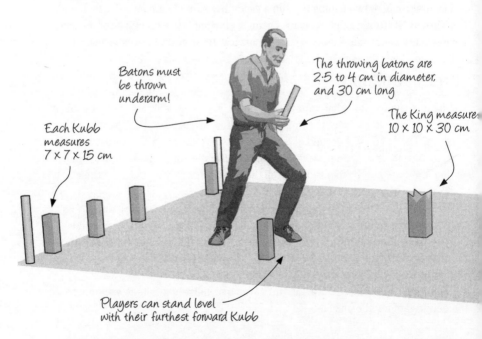

Batons must be thrown underarm!

The throwing batons are 2·5 to 4 cm in diameter, and 30 cm long

Each Kubb measures 7 x 7 x 15 cm

The King measures 10 x 10 x 30 cm

Players can stand level with their furthest forward Kubb

The aim of the game is to knock down all the Kubbs in the rival half of the pitch and then topple the King.

Team A start by throwing their batons underarm, end over end (no sideways, helicopter throws allowed), attempting to knock down as many of Team B's Kubbs as possible.

Before Team B can retaliate, they must throw any fallen Kubbs into Team A's half of the pitch between the King and the baseline[1]. Team A then stand up those Kubbs – now called Field Kubbs – where they landed.

Team B must knock down these Field Kubbs before they can go for the baseline Kubbs. It's fine if a baton knocks down more than one Kubb. But any baseline Kubbs accidentally knocked over before the Field Kubbs are toppled should be set upright again, unless the last Field Kubb has gone down with that very throw.

Team A must now throw any fallen Kubbs back to their opponents' half. If there are any Field Kubbs still standing on their side of the pitch, however, they can stand level with the furthest one when throwing their batons[2].

Turns continue until one team has knocked down all their opponents' Kubbs. The players must then retreat to the baseline and use the rest of their turn to try to knock down the King and win the game. (The King can only be toppled in the very first round if two batons are left, a pretty unlikely event.)

The joy of Kubb is that players' fortunes wax and wane. One moment you're sure you're about to lose, the next you're on top again. Sometimes games are over in a trice, other times they last 20 minutes or longer[3]. It's one of those games that doesn't really make sense until you play it – and then it's hard to stop.

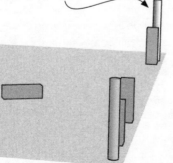

Corner poles mark out the playing area

1. They get two chances to throw the Kubbs back; if they miss both times, the other team places those Kubbs anywhere in their half a minimum of one baton's length from the King or a corner marker.

2. Kubbs themselves, however, must always be thrown from the baseline.

3. A good variation is to allow thrown Kubbs that hit each other to be built into towers – it makes them much easier to knock over, and can speed up sluggish games.

The Centipede

This variant of the *Wheelbarrow Race* is even sillier and more droll. It's best played on soft ground or even indoors if there's enough space. You need a couple of teams, each with a minimum of four players. Try to ensure that they are evenly matched, splitting kids of similar ages and adults.

Both teams should line up in a row and then get onto their hands and knees. With the exception of each leader, the players should put their hands on or around the waist or hips of the person in front. At the command, they head towards the finish line as quickly as they can. If the centipede breaks, the team must stop and reconnect before proceeding.

To make it harder, you can use a marker such as a tree or pile of clothes and make the two teams go around this before returning to the starting line.

Pass the water, please

If you've a good many kids to entertain outside on a hot day, why not recreate something of the atmosphere of *It's a Knockout* with a game that's messy, frantic and enormous fun. (Who says we watched too much TV when we were kids?) You'll need a paddling pool (any large water container will do), two identical buckets, two identical sponges and a bunch of children prepared to get very wet.

To think I left the Great Barrier Reef for this...

Arrange them into two lines leading away from the paddling pool, with an empty bucket at the head of the line. On the word 'Go', the person nearest the pool in each line saturates the sponge and then passes it along the line until the last person squeezes what's left of the water out into the bucket.

The sponge is then passed back to the paddling pool end – no throwing! – to be refilled. The winning team is the one that fills its bucket first.

FASCINATING FACT

What animals have the subspecies Pink Vase, Red Beard, Organ Pipe, Loggerhead and Boring? You're not going to believe this – but it's the sponge. Yes, sponges are animals. (Except for the polyester ones.) When you buy them in shops, all the living tissue has been removed: you're washing your face with their skeleton.

Double Blind

A great, raucous game that can be played in the park, on the beach, or in any wide open space where the neighbours aren't going to complain about the noise.

Split up into two teams: each team chooses one person to be blindfolded (a jumper over the head works well if you haven't got any scarves to hand). Both blindfolded team members have to be guided, by shouts from their fellow team members, around an obstacle (a tree, for example) and back to the rest of the team.

Here's the fun part: both blindfolded competitors are trying to complete the course *at the same time*, with everyone on both teams yelling instructions simultaneously.

Not, perhaps, a game to be played near rose bushes or on motorway verges.

What's the time, Mr Wolf?

This is an alternative to *Musical Statues*, a game that tends to degenerate into 'You moved', 'No I didn't', 'You're out,' 'I'm not playing' arguments. Appoint a Wolf, a role for which Dads are eminently suited as it gives such scope for their untapped ability to overact shamelessly.

The Wolf stands with his back to the other players, who should begin at least 20 feet away. They call out, 'What's the time, Mr Wolf?' and the Wolf turns and shouts out a time, which must be something o'clock. The players advance a corresponding number of steps towards the Wolf. If he says 'Two o'clock', for instance, they move two steps towards him.

As they get nearer to the Wolf and the tension rises, the players all know that the next time they ask, 'What's the time, Mr Wolf?', they might get the answer 'DINNER TIME!' from a slavering Wolf who now chases them, trying to catch one before they reach the safety of the starting line. Depending on local rules, the person caught may become the Wolf or not.

Charades

This is one of the all-time great games for a decent-sized group. Kids love it. But we often find games are spoilt because of vagueness over the rules.

There should be two teams with adults and kids evenly split. One person must act, silently, a charade chosen by the other team. It can be a book (mime opening a book), a song (mime singing), a play (curtains drawing apart), a TV show (draw a box in the air) or a film (an old-fashioned hand-cranked movie camera).

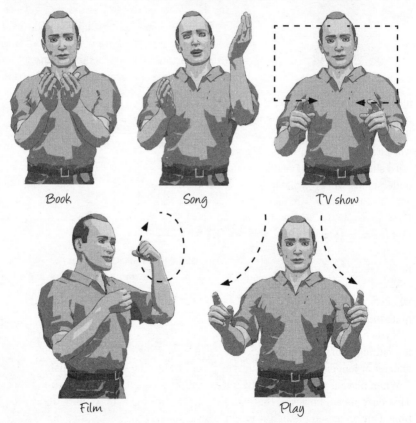

Book   Song   TV show

Film   Play

If only adults are playing, suggestions might be as fiendish as *The Shorter Oxford English Dictionary* but, if you want to keep kids happy and absorbed, it's better to choose stuff they know well, such as favourite books or movies.

The mimer should indicate with their fingers the number of words in the title,

3 words   2 syllables   Little word

including 'a' and 'the'. They can act out the whole thing (use a grand sweeping gesture to indicate you're going to do this), any of the words or part of any word. Words don't have to be acted out in order, but the mimer should indicate which word it is by holding up their fingers again.

To show how many syllables a word has (ensure before starting that everyone understands what a syllable is), put that number of fingers on the forearm. To act out a particular syllable, show that number of fingers of the forearm again. Four fingers in the air, three on the forearm followed by two on the arm indicates that they are to act out the second syllable of the fourth word, which has three syllables. If there's a little word (such as 'a', 'the' or 'of'), show which it is with fingers then draw the index finger and thumb together.

When someone guesses the right word, the mimer should point and nod at whoever got it right, giving a rapid wave of the hand if the person is close, but not quite there.

If you can't think how to act out a word you can try something that sounds like it – putting your hand to your ear indicates 'sounds like'. If the word needs to be shorter or longer, move your hands as if you're showing the size of a fish.

When playing with two, alternating, teams, everyone takes their turn in order. This does mean, however, that half the players are just sitting there at any one time. Our preferred method is for one player to start the ball rolling, performing a title given to him by someone else (probably Dad); thereafter, when a player guesses the correct title, it's *their* turn to act out a title, which is written down for them by the player who's just performed. If someone isn't getting enough turns, Dad can opt to slot them in as appropriate.

The Flippin' Kipper

The kids should cut out paper, newspaper or tissue paper in the shape of a fat, kipper-like, fish. All contestants must place their fish on the floor and stand behind it. On the word 'Go!', they must flap a sheet of card or a magazine madly to make their fish head towards the finishing line or, alternatively, a plate onto which the fish must land. A great party game.

Who's in the Hat?

The problem with many games that involve trivia-style questions is that most children are at a massive disadvantage to the adults, having had far fewer years in which to accumulate the sort of nutty knowledge that is mainly useful only for playing trivia quizzes.

Most kids, however, *are* familiar with a prodigious number of celebrities and pop stars, making *Who's in the hat?* a splendid family game. You'll need a one-minute timer (plundered from another board game if necessary).

Divide the players into a couple of equally able – or unable – teams. Each player writes five names of well-known people, who can be fictional, on slips of paper and drops them into the hat. One player from each team must then, without mentioning the name of the people in any way, try to get their teammates to guess who they're talking about. Each name guessed in the time wins the team a point.

Take it in turns until all the names are used up. A great spin on the game as it's traditionally played is to put the names back in and do it over: this time, however, players are restricted to saying just one word. Since this word will probably be drawn from the previous, lengthy explanation, it's a test of memory and conciseness to see who can remember to whom those three words apply.

And when that round is over, do it once more, but this time you can't use any words at all – just gestures.

Ibble Dibble

To our surprise, this utterly ridiculous student drinking game works brilliantly even without the injection of copious quantities of alcohol. You do, however, need to remember to save a cork or two from your last bottle of wine. Before the game commences, this needs to be burnt on the outside by being held in a flame. Let the cork cool down, and be sure not to burn plastic corks!

Form your players into a circle and assign each player a number in order. The first player must say, word perfect, *'Ibble Dibble Number One with no Dibble Ibbles, calling Ibble Dibble Number...'* At this point they choose another player, calling them by their number, and continuing, *'...with no Dibble Ibbles.'* That player, say Number Three, must continue, *'Ibble Dibble Number Three with no Dibble Ibbles, calling Ibble Dibble Number...'* and choose another player, and so on.

Any mistakes and the error-prone player must have their face marked with the cork. Each player must add the number of the marks on their own face as well as the number of marks on the player

After the kids have gone to bed, the game can be played in its original form

they are calling. Every error means another black mark. So player two with three marks must say to player five with one mark, *'Ibble Dibble Number Two with three Dibble Ibbles, calling Ibble Dibble Number Five with one Dibble Ibble'*, and so on. As things go on, it becomes ever harder to remember how many marks you have on your own face and, while the marks might begin by being spots on the cheeks, they may later be on the nose, or black eyes, or moustaches.

And once the kids have gone to bed, the adults – no doubt needing another burnt cork – can open a bottle and play the game as it's meant to be played, with drinks as forfeits for mistakes.

Island Hopping

Take the cushions off your sofa. Place them strategically around the room – or interspersed through several rooms, if you have enough cushions – and challenge your kids to get from one end of the island chain to the other, without stepping on the floor. It's a great indoor physical game, as long as you remember to remove any priceless Ming vases and family heirlooms first.

Outdoors, the same game can be played using towels or clothing. If your partner objects (*if???*), you can try using newspapers, as long as it's not too windy. If you have any trees handy, these can be used for swinging on to overcome larger gaps.

To extend the game further and make it more of a challenge for a wider age range, start with a large number of islands and then remove them, one at a time, after each successful completion of the chain by all the children playing. Even younger kids will enjoy watching their elders making their way across a course that defeated them.

The jelly game

With everyone in a circle, a die should be thrown in turn. If anyone gets a six, they must don a waiting hat, scarf and gloves and try to eat their way through a bowl of jelly with a knife and fork. If you want to make it truly fiendish, then mittens or oven gloves can be used.

Only one minute is allowed before the die is thrown again. The game ends when the jelly does. Often played with a bar of chocolate instead of the jelly, it's a simple party game that kids find hilarious. You can also put the gloves to use in *Pass the Parcel* to make it that much trickier.

11 Kindergarten kids

IF YOUR KIDS ARE STILL IN NAPPIES and endlessly fascinated by a revolving mobile tinkling 'Twinkle Twinkle Little Star', the chances are that even your best-rehearsed magic tricks will go unappreciated. But at some stage, babies change into children and you can wheel out some of that Dad Stuff you've been desperately waiting to try.

Younger children are a less demanding audience than their older siblings. You don't need to be an expert at slight of hand to pretend you've plucked off their nose by sticking your thumb between your first and second fingers. The downside, however, is that they will want to experience their favourites again... and again... and again.

The younger kids are, the more physical they'll want their games to be. But that's OK: you're still young yourself and in your prime. They won't have crushed the life out of you for a good few years yet.

This Is the Way the Ladies Ride

There are countless nursery rhymes and songs with accompanying actions to delight younger children. 'Round and round the garden', for instance, seems to be hard-wired into all adults' brains.

'Round and round the garden, like a teddy bear (walk your fingers on the child's palm); one step, two step (walk your fingers up their arm), tickly under there' (tickle them under the chin, arm or on the tummy).

Of the action songs, our favourite is the knee-bouncing rhyme, 'This Is the Way the Ladies Ride'. It has the great merit that you don't really need to sing but can instead do a Rex Harrison 'can't sing, won't sing' impersonation.

Let the rider hang onto your hands as you raise your legs onto your toes in time with the words, four times to each line, so that each lift of the legs coincides with the stress of the words.

A gentle bounce should accompany this verse:

This is the way the ladies ride
Trippety-tee, trippety-tee
This is the way the ladies ride
Trippety-trippety-tee.

Lift your knees higher:

This is the way the gentlemen ride
Gallopy-gallop, gallopy-gallop
This is the way the gentlemen ride
Gallopy-gallopy-gallop.

For the last verse, make the riding 'terrain' really rough:

This is the way the farmers ride
Hobbledee-hoy, hobbledee-hoy
This is the way the farmers ride
Hobbledee-hoy and down in the DITCH.

On 'DITCH' move your knees apart so the child falls a little way. Repeated a few times, it's amazing how tiring this can be. For you, that is, rather than for the child – who'll still be begging for more after twenty minutes.

Instead of giving up before they are sated, why not think of it as exercise without the hassle or expense of gym membership?

The Tickle Robot

On your palm, draw the numbers 1 to 4 and the letter R. Stand stock still, with a vacant expression on your face, gazing into the middle distance (fathers of young babies will find this comes quite naturally). Robot though you may now be, you are a robot in standby mode.

Encourage a child to experiment with pressing the numbers to see what happens. As a number is pressed, come to life, standing tall but with your control pad (hand) still in reach. Another press and you should advance towards your 'controller', your aim being to pick up, tickle or do whatever you think the child will like. Change your actions as they press the buttons unless they press the 'R' for 'reset' button, in which case you should return to standby mode. Move in jerky, robotic spurts, and try to keep your face entirely passive – this really helps the robotic effect.

Young kids seem to love the playful scariness of the tickle robot. You know you've got it right if, moments after claiming they can't face being tickled any more, they press another button. Once they've got the hang of it, you don't even need to write on your palm; just holding out your hand should alert them to the game. You can add endless variations and wind yourself up with an imaginary key if this helps move the action along.

Find me a yellow flower...

...a red leaf, a stone the size of your thumbnail and a twig the length of your little finger. Ready... Go! And off they scamper to do your bidding, leaving you to enjoy that post prandial cup of coffee while you chat with your friends. It's an activity that requires absolutely no effort on your part, and will keep the little darlings happily occupied for ages.

The garden on a plate

A good activity on a sunny day. The aim is to plunder the garden for bits of grass, earth, interesting leaves, small flowers and twigs, and to build a garden using a plastic plate as a base. It encourages creativity and small children take a real pride in their creations.

Simon Says

We all remember this one from our childhoods, yet it's just as much fun for kids as it ever was. They have to do everything you tell them – putting their hands on their shoulders, sticking out their tongues, standing on one leg – as long as the command begins 'Simon says'. If it doesn't, then they must *not* obey the request, which makes it particularly enjoyable if it's 'Go and get a chocolate biscuit from the cupboard'.

In Simon's household, the children always do everything he says as a matter of course. Or so Simon says.

Smashing fun

You've spent an hour and a half building a spaceship out of Lego bricks. The creation is finished, and it's a stunning work of engineering. The problem is: what do you do with it now? You can't really keep it, partly because there's nowhere to put it and partly because you're going to need the bricks again for the next creation. But mainly, of course, because it really isn't *that* good a model, and you know you could make a much better one next time around.

The best solution is to treat it the way you'd treat any spaceship, and throw it through the air. Sure, it will smash on impact – but that's exactly the point. Kids get told off every time they break household objects, so it's a great treat for them to be told they're allowed to destroy something for once, especially something as destructively extravagant as a thousand-piece Lego model.

The leaning tower of Lego

Now that you've got a floor full of Lego bricks, what better use can you put them to than to make a tower as big as your child? If they're young enough to have Duplo, use these as the base: for, amazingly, not only can you build Duplo on top of Lego, you can also build Lego on top of Duplo. These toy designers really thought that one out.

Kids are amazed when they manage to create something bigger than they are – it's a kind of benchmark of what's within their reach. It's a fairly mindless activity, so you can easily do it at four o'clock in the morning (or whatever time your sleepless toddler has woken you up).

When the model's finished – topple it over and smash it, of course. Then they can have a go at building it again themselves, while you 'rest your eyes' for a few minutes on the couch.

The handkerchief rabbit

Open out a handkerchief and run it through your closed hand, making it long and thin. Tie a knot a third of the way along and fluff out the smaller section. This will be the rabbit's ears (even though there's only one of them).

With the ears pointing up your arm towards your elbow, cradle the rabbit in the palm of your outstretched hand and stroke it with your other hand to conceal what you're doing. With the middle finger of your rabbit-holding hand, flick the knot to make the rabbit jump along your arm.

As the rabbit jumps, affect surprise and, delaying just a fraction of a second, pull the naughty rabbit back down by its tail. Stroke it again for a while to calm it, only to find it jumping away again when you least expect it. Although this is something younger children love, it is surprising how fascinated by the rabbit even supposedly cool teenagers can be.

If you don't carry a handkerchief, it will work with cuddly toys that are big enough to hide your fingers but small enough to travel up your forearm.

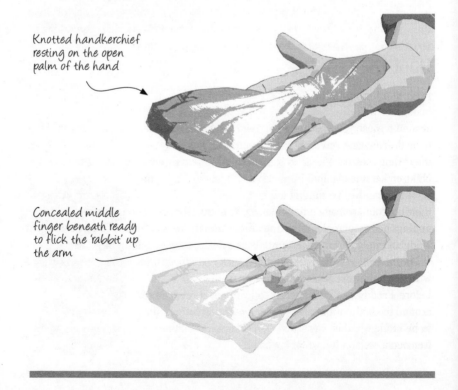

Knotted handkerchief resting on the open palm of the hand

Concealed middle finger beneath ready to flick the 'rabbit' up the arm

Teensy Rider

Sit the child on your knees, facing away. Hold up your arms, fists clenched, for them to grab hold of your fists.

They're now holding the handlebars of a powerful motorbike, the noise supplied by you. Faster and faster you go, leaning into ever steeper corners, going up steep hills only to plunge down the other side, hitting potholes, bumping along dirt tracks, even attempting the odd jump. You can also be a roller-coaster, with your folded arms as the safety bar.

Not surprisingly for beginners, almost all rides end in a crash. If, when they hit their teens, they start wearing bike leathers, don't blame us.

Hunt the Fluff

It really did used to be *hunt the fluff*, in the days when young Simon had a fluffy bedspread and Mrs Smith came to babysit. There aren't many fluffy bedspreads around now, so you might prefer to call the game Hotter or Colder. It doesn't have to be fluff anyway. Anything tiny will do. At bedtime, get the child to hide whatever they want you to look for in their room. It's a great way of making recalcitrant children keen to clamber into bed.

Only once they've snuggled down should you hunt for it. As you prowl around their bedroom peering into nooks and crannies, they need to tell you when you're getting 'hotter' or 'colder' or, ultimately, 'boiling' or 'freezing'. You can spin it out by deliberately going the wrong way and misunderstanding them.

The other way of playing the game, of course, is to make the child do the hunting while you give directions. Steve uses this method for prolonging the anticipation before Freddy and Joe open their birthday presents, by first concealing them around the bedroom. It's become so popular that they'll even ask for their presents to be hidden in this way – and it's certainly one way of slowing down the annual frenzied attack on the wrapping paper.

Snake – open and close the mouth

Wolf – make the ears twitch

Panther – that mouth can bite!

Shadow puppets

Fun and easy to do, with a little practice. For very young children, try sitting on the floor cross-legged with them sitting in your lap directly beneath a ceiling light (halogen down-lighters are best), and perform the shadows on the floor in front of them. It's much more immediate than projecting onto a wall.

Some of these require two hands, and they're harder to do (and won't work

Old man – waggle your ring finger back and forth to make the eye move

Greyhound – use your little finger to open and close the mouth

Snail – make those antennae wiggle!

when your child is in your lap). But with the single-handed shadows you can do a different one with each hand, and make them fight each other. Also try simple shadowplays, such as making a basic shadow of your outstretched hand – the fingers can pop open one by one – and having one of the animals 'eat' the fingers one at a time. Younger children find this hilarious.

Wiping the smile off your face

Move your flat, open hand from the top of your head to your chin quickly, changing a smile to a frown as you do so. Bring the hand back up and smile again. It's a particularly good ruse for cheering up small children who find themselves affronted or just in a bad mood, and will even work reasonably well with older kids. Getting kids to smile is the first step in helping them to get themselves out of a strop.

Just remember where you are. It may work wonders with little ones, but it's likely to cause bewilderment if you're with your mates in the pub.

Dad, the action toy

Press your nose and have your tongue pop out. Pull your right ear and, simultaneously, bend your tongue to the right, as if it's the ear tug that is doing it. Pull your left ear and have it go the other way. Press your nose again – and the tongue disappears.

A nice variation is to press your nose, tweak your ear or operate another control point, while making an entirely unrelated part of your body respond to the action. A leg could pop up, a foot start tapping, an elbow twitch, and so on. You should try to express complete surprise at these effects, as if they're entirely involuntary.

After a while, your child will probably want to operate the 'buttons' themselves. Let them – unless they're in their teens and angry that you won't let them have their ears pierced.

 It's a Dad's world

WE'RE THE FIRST TO ADMIT that there are some things Dads just aren't biologically cut out for. If it was left to us, our children would still be wearing clothes they grew out of three years ago and begging us never to dish up beans on toast again.

But there are some areas in which Dads excel. With our trusty Swiss Army penknives always at the ready, you can be sure that Dad will fix that broken gadget – or, at the very least, tell you that it's so far beyond repair that you *have* to get a new one immediately, especially since there's a new souped-up turbo version available at a special introductory price.

Dads are also expected to be able to teach their kids to do things. The trouble is, we have to learn them first, so a bit of secret practice is needed when everyone's gone to bed. That way, when your child says 'Dad, can you juggle?', they'll be truly impressed when you toss the contents of the fruit bowl in the air and catch them all on the way down.

How to teach a child to ride a bike

'Of course I won't let go,' fibs even the most doting Dad, puffing away madly as he runs behind his child's bike. A moment later, he takes his hand away, praying that the child will stay upright. Some do. Some don't. The loss of trust between those who fall and their fathers is psychiatry's future gain.

Lower seat using the nut underneath the saddle

There is a better way. Children are instinctively able to 'scoot', so get them

Take the pedals off at the front gear wheel

used to the bike by scooting first. Once they grow out of riding with stabilizers to keep them upright, remove the bike's pedals with either a spanner or allen key, depending on the bike. Then lower the seat until your child can sit with both feet comfortably flat on the ground.

Remember where you put the pedals when you take them off!

Child's feet should be able to touch the ground

Now they can scoot along using both feet, lifting them from the ground between pushes. This way, they learn how to balance and turn on two wheels without simultaneously having to cope with the destabilizing circular motion of the pedals. Once they are happily scooting and turning, you can replace the pedals, knowing that the child is already adept with every other aspect of the bike.

How to remember your kids' birthdays

One thing you must never, ever, *ever* forget is your child's birthday. It's perfectly possible that they will help you out, reminding you of the forthcoming date at frequent intervals and offering helpful hints as to suitable presents. But this can't be relied upon, so Dads are forced to use such unreliable things as memory, diaries, electronic organizers and the like.

Credit and debit cards have four-digit PIN numbers that can be altered to any combination, so why not amend your number to that of your child's birthday? That way, you're very unlikely to forget.

More than one child? Simple. Get another credit card for each successive addition to the family. You'll need them.

How to bark like a dog

It is surprisingly easy to learn to bark. With a little practice, you'll be able to summon up a dog that will fool not only kids, but quite a few canines as well.

Spot the difference

Get a deep 'rrrr' vibrating at the back of the throat. As you're doing this, you should say the word 'rough' loudly, emphasizing the latter 'uff' part of the sound. The 'rough' should come out very quickly, like a mini-explosion. Make sure you open your mouth wide as you do it.

Experiment with pitch until you find the level that best suits you. We're both yappy mongrels rather than Crufts contenders, but you may find your inner dogginess is something more substantial.

It might be best to practise somewhere quiet – like a padded cell. Even as expert barkers, the first one each time can be under par. So we prefer to bark offstage, enticing curious kids to come running. When they arrive, they find us already looking for the dog they heard but which, mysteriously, can't be found.

How to untangle puppet strings

In a perfect world, children would tidy their puppets away with the strings neatly gathered together and elegantly looped over the control bar.

Sadly, the world of children is rarely so well ordered. So it's up to Dad to sort out a tangled mess of strings… again. What's most frustrating is that you know it must be possible to reverse whatever's been done, but it isn't long before your brain is reeling in a way it hasn't since you last played with a Rubik's Cube.

The tangle often results from nothing more than the control bar being flipped over when the puppet was put away and then flipped once more when it was picked up again. The first thing to do is see if turning the bar over will sort it out.

If it doesn't, then unsnag the strings from the puppet and the bar so you have only one loose knot of strings in between to sort out. Instead of pulling at them aimlessly, choose one of the strings – say the rear one – and try to get that free. If you can, use it as a pivot, twisting the bar one way and the other to untwist the other strings.

If this doesn't work then remember the Dad's maxim: if at first you don't succeed – cheat. Untie one or more strings from the control bar, sort them out and then refasten them. If you need new string, fishing line works well. And in future, only buy modern puppets with readily detachable, colour-coded strings.

How to untie stubborn knots

Shoelaces, swimming costume cords and the like have a nasty tendency to get badly knotted up, particularly when the knots have been tied by small fingers in a hurry. To a child, the untying process involves pulling any stray ends they can find – which only makes the problem worse.

The solution is to rub the knot firmly between your thumb and forefinger, using a slight rotary motion with your thumb. This action can generally persuade even the most awkward knot to yield to your touch.

How to tie shoelaces so they don't come undone

Walk down the road with a gang of children and you can pretty well guarantee that at any given moment at least one is kneeling down doing a shoelace up. It slows down family outings more than anything else, yet it's wholly avoidable.

Begin tying the shoelace as normal with the over and under starting knot. The next stage is usually to make a loop from one of the laces, then wind the other lace around it before poking it through the opening to make a second loop.

Instead, get them to wind the second lace around the first loop not once but twice before poking it through the opening. This shoelace won't come undone until you want it to.

How to keep a cardboard box closed

You want the box shut but you've no tape to hand, or you're deluded enough to think you're only putting it away for a short while. Easy when you know how.

Choose to go clockwise or anti-clockwise. Take one flap and overlap the next flap slightly. Keeping that corner in position, ensure that the second flap goes outside the next flap around, again overlapping it slightly. Do the same for the other two corners.

Once you've ensured that each flap overlaps the successive corner, begin working all the inside flaps downwards.

The cardboard will tend to bend a little, but suddenly you'll find all the flaps dropping into place at the same time and, *voilà* – a perfectly sealed cardboard box.

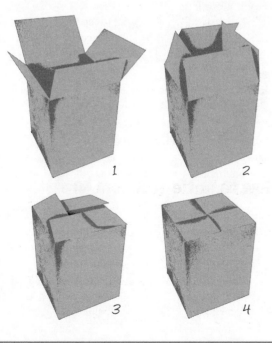

How to juggle

If you've always wanted to juggle, learning so you can entertain your children is the perfect excuse.

Proper juggling balls can be handy. They're like spherical bean bags and have a welcome tendency to stay where they land, so you don't spend half your time hunting around under the sofa. You can learn comfortably with bean bags, or any softish balls two to three inches across. It's best not to use fruit just yet unless you fancy explaining why everything in the bowl is so badly bruised.

Get used to holding three balls right from the start. Hold one in the palm of your right hand. Make a curved V-sign with your left hand, and put one ball in it and another in the palm, held there by your thumb and third and fourth fingers.

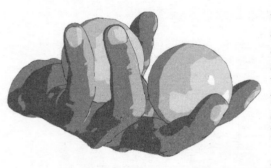

The first stage is to practise throwing the ball in your left V up and to the right so it describes an arc, peaking around your eyeline, and dropping into a corresponding V in the right hand. Then throw it back the same way. The aim is to do this over and over again while looking ahead, not at your hands.

Get used to moving your hands from the outset. Your left hand should move anti-clockwise from your point of view, largely from the wrist, the right hand clockwise. It isn't quite a circle, more the flatter sort of wave a lazy pantomime King would give the plebs from his cardboard carriage. This is how you avoid the balls hitting each other in the air.

In stage two, just as the first ball hits its peak, you should throw the ball from your right hand to your left hand. Initially, it doesn't matter if you're almost putting it in your left hand, just so long as you get used to getting rid of the ball and getting your hand back into position in time to catch the ball heading to your right hand. You should only progress beyond this stage, though, when both balls are reaching your eyeline every time.

The third stage is to add the third ball, throwing it as the second reaches its apex. Catch each one as it lands so you end up with two balls in the right hand and one in your left. When you have perfected this, try to keep going, throwing each ball as the one heading for that hand reaches its apex.

Don't be stingy with your throws. Although it's tempting not to throw the balls very high, in fact the higher they're thrown (within reason) the easier it becomes.

You'll be tempted to walk forwards to chase your balls as they fly through the air: try juggling while facing a wall at first, to prevent this happening.

Learning to juggle takes time and practice – a lot of it – but once you can do it, it's like riding a bike; you can do it for life. It might be best to become proficient with three balls before you move on to juggling swords, flaming torches or chainsaws.

The painless way to learn to ski

Making people learn to ski by balancing them precariously on two long planks of wood plonked down on slippery snow is akin to trying to get kids to ride a bike without going the stabilizer route first. It's not only tricky, but could put somebody off for life.

Instead, ask your instructor – or the children's – to start off with snow blades. They're much shorter than conventional skis so everything is easier: keeping your balance; manoeuvring; even getting up again when you fall over. With blades, confidence – and ability – comes more quickly. When you've got the hang of it, it's then fairly easy to transfer to proper skis. Kids already adept on roller blades should find ski blades an absolute doddle.

Using this method, Simon – hardly the sportiest of individuals – went from novice to tackling a couple of black runs in just four and a half days. Showing off? Sure, but everyone else is bored of hearing about it so it's your turn now.

Misconceptions

You don't always have to tell your children the truth. Sometimes a white lie is better than exposing them to the harsh realities of life. Sometimes, though, it's just plain fun to mess with their heads by telling them some outrageous whoppers.

Here are a few of our favourite misconceptions spread by mischievous parents. We'd like to think some people reached adulthood still believing that:

- Some breeds of cows have two legs shorter so that they can graze more easily on hillsides. On the flat, they simply go round in circles.

- Sheep are just woolly pigs.

- Just as hens lay eggs, so pigs lay sausages.

- Pigs can fly. But they're very lazy so they don't do it often.

- Sheep's wool shrinks when it rains and peels off so the farmer can collect it.

- Zebras are horses that have been painted with stripes so the farmer knows who they belong to.

- Electricity pylons are spaceships left behind after a Martian invasion was defeated.

- Birds don't get electrocuted when they land on pylons because they have rubber feet (or else hop quickly from leg to leg so they don't make a circuit).

- Bees make honey and wasps make jam.

- Rabbits can fly by flapping their ears very quickly.

- There's a parallel universe the other side of mirrors where people exactly like us do exactly the same things.

- It will be much easier to travel to Australia when they finish the tunnel through the middle of the Earth.

- Your toys come alive when you're asleep.

- By staying in the bath when the water's running out, you risk going down the plughole with all the rest of the naughty children.

- A little man lives at the back of the fridge to turn the light on when we open the door.

Broken or battery?

When something stops working, how do you tell whether the battery has run down or if it's kaput? It's intensely irritating to buy yet more batteries for some power-greedy gizmo, only to discover it has given up the ghost for good (usually the first week after the warranty runs out).

Battery testers are useful, but aren't so handy for devices such as watches that need specialist help to replace their batteries. Instead, place the object somewhere with a source of gentle warmth, like an airing cupboard or on a radiator. If a watch, warmed overnight, starts working again you know that all it needs is a battery replacement.

Ovens, conventional or microwave, are not suitable places to put batteries. In fact, doing so can be incredibly dangerous. So don't do it.

How to teach a child to skip

To teach a child to skip, get them to throw the rope over their head so it lands on the ground in front of them. Have them step forward over it. Then get them to do it again… and again… and again.

When they are adept at this, get them to jump forward over the rope each time. Speed the process up until suddenly they're skipping.

How to appear in family photographs

In every family, however technologically competent, there's usually only one person who takes responsibility for the camera. Whether it's a Dad or a Mum, they'll be the one who takes it along on holidays, to the beach, or gets it out on birthdays – which means they're guaranteed never to appear in family photographs.

All modern cameras have a self-timer, as do some phone apps, which give you just enough time to run around the back and pose with your family. But unless you carry a tripod in your pocket, you'll find that setting up the camera is a nightmare.

A cushion, pillow or even a bunched-up sock makes a good 'tripod', allowing you to support the camera and angle it towards the scene. Some enterprising camera shops are even selling overpriced bean bags precisely for this purpose.

Arrange your family in front of the lens, making sure they leave a space for you to slot into. Then – and here's the important bit – *angle the camera up* a

few degrees. You're likely to be the tallest person in the photograph, and if you compose the scene perfectly for the arrangement without you in it you'll find all your pictures have the top of your head cropped off. Press the shutter, and then run like hell. And remember to smile: most of Steve's family snapshots show a perfectly composed grouping with a flustered, panicked Dad peering anxiously at the flashing timer light.

How to make a barbecue without poisoning your family

If there's one thing above all else that sorts out Dads from Mums, it's the barbecue. As soon as the weather turns nice, Dads who had trouble even finding the kitchen all through the winter suddenly start comparing marinade recipes and stocking up on wooden skewers.

Every Dad has his own distinctive barbecue ritual. We don't want to cramp your style. But there are a few pointers to make the experience less stressful.

First, light the barbecue a long time before everyone starts feeling hungry. Even the most carefully prepared pyre will take 45 minutes to reach full strength, and if you wait until you've opened your second beer you'll find your kids have already escaped to McDonald's. (Avoid those all-in-one charcoal bags. They're done long before the food.)

Barbecued sausages always go down well, but if they're charcoal on the outside and salmonella pink on the inside you risk them coming up again in the middle of the night. Your safest bet is to *boil* sausages for ten minutes first: that way you know they'll be cooked all the way through, so you can just take them off when they change colour. Boiling chicken portions doesn't work so well, but stick them in the microwave for ten minutes first and you'll ward off the worst of the unfriendly bacteria.

It's a sad fact, but barbecues always reach their peak just when you've finished cooking. But there's still time for your *pièce de résistance*: the barbecued banana. Here's the recipe: take a banana. Don't peel it – it's ready-wrapped. Bung it on the barbecue. Take it off when it goes black. And that's it. Implausible though it sounds, they're truly delicious.

The wonders of candle wax

You may have thought candles were only used for grown-up dinner parties, but the resourceful Dad will press all those one-inch stubs into service long after the guests have departed.

Rubbed on saw blades, the wax will ensure they cut smoothly through even the toughest wood. Rub a candle around a screw before driving it into a piece of wood or a Rawlplug, and it will screw home that much more easily. Best of all, though, is to rub candlewax on the metal runners of your kids' sledges – they'll glide over the snow even faster.

Knots: bowline

This is a great way of making a loop at the end of a rope. Tough and easy to make, good for swinging from a tree. This one's known as the King of Knots, and is recommended by the FAA for tying down light aircraft.

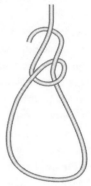

Make a small loop in the rope

Pass the end through the loop

Pass it under the top end...

... then through the loop and tighten

Knots: clove hitch (1)

A very good knot for attaching ropes to tree branches. This one's also useful for tying ropes onto a pole when you can't easily get to the end of the pole. Don't use this one where the pole can twist, or the knot will slip.

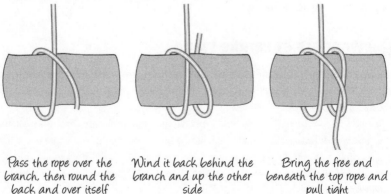

Pass the rope over the branch, then round the back and over itself

Wind it back behind the branch and up the other side

Bring the free end beneath the top rope and pull tight

Knots: reef

The easiest way to join two ropes together. It's really just two opposing granny knots, but here's the correct way to make it so it won't easily come undone.

Make a loop with one rope, bring the other beneath it

Lift the second rope over the first...

... and around the back of it

Bring the free end through the loop and tighten

Knots: clove hitch (2)

Unlike the first clove hitch, this one's easier to tie when you *can* get to the free end of a pole or tree stump. Best for tying up boats, as it can be lifted off easily.

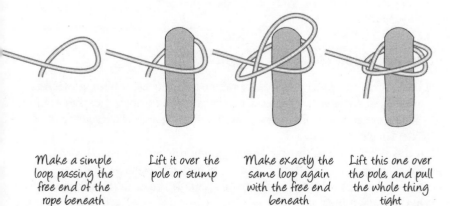

Make a simple loop, passing the free end of the rope beneath

Lift it over the pole or stump

Make exactly the same loop again with the free end beneath

Lift this one over the pole, and pull the whole thing tight

How to get children to go to sleep

The art of telling bedtime stories is one that's in danger of dying out, as live narrators are increasingly usurped by CDs and downloaded stories.

But storytelling is a great way of getting children – particularly younger ones – to relax and into a drowsy condition where they're ready for sleep. It doesn't have to be about enchanted forests, fairy princesses and magical beasts: the stories kids like best are those that describe their own lives.

Always begin with 'Once upon a time'. It's a time-honoured tradition that will immediately put them in the right frame of mind for what's to come, and should get the eyelids drooping straight away.

After that, we find the best method is to talk through the events of the day, step by step, beginning with breakfast (or teeth cleaning, face washing and sock-finding, if you think you're going to be in for a long session) and then continuing through each meal, outing and activity. It may sound dull, but that's the point: resist the temptation to embroider the facts.

Here's the clever part: when you get to the present time in your narrative, just *keep on going*. So deal with getting into pyjamas, climbing into bed, then discuss Dad telling the story, and talk about how the child rolls onto their side, closes their eyes, and slips into a deep, deep sleep. With any luck, by that stage they'll simply follow the instructions and will be fast asleep.

Even if they don't drop straight off, the exercise will have helped them to sort out the day's activities into a logical and categorized order, encouraging relaxation and drowsiness. And the feeling of satisfaction you get when tiptoeing from the room is boundless.

The painless removal of splinters

In the majority of splinter episodes, there's no necessity for needles or tweezers. Providing just a little of the splinter is protruding, reduce tears and fears by simply sticking a piece of Sellotape over the splinter. Peel the tape off carefully and the splinter should come with it.

If this solution doesn't work, then try a fine pair of tweezers. Research the splinter-aquiring incident first: a little elementary deduction as to the angle of entry should ensure that all your efforts go towards pulling the thing out, rather than pushing it further in.

First aid: the psychological approach

When children hurt themselves, the one thing they want is a Mum. Any Mum will do, as long as she's huggable and carries one of those paramedic kits all Mums seem to keep in their handbags (aspirin, arnica, plasters, slings, bars of chocolate and so on.) But what's a Dad to do when there's no Mum to hand?

As long as the child isn't actually bleeding copiously or unconscious, the chances are the wound or bruise is more a question of hurt pride than injured bones. Humour, we find, really can be the best medicine.

That's not to say that you should laugh at their misfortunes: far from it. Take each incident perfectly seriously. Begin by looking at the bruised elbow, for

Stage 1   Stage 2   Stage 3

example, and scratching your chin. 'Hmm,' you say, donning your best bedside manner, 'can you do this?' Bend your own elbow, or touch a finger to the affected part. Sniffling, the child will follow suit.

'OK,' you continue, 'how about this?' Perform something slightly silly – such as crossing your arms behind your back, or scratching your ear. This stage should just be within the bounds of medical possibility. Keep this up, performing sillier and sillier actions – sticking your fingers in your ears is a good one – all the while keeping a straight poker face. Before long, it's your child who will be laughing, and they'll forget they were ever injured.

Best to know where the local hospital is, though, just in case.

If it's broken – fix it

Few abilities define the competent Dad as much as the ability to mend things when they go wrong. What's needed is a heady mix of experience, confidence, and a willingness to take things apart on the grounds that if they're broken anyway, you can't make it any worse.

Heads will roll

The plastic heads of Action Man, Barbie and Bratz dolls seem to fly off with the merest provocation, and all your pressing and grunting won't get them back on. The trick is to soften the neck aperture in really hot water for a few minutes first: this should make it pliable enough to slip the head back on.

Stopped watches

Look for a small indentation

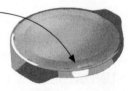

Good watches need a special tool to get them undone. But experienced Dads won't buy their kids decent watches, knowing that they'll be lost almost immediately anyway. Cheap watches look like they unscrew, but the backs can be often prised off with a knife: look for a tiny raised portion about a quarter inch long on the rim, which conceals a slight gap below it. If you get the back off, most often you'll find the problem is simply that the battery is loose.

DVDs

If your DVD is skipping, it may well be dirty rather than scratched. Wash it under warm water, and dry with a towel from the centre outwards – not around in a circle, as this is more likely to deepen any scratches there may be.

Chairs and small tables

You spend mealtimes begging kids not to tip back in their chair, and then the whole thing collapses. Except it's always *your* chair that breaks, not theirs. Use a quick-drying wood glue, but don't try to squeeze it into tiny gaps: pull the whole chair apart, and start again. If you don't have any clamps, tie the chair up with string and wind a stick through it to tighten the string until the wood glue has fully set (overnight is best). Then swap your chair for one of theirs.

13 Rainy days and Sundays

SUNDAYS AREN'T WHAT they used to be. Time was, the day would stretch out endlessly before us, with nothing to do but hang about with our parents. Now, of course, Sundays are just like Saturdays, and are largely devoted to shopping.

We can still find ourselves at a loose end at home on a Sunday – or on any day when it's too wet, cold and miserable to play outside. These are the times when a Dad's resources are most tested: sure, you can just plug the kids into the latest movie download, but there's a lot of fun to be had that doesn't involve screens.

You don't need much equipment to entertain bored children. We've assembled a range of games, activities and building projects that can be completed using everyday household items.

Of course, it helps to stock up on the essentials: a packet of balloons, a set of marbles, and the usual array of old cardboard boxes, sticky tape and glue. It doesn't take much organisation to provide an entertaining afternoon for your kids.

Camera games

Most of us have either a digital camera or a phone that's capable of taking pictures. There are many great games you can play with these: here are a few of our tried and tested favourites.

Spy camera

Our favourite games for a Sunday afternoon are those which involve the kids rushing around while Dad stays sitting in an armchair. This one requires only a small amount of initial Dad activity.

Take your mobile phone and half a dozen toy soldiers. Position the soldiers in various positions around the house, in plain view but tucked into unlikely places. They should be visible without opening drawers, but not so obvious they can be seen immediately.

Photograph each one in location with your phone, then show each of the photos in turn to your kids: their task is to locate each of the soldiers. If you prefer, just give them your phone and let them get on with it (but don't be surprised if they spend the whole time phoning their friends in Australia).

Taking extreme close-up views of their location makes the job much trickier, though occasionally it can be too difficult. We've found a good alternative is to photograph each soldier with a fair bit of background (enough to give the game away) on your digital camera. Then, when you show them back the images, begin with them zoomed all the way in. If they don't get the location straight away, you can zoom out step by step until they're able to tell where the soldiers are hidden.

Spot the body

Give each child your phone or camera in turn, and tell them to go off into another room and photograph part of their body. (You may need to censor the photos before general viewing takes place, just to make sure none of them have taken the kind of pictures that could get Social Services involved.)

When all the pictures have been taken, show them around: the task is to guess whose body each photo belongs to. It helps if you can rig your phone or camera up to a TV so they are large enough for everyone to see them.

Photo scavenger hunt

Kids seem to get their own mobile phones or digital cameras at a frighteningly early age these days. If you have a bunch of kids who all have their own phones, you can organise a scavenger hunt for them. Prepare a set of tasks to complete: they have to take a photo to prove they've done it. If not all the kids in your party have their own phones, organise them into teams with at least one phone or camera present on each team.

Depending on the age of the children, you can gauge whether to send them on tasks that involve leaving the house. Here are suggestions for some of the activities they could be asked to photograph:

- as many kids as can fit in one bath/armchair/under a bed at one time

- standing on one leg, holding each others' free feet

- wearing hats, coats and sunglasses backwards

- pulling the silliest faces they can

- shaking hands with someone in uniform

- wrapped up in newspaper

- acting out a scene from a movie they all know

- scoring a goal with a balloon football.

Climbing the wall

We remember fondly that old Batman TV series, which had none of the whizz-bang special effects available to the recent Batman movie series. Then, if you saw Batman and Robin appearing to be climbing a wall with a bat rope, in reality the only special effect you were watching was a wall built on the floor, with the very un-special effect being that the camera was tilted on its side. It shouldn't have worked, but somehow it did – and this is one you *can* try at home.

It's a great time filler, and easy to do. Choose a clear piece of floor that could pass for a wall, and have your kids make as if they're having great difficulty climbing it – while you film them, with your camera held on its side. If you can make a fake window from pieces of wood or cardboard, it will greatly add to the effect. A perfect afternoon's entertainment with a video camera.

Being a pawn was bad enough – now I'm just cannon fodder

Combat chess

This is a game Steve invented when he was a student, and he's been playing it ever since. Take an old chess set that you don't mind getting a little battered and arrange all the pieces clustered around the king, one colour at each end. Make sure all the pieces fit within an area four squares wide, so you have room on each side of them.

Stack books on end down each side of the board to catch stray pieces. If you can find some large sheets of cardboard, use these as walls at each end as well; hold

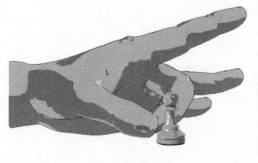

them up when it's not your turn to fire, and take them down when it's your go.

It's now your task to knock over your opponent's king (and any other pieces in the way, of course) by flicking your pawns at it from behind the baseline. The trick to doing this is to press your index or middle finger against your thumb, *in contact* with a pawn: that way, when you release your thumb, it won't hurt your finger. If it isn't in contact with the pawn at the start, the act of hitting the pawn will hurt after a while. Take it in turns to fire pawns at each other's chess pieces. The board will quickly fill up with fired pawns and fallen pieces, but don't be tempted to take them off: the only 'rule' is that *all casualties must remain on the battlefield*. The added confusion caused by so much debris littering the board makes the game more fun as it progresses.

If you run out of pawns, you're allowed to stand up and fire any pawn on your side of the board – but you have to fire it from where it is lying. It's a raucous game, and marginally less mentally taxing than real chess.

There are two skills to this game. One is learning how to fire the pawns accurately, and the other lies in working out the best defensive placement of your pieces.

One word of recommendation: when a pawn flies off the table, as it surely will, pause the game and find it immediately. Otherwise you run the risk of losing a great many pawns very quickly indeed.

Tutty's Bulletin

A while back we heard of this great game, played in an office in Hull. It appears that there was a stationer, Tutty's, which produced a newsletter considered somewhat tedious by the employees of one office. So they formulated a game, the aim being to 'give' the newsletter to a colleague without them realising.

It might be secreted in their coat before they put it on, or in a file that they might then pick up. Cue giggles all round as the mark realised that they had unwittingly taken possession of Tutty's Bulletin. Apparently, so popular was the game that it has kept going for over twenty years, being passed from generation to generation of new office workers.

We think a family version would work wonderfully. You need to find something very distinctive and relatively easily concealed, such as an oddly coloured handkerchief or a peculiar toy or figurine. Somebody must be present when the object is discovered for a point to be scored.

If the mark discovers the object when they *aren't* observed, they can go on to hide it on or among the possessions of somebody else. We've both started the games in our households, though we don't honestly imagine that we'll be able to keep it going for anything like twenty years. But who knows? Maybe we will still be playing it with our grandchildren.

Peatime pickup

Although it sounds like a recipe for disaster, we're assured by very good friends of ours that a handful of annoyingly boisterous young children can be occupied for some time if you empty a big tub of dried peas, or something similar, onto the floor. Each child should be given an identical-sized container and a prize offered to the one who gathers up the most number of peas.

Retire to an armchair somewhere far away with the paper and a cup of tea as they compete to see who can get the most into their container. If it doesn't work, blame our chums, not us, and get out the Hoover.

This isn't doing our viewing figures any good

Don't watch that, watch me

We all know how compelling TV is for kids – but here's a way to make a game out of them *not* watching it, while teaching them just how compulsive the moving image really is.

Face your child, with the TV to the side of you. Look at each other's eyes. The game is to see who can hold out the longest without turning to look at the screen. It's much harder than it might seem, especially if the sound is left on: while it's just possible to ignore what's going on at any one time, as soon as the scene changes the need to see what's going on will quickly become unbearable. Give them a prize if they manage a minute!

Flat people

If you want clothes that make you look thinner, this is the way to do it.

Get the kids to arrange an outfit of clothes – top, trousers and shoes, with gloves for the hands – on a sofa or chair so that when they go behind the furniture, it looks as though they're a two-dimensional person. It works particularly well when you view it later as a photograph. This is so quick and simple to do that it's now one of our firm favourites.

Spin things out by getting a group to compete to see who can come up with the worst or most outrageously dressed flattie they can.

Bicycle noises

Split a few drinking straws lengthways, then cut them into 2cm long pieces. Slot them around the spokes of a bicycle wheel, and they'll make a great rattling noise as they slide up and down while your kids ride along.

For even more noise, tape a piece of stiff card to the rear frame so that it scrapes on the spokes of the back wheel as they cycle. Sounds just like the motorbike they've always wanted – with the advantage that the card should wear out before the noise begins to drive you crazy.

Marbles

Although you rarely see marbles played now, it isn't so long ago that these small glass globes containing coloured shapes could keep children occupied for hour upon happy hour. The Ancient Romans and Egyptians had them, made from stone or clay, and marbles feature in Shakespeare. Our language still recognises their influence, with phrases in common parlance like 'losing your marbles' and 'knuckling down to it'.

Indoors

There are an amazing variety of marble games. The one we used to play indoors was usually for two, though up to four could join in. With the furniture left in place as obstacles, each player starts from the same corner and has one roll. Unlike some marble games, the marble isn't flicked but rolled from your hand.

In turn, the players roll their marbles, releasing them at the spot where they ended up, the aim being to hit their opponents' marbles, either winning them or scoring points depending on mutually agreed rules. If you hit a marble, you get another roll but you must 'play away' and can't hit an opponent on that shot. Some winning strategies include trying to hide behind furniture legs to ambush others, and tempting others to play their marbles too close to a wall where they'll be easier for you to hit.

He'll never find us here, lads

Outdoors

Outside, the most popular variants usually involve a circle (a stick of chalk is handy) up to ten feet across, depending on the age and skill of the players.

In Ringo or Ring Taw, two players decide who begins by 'lagging' – throwing marbles from one tangent of the circle ('the lag line') to see who can land a marble nearest to the opposite tangent ('the pitch line').

At the centre of the circle, a number of smaller marbles (which are known as 'ducks', 'mibs' or 'migs') are placed in the shape of a cross. Players must 'knuckle down', keeping one knuckle in contact with the ground as, with their thumbs, they flick a larger marble, known as a 'tolley', 'shooter', 'masher' or 'taw', from any point on the circumference of the circle.

The aim is to knock another marble out of the ring while keeping their own tolley within it. If they succeed, they take that marble and continue where their shooter came to rest. If their tolley goes out of the ring, however, while they score any marbles that were knocked out, their turn is over.

Play also switches to the opponent if a tolley stays in the ring but no marbles are knocked out of it. For the initial go, from any point at the edge of the circle, the opponent can aim at the marbles in the cross, at the rival tolley or at any stray marbles.

If their tolley is already in the ring, they play from that spot. If anyone succeeds in knocking their opponent's tolley from the ring but stay in it themselves, their opponent is out of that game and must relinquish the marbles they've won.

It should be established at the outset whether playing for 'fair', in which case marbles are returned to their original owners, or 'keepsies', where winners keep the marbles they've gained.

Among the many marble buzzwords are 'fudging' or 'hunching' (using your shooting hand illegally), 'cabbaging' (shooting from the wrong place) and 'histing' (not having your knuckle in contact with the ground).

The British and World Championships take place each Good Friday at the Greyhound Pub in Tinsley Green in West Sussex, as they have done every year since 1932. There are two teams of six, each with 49 marbles placed in the elevated ring. The captains see who starts by 'tolleying off', dropping their marbles from their noses, trying to get closest to the edge of the ring. The first team to get 25 points wins.

Coin games

Remember how you could keep yourself amused for hours at school with a few coins from your pocket? Pass the tradition on, reminding your kids they don't have to spend their pocket money the minute they get it.

Pitch and toss

Known in some unimaginative corners as 'coinie', this once common playground game is for any number of players. Everyone stands in a line facing a wall, each armed with a coin of the same value. The object is to throw the coins so they land as close to the wall as possible. It should first be established if coins must hit the wall first and bounce off or not. Points are won either for being nearest or for the first three with descending scores. The first to a certain total is the winner.

A different game, confusingly also usually known as Pitch and Toss, involves throwing two coins in the air from upturned fingers of the same hand. If the result is two heads, the thrower wins. Two tails (sometimes known as 'two bikes') is a loss for the thrower. If it's one head and one tail then nobody wins.

This was once such a popular gambling game among adults, particularly miners, that it was made illegal and discovery was punishable with heavy fines. It's even mentioned in Rudyard Kipling's famous poem 'If'.

Penny rugby

The playing surface should be a bench or table with open opposite ends so that a coin can fall without hindrance. The two players sit opposite each other. The first starts with a coin half on and half off the playing surface. Their aim is to get the coin into a similar position on the opponent's side of the table, partly off the playing surface but without falling off. The player should initially hit the coin smartly with the side of their hand. They then have one more go flicking it with their finger to get it into position. If they succeed, they get 5 points.

If the coin falls off, the opponent wins a point. If the player fails to get it to the edge with their two goes, the opponent takes their two attempts from where the coin ended up. If a player is successful in getting the coin over the edge without falling, there's a two-stage conversion process. First, they must lean across the table and, with their middle finger, flip the coin into the air and catch it either with that hand or by clapping their hands together, depending on house rules.

If successful, the opponent must use their hands to form a goal, with their little fingers down, index fingers touching horizontally and thumbs vertically up. The goal attempt is made by putting the coin between the player's thumbs. With their forefingers on the table, they must flick the coin up and try to get it between the two uprights above the crossbar, for which 2 points are scored. Some rules have it that the player must first spin the coin on the table, catch it between their thumbs and instantly try to score as before.

If you want to make the game really complicated, use three coins originally set up in a triangle with a single coin towards the attacking player. They must flick this to part the other two and then make a 'run' up the table, always flicking the nearest coin through the other two in an attempt to get one coin hanging off the opposite edge. If at any stage a coin goes off or a player can't get the nearest coin through the other two, their turn ends and the coins are passed to the other player for his turn.

In the soccer variation, the goal is formed with touching index fingers forming a crossbar and thumbs the uprights (or vice versa for more skilled players). Local variants may allow another finger to act as a goalie, defending the goalmouth. The goal attempt is made by flicking the coin along the surface. Before an attempt at goal is allowed, the player must first succeed in the flipping up of the coin or catch the spinning coin between their thumbs or even both.

These games usually finish when the school bell goes.

Coin football

Everyone knows that the true purpose of school benches, tables and desks is for playing coin games on.

We wasted days of our lives playing coin football while waiting impatiently for the invention of computer games. The ball is a penny, while the two players are each represented by a two-pence piece. Starting in the centre, the first player strikes the ball with his player three times in an attempt to get it into the goal, usually represented by a pair of books of similar dimensions.

Players can't score straight from the centre spot and if they miss the ball at any point, play passes to the other player.

Card games

Everyone has a pack of cards somewhere about the house. Here are some entertaining and exhilarating games for children of all ages that should postpone their interest in online poker for a while.

Racing demons

This boisterous card game is like a competitive version of Patience. You need as many packs of cards as there are players (three to eight is best) and each pack must have a different design on the back. Bearing in mind how frantic the game gets, it's best to use scruffy cards rather than the pack you're keeping for your next bridge evening.

Unless you have a large table, it's best to play on the floor. Each player puts their hands flat on the floor either side of their pack of cards. At the word 'go', each player – as quickly as they can – counts out twelve cards face down, putting a thirteenth face up on top. They then deal four cards face up in a line to the right.

Players then go through the rest of their cards, three at a time. If anybody has an ace in front of them or turns one over, it's placed in the central playing area. Anyone with the two of that suit can then put it down, using only the hand that isn't holding their cards. But everyone is in competition with each other, so it's the first to notice and slam their card down who gets it away. Anybody completing a run of one suit, from ace to king, grabs the whole pile.

The game continues until one player gets rid of their pile of thirteen cards, though they may still have cards in their hand or on the floor in front of them. They call 'stop' and scoring begins. For calling 'stop' you get 10 points. You get 5 points for each pile you have won but lose a point for each floor card you haven't played.

Each player must then gather in all the cards they haven't played and set them aside. Then all the cards that have been played are gathered up and sorted into the different packs, adding the number you played to your score.

Racing demons is usually played over several rounds. If a stalemate is reached and nobody can play any cards at all, which sometimes happens, house rules usually allow everyone to put the top card in their hand to the bottom before recommencing counting in threes.

Demolition

This is another game where you want to use an old pack of cards. You need a demarcated playing area. An old-fashioned square card table is ideal. If playing on the floor, it needs to be somewhere where you can mark out a circle.

All the cards should be spread out face upwards in the playing area, with somebody who isn't playing to act as a caller. The players sit in a circle around the cards, either at chairs if at a table or cross-legged on the ground. The caller announces a card and the players must quickly locate it and drag it off the table or out of the circle, using only one of their middle fingers.

Unless somebody is very quick off the mark, the chances are that more than one player will compete for a card. The caller is allowed to call out the name of another card at any time, so players who are in mid-tussle may suddenly switch their interest to another card they think they can snaffle without competition.

The winner is the player to collect the most cards.

Pack of animals

Players must name an animal and demonstrate the noise that animal makes. Each player in turn takes a card, placing it face up in front of them. If anyone puts down a card that is the same rank as another exposed on the table, that player must say what animal he or she is, but then make the noise of the player of the *other* card.

If they make a mistake, they must take all the cards on the table. Get it right, though, and the cards go to the other player. Play continues with the person to the left of whoever picked up the cards. The object is to have as few cards left in your hand as possible.

Cheat

Divide the pack equally between all the players. The aim is to get rid of all your cards. The first player places as many cards as they like face down, saying what the cards are – for example, 'three queens'. The next player has to place cards either above or below that one in value: such as 'two jacks' or 'four kings'.

Of course, if you have a king and another player calls 'four kings', you know they're cheating, so you call out 'Cheat!' You all then examine the pack: if they were cheating, they take the whole pack of face-down cards; if not, you take the pack yourself. Try to keep track of who's placing which cards!

The magic touch

A good magician never reveals his tricks. We must be lousy magicians, then. Here's a selection of easy-to-do but impressive tricks to amaze your kids.

Now you see it...

Some children have an amazing ability to make loo paper vanish (leaving you to discover the fact only at the crucial moment). But here's a simple trick you can do virtually anywhere with a square of it, or a tissue or paper napkin.

Scrunch up the sheet of loo roll into a little ball, keeping it hidden in your hands. Tell the child you want them to make it disappear, using only the power of their mind. Get them to blow on your hands and then ask them to concentrate as, moving your hands as if still scrunching it, you shake them about, moving them above their head or to one of their ears and back again. Do it more than once if you like. Ask them to blow on your hands once more and then open them up to reveal that the loo roll has gone.

The secret, if you can give such a label to something so ludicrously easy, is to use the momentum of your hands moving out of their line of sight to drop the loo roll behind them. For that reason, the trick only really works on a one-to-one basis. Naturally, the paper needs to be silent, so old-fashioned Izal squares won't do (did they ever?) nor will bog-standard (sorry!) writing paper.

The vanishing coin

Sit at a table, facing your kids, with a coin in each of your upturned palms. Flip both hands over so they're face down on the table, then slowly lift the right hand: there's nothing beneath it. Then, with perhaps the odd magic word, reveal that the coin has reappeared beneath your *left* hand.

It's an easy trick, that requires only a tiny amount of practice. As you flip your hands over, throw the coin from your right hand to be caught beneath your left. It's easier than it sounds, and we haven't met a kid yet who's able to spot it flying through the air: this is a case of the quickness of the hand, quite literally, deceiving the eye.

Starter for ten

Using whatever mumbo jumbo and razzmatazz you choose, tell a child you can tell what date is on a ten pence coin they produce from their pocket. You don't need to see it, just for them to hold it in their hands.

All you need do for this trick is remember to specify a *ten* pence piece (better hope you've given them one in their pocket money) and the date 1992. This is when the smaller ten pence pieces were introduced and, as a result, about half of all ten pence pieces currently in circulation still date from then: you've got an even chance of getting it right first time. Of course, this isn't a trick that can bear much repetition.

You could, of course, cheat and memorise the dates of any other coins you give them. But we would never suggest doing that. Then it wouldn't be magic.

The flicking coin trick

This is a neat trick which, once practised, needs no preparation and very little equipment, just a playing card and a heavy coin. A one-pound coin is fine, but it's actually easier to perform the trick with a two-pound piece and, what's more, it looks more impressive.

Clench one hand into a fist but with your index finger pointing vertically upwards. On this you must balance the playing card with the coin in its centre, ensuring that it is exactly over your fingertip.

Now you must flick the playing card away, leaving the coin in place on your finger. Although it *should* be possible to flick the card away lengthways, we've never managed it. But to us it looks just as impressive flicking it sideways. You must be careful, though, not to follow through on the flick so far that you hit the coin. Not only does it spoil the trick but it hurts, too!

You'll need to practise a bit before you try this in public. Ensure that your flick is in line with the playing card and not pushing it up or down. The hardest part, to be honest, is not the flicking at all, but getting the two balanced properly on your finger.

If you don't have a playing card to hand, you can use a business card though, being smaller, it's not as impressive. We've tried with credit cards but all those raised digits make it a little too tricky to be reliable.

Pick a card...

Whether you shuffle the pack of cards in front of
your audience or not, before the magic commences
you must 'box' the pack by turning the bottom card the
other way up. Keeping that card in line with those above it,
fan out the rest of the cards with the faces downwards. Now you
get to say those truly magical words: 'Pick a card, any card.'

Let the child take the card and show it to anyone they like while you, as naturally
as you can, turn the pack the other way up in your hand. Thanks to the card you
turned over, it will look as though the pack is still facing down. Keeping the pack
together, ask your guinea pig to push the card back anywhere in the pack.

Get them to tap three times on the cards, muttering some hocus pocus if you
think it will help. Ask them to confirm their card with the others while you take the
chance to turn the pack over once more. Ask if they'd think it was magic if their
card, and only their card, was face up. Fan through the pack and, lo and behold,
there their card is, the only one facing upwards.

Don't forget, though, that the bottom card of the deck will also be face up, so
don't inadvertently show it.

...any card

Hold out a pack and tell them to pick a card, which they'll look at and keep hidden
from you. 'Tell me what it is,' you tell them. And they do.

'Correct,' you say, acting mystified that they aren't terribly impressed. There's
no pleasing some children.

Domino delight

Give your kids a set of dominoes. Tell them that you're going to leave the room,
and while you're out they must arrange all of them in a single line, so that the
number of spots on the right side of each domino matches the number on the left
of the following domino (in other words, as the game is played). Without coming
back into the room, you'll be able to tell them the number of spots on the dominoes
at each end of the line.

The trick: take one domino away before they begin. The spots will match the
domino you've taken. Sneaky, but very effective!

Greengrocer's grin

Sitting in a circle, everybody chooses a fruit or vegetable they'd like to be, the weirder and more exotic the better. A player must say the name they've picked twice, followed by that of another player's fruit or vegetable. That player must then say the name of their fruit or veg twice and then somebody else's once and so on and so on.

If any player shows their teeth, however, they are out of the game so – while keeping their own teeth hidden – players are also trying to make the other players laugh or otherwise lose their composure. A variation of this is for the players, while avoiding showing their teeth, to name a vegetable or fruit that hasn't yet been mentioned, a progressively more difficult task.

Why is James wearing odd socks?

Give every player (there should be an odd number) a strip of paper and something to write with. Each person should write down a question beginning with 'Why?' about one of the other players. The questions are mixed up and handed out again, this time for everyone to write an answer to the question on the back.

A player should read out the question on their paper but the person to the left should read out the answer that's on the bit of paper they have. A little like Consequences, the answers can be bizarre and occasionally surprisingly apt.

How did he die?

Players sit in a circle. The first person asks the second, 'Did you know Uncle Arthur died?' The second says, 'No. How did he die?' The first then chooses something about the death that the players can perform, such as, 'He died with one eye closed.' They must close one eye and keep it closed.

The second and third player now go through exactly the same exchange, ending with the second player closing their eye.

When it's the turn of the first player to speak again, they must add another trait, keeping the first one. Perhaps Uncle Arthur died 'with one eye closed and screaming loudly' or with a stammer or shaking uncontrollably. Anybody getting it wrong as more and more of Uncle Arthur's unfortunately deadly afflictions are piled on, is out of the game. Of course, if your kids *do* have an Uncle Arthur, you might like to change the name of this game to avoid complications.

14 Out to lunch: kids in the restaurant

ONE OF THE GREAT JOYS of seeing our kids grow up is that they can begin to participate in more adult activities with us. The day eventually comes when you can return to restaurants that serve real food, rather than burgers and chips hurriedly gulped between visits to the in-house ball pond.

Restaurants do have to be approached with care, of course. Even the most patient child will have trouble sitting still while waiting for their food to arrive. We favour beginning with restaurants that involve no waiting at all – such as those serving sushi on conveyor belts, or help-yourself buffets.

There will come a time, though, when you've ordered your food, the drinks are with you, and you need to pass the time until your meals arrive. This is where Dad can shine: keeping kids amused and entertained in public is the sign of greatness. We've got a range of solutions to help you on your way, along with a more radical suggestion for when service is sluggish and you need to attract the waiter's attention by any means possible.

Games and puzzles

Nothing keeps a child's mind occupied as well as a puzzle. Here's a selection of diversions that are particularly good for playing in restaurants, as they need only the items to hand and cause the minimum amount of disruption.

The coin puzzle

An easy trick to reveal, but one which is hard to puzzle out. Take two pound coins and place them about eight centimetres apart on the table (it *has* to be a table with a tablecloth for this trick to work). Place a thinner coin – 2p, 1p or 5p – between the two pound coins. Now turn a glass upside down and place it so it's resting on the two pound coins, with the other coin unreachable beneath the glass.

The challenge is to get the small coin out from under the glass without touching the glass or either of the pound coins. And that includes not touching them with cutlery, so if they try to slide a knife blade beneath the glass they'll lose when it tips the glass over.

The solution is utterly straightforward: simply scratch the tablecloth with a fingernail, directly in front of the glass. Each time you scratch the coin will creep towards your finger, until it eventually comes right out from under the glass.

Menu games

Kids choose quickly in restaurants: adults can take longer to compare the merits of each dish on offer. To keep them occupied while you make up your minds, have them search the menu for a particular word, or look for the most expensive item (but don't necessarily encourage them to order it). If you're in a posh restaurant, get them to find the most expensive bottle of wine – they'll be amazed.

There are endless variations on menu searches. You could assign them each a colour – red, brown, white and green are good – and have them search the menu to find as many items as they can that match their chosen colour. You may not ever get your children to *eat* their greens, but at least this way they'll get an idea of what they are.

A good menu game to play while you're waiting to be served is the Missing Words game: you read out a menu description, and they have to guess the one word you've missed out. It's going to be tricky if the missing word is 'coulis', or 'ganache', or 'fricassee', or any one of the dozens of fancy expressions restaurateurs use to justify their inflated prices; but it can be funny if, for instance, you're going through the children's menu item by item, and the one word you keep missing out is 'chips'. Remember, this is a game designed to amuse, not a challenge to test their culinary knowledge.

Fork balancing

Give your kids two forks and a toothpick. The challenge is to balance them all on the neck of an open bottle so that only the toothpick is touching the bottle.

You may want to clear a little space around the base of the bottle before starting this one, as in the first few attempts the forks are bound to fall. It's best if there's a tablecloth to muffle the sound of crashing cutlery!

The solution: first, knit the forks together so that their tines interlock. Press them together to make a firm joint. Then wedge the toothpick into the fork assembly so it holds hard. All you have to do now is to rest the toothpick on the edge of a bottle or a glass and the cantilever action will make the forks stay in place, perfectly balanced.

If you're feeling really ambitious, try resting the forks on *two* toothpicks. Build the assembly with one pick, as described above; then place the second so it rests just inside the neck of a bottle, and balance the other toothpick (and the forks) on the other end. Amazing when it works!

What can we make at this restaurant?

A good waiting game is to see how many words you can make from the letters that make up the name of the restaurant you're in. It's an anagram game, but with a twist: your kids score extra points if they can make up items of food from the letters in the restaurant's name. Just in case you happen to be playing there, McDonald's contains all the letters needed to spell Almonds, Salmon, Damson, Clams, Soda and Cod.

An easy one if you happen to be in somewhere like The Hungry Hippo All You Can Eat Burger and Pizza Emporium, but a little tricky if you've ended up in a branch of Wimpy (and you should think yourself lucky that Pizza Pizza is only popular in Canada).

Some sort of prize should be given if a child manages to think up an anagram that uses all the letters in the name: McDonald's is an anagram of Damn Clods, for instance, and Hard Rock Cafe makes Fake Car Chord. (It also makes For Crack Head, but you might want to keep this to yourself.)

Lean on me

You'd never want to do this in a stuffy restaurant, but it can be great fun if your waiter has already established a bantering rapport with the children. You might also consider it if you've complained about the table being wobbly and feel that too little has been done to rectify the problem.

When the waiter is out of sight, use salt to raise one side of various objects such as place mats or the salt and pepper shakers, if they're of suitable design. The aim is to get several things on the table tilted at about the same angle. When the waiter returns, the entire family should be leaning in line, the aim being for everybody to behave completely normally – or at least what passes for 'normal' in your household.

In fact, the real struggle is not to burst out laughing almost instantly. Try going through the whole ordering process with the children and somebody – possibly you – is bound to giggle before it's done.

This Leaning Tower of People also works well when dining with your relatives, providing they have a good sense of humour. It could be ages before granny realises just what's odd about the scene around the dinner table.

Hot air wrappers

If you are ever *en famille* in an Italian restaurant that serves those lovely almond-flavoured amaretti biscuits, make sure you hang on to the thin paper they usually come wrapped in (though not the thick, waxy wrappers you occasionally get).

Shape the wrapper into a cylinder along its longer side and place it on a plate or saucer. Light the top of the paper. The flames will steadily burn downwards. Just before they reach the bottom of the cylinder, the lift from the hot air will be sufficient to float the delicate paper, still burning, several feet up in the air. Use the plate or saucer to catch the ash as it floats back down.

There can't be an Italian waiter anywhere who hasn't seen this trick and, having heard tell of smoke detectors being set off, perhaps it's best either to check first that the staff don't mind or else take the wrappers home and try it there.

If you never encounter amaretti biscuits, you can also use those teabags that come with a string attached. Remove the string and the staple that attaches it to the bag. Pour out the tea into the pot, after warming it of course, so you can have a nice cuppa.

Unfold the teabag and you will see that it's really a long cylinder. Keeping it as cylindrical as possible, place it on a plate or similar and light the top. It works almost as well, though you don't get to enjoy the lovely biscuits or the green or blue-tinged flames that come off the amaretti paper.

Pizza toppings

Each child has to make up a pizza, each ingredient beginning with successive letters in their name. Easy if their name happens to be Tom (tomatoes, olives, mozzarella); less palatable, but still edible, for a Martha (mushrooms, anchovies, radish, tea leaves, ham and apples).

Spare a thought for all the kids out there named Max and Zoe, though, as they'll end up gnawing their way through xylophones and zebras.

The amazing vanishing teaspoon

Tabletop magic is always appreciated, even when it's fairly obvious how the trick is done. Of course, the more bravado and stagecraft you can bring to this, the better it will go down. Check you aren't wearing a T-shirt *before* starting this trick.

Hold a teaspoon in your hand as shown, and cover your hand with a napkin (a cloth one will work best, if you're in a posh enough restaurant). As you put the napkin in place, let the teaspoon drop down into your sleeve; raise your forefinger to take its place, and it will look as if the spoon is still there.

Whip the napkin away with a flourish, folding your finger down as you do so – and ta-ra! The spoon has magically vanished!

Of course, you're now left with a spoon up your sleeve. Stand up, and pick up an empty glass from the table, using the hand that has the concealed spoon. Cover the glass (and your hand) with the same napkin, say a magic word, and allow the spoon to slip out into the glass with a magical chinking noise. Take the napkin away, and the trick is complete.

The three cup trick

You may well have seen this trick performed on street corners by tricksters who are expert in taking money from gullible passers-by. Here's an easy version which will enable Dads to win back pocket money from gullible children.

You need three clean cups and a pound coin. Don't be tempted to use cups that have had coffee in them or you'll leave nasty stains on the tablecloth.

Turn the cups upside down on the table. Place the coin under one of the cups, and ask your kids to watch carefully so they can tell you where the coin is.

Shuffle the cups around at random, using both hands. Then, as you move the cup containing the coin forwards, tilt it away from you slightly so the coin slips out from behind it.

Keep on moving your hand and the cup forwards, and trap the coin beneath your palm. It should stay in place as you move your hand around the table top, as long as you don't move it too far. This is the most difficult part of the trick: make sure you do something flashy with the other hand at this moment, to distract attention from what you're really up to: perhaps waggle your fingers, or rattle the cup you're holding in it.

Then, while you switch to grasp a different cup, release the coin that's trapped under your palm. All you have to do now is to tip *that* cup forward as you pull it back, to allow the coin to slip underneath it.

Like all magic tricks, this one does benefit from some practice before you attempt it in public. It works best on a table with a tablecloth, which will muffle the tell-tale sound of pound coins scraping on wood.

Tippit

Apparently a Welsh game also played in parts of Europe, Tippit needs two teams of three, a table and a small coin. It's a good one for pubs and restaurants if there are enough of you, though we've also heard of it being played at parties and using marbles or nuts instead of a coin.

The coin is tossed to see who goes first. That team hide their hands under the table, passing the coin between them until, when they are ready, the middle player knocks on the table three times.

The players put their six closed fists – one of which contains the coin – on the table. The other side can confer amongst themselves as they try to work out which fist contains the coin. The middle one must name a player and say one of two things. They may order them to 'Take your right/left hand away' and the designated player must open that fist and, assuming there's no coin there, remove it from the table. If the coin *is* there, the team hiding the Tippit have won that round. They score a point and hide it again.

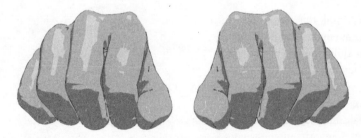

Alternatively the leader of the seeking team may point at a player and say, 'Tippit in your right/left.' That person must open their hand to show if the Tippit is there. If it isn't, the hiding team have won their point and have another go.

If, however, the Tippit is in the chosen fist, the seekers score a point and the coin passes to them, who now have to hide it. Tippit is generally played until one team has eleven points.

Tippit makes for a fun family game as players have to do their utmost to convince the seekers to pick the wrong hand, while those looking for the coin may indulge in staring contests in an attempt to make the hider of the Tippet crack under the psychological strain! Children not yet certain of the difference between their left and right will find they quickly learn. As with so many pastimes, it's easily adaptable into a drinking game when the kids have gone to sleep.

The barfing tomato

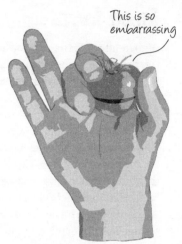

This is so embarrassing

Get hold of a cherry tomato (one of those really small ones) and cut a horizontal slot in it. When you hold it in your hand, you can make it 'talk' by squeezing your fingers together.

Doing your best ventriloquist voice, make it say something like: 'I don't feel too good... must have been something I ate... oh, I think I'm going to throw up... here it comes... eeurgh!'

On the final 'eeurgh!', squeeze your fingers and thumb together and the tomato will barf its contents out of its mouth. Sounds disgusting, and it is. Which is why kids love it, of course.

Peppercadabra

You'd think that if you mixed salt and pepper together, you wouldn't be able to separate them again without tweezers and a good deal of patience. So challenging your children to do just that should keep them occupied for a while.

Pour some salt onto a plate and then add a little pepper on top. The fine stuff that comes in packets is best but ground pepper will work too, just so long as the pieces aren't too big.

Naturally, separating them again is a trick. If you have a plastic comb, smarten yourself up by combing whatever's left of your hair a few times. It will cause static electricity to build up on the comb. Hold it over the salt and pepper and the static on the comb will pick up the grains of pepper, which are lighter than the salt grains. If you haven't a comb, anything else that will take a charge will do, such as a balloon rubbed on a jumper. Easy when you know how.

Food facts

A great Dad is recognised by his ability to pluck fascinating facts out of the air to suit any occasion. And few occasions are as good as being in a restaurant, when you have a captive audience eager for food-related trivia.

Pizza

People have been putting food on discs of bread for thousands of years. Virgil mentions them in the *Aeneid*, for instance, and archaeologists have discovered buildings in Pompeii that look surprisingly like pizza restaurants. Pig's blood was a popular topping.

The version we have today, with a cheese and tomato base, was invented by Raffaele Esposito in Naples, in around 1830. His restaurant, now named Pizzaria di Brandi, is still serving pizza today.

In 1889 Esposito was commissioned to bake a special pizza for the visit of King Umberto and Queen Margherita of Savoy. He made it in the colours of the Italian flag – green, white and red – using basil leaves, mozzarella and tomatoes. You can still buy this concoction in any pizza outlet, and it's called a Margherita.

Hamburgers

Street stalls in ancient Rome sold cooked meat in ciabatta. In the 12th century the Mongol horsemen of Genghis Khan needed food that was easily portable, and which could be eaten with one hand while holding the reins with the other; they used to place ground-beef patties between the horses and the saddles, where they would be tenderised as they rode along. When Genghis's son, Kublai, invaded Moscow in 1238, the Russians were so impressed by their raw ground meat that they called it *Steak Tartare* (Tartar was the Russian name for a Mongol).

German ships visiting the Baltics brought the idea home, most notably to the port of Hamburg – hence the name, just as other German cities have given us frankfurters and Vienna sausages. Hamburgers were never made of ham.

An early recipe for 'Hamburgh Sausages' was published in England in 1758 in *The Art of Cookery Made Plain and Easy*. Hamburgers were served between two pieces of bread, until Walter Anderson invented the burger bun in 1916.

Hot dogs

Sausages are one of the oldest forms of processed meat: Homer mentions them in the *Odyssey*. The hot dog as we know it was apparently invented in Frankfurt, Germany in 1487; the city celebrated the 500th anniversary of the frankfurter in 1987. The American National Hot Dog and Sausage Council (yes, there really is such a thing) asserts that the hot dog was invented by Johann Georghehner in the 17th century.

In the 1830s a rumour spread that stray dogs were rounded up and made into sausages, and frankfurters came to be called dog sandwiches. The 1860s song *Where Oh Where Has My Little Dog Gone* contained the following verse:

Und sausage is goot: Baloney, of course,
Oh where, oh where can he be?
Dey makes 'em mit dog, und dey makes 'em mit horse:
I guess dey makes 'em mit he.

In 1870 a joke appeared in American newspapers: 'What's the difference between a chilly man and a hot dog? One wears a great coat, and the other pants.' This is the first known printed reference to hot dogs.

Sandwiches

The first recorded sandwich was made by the rabbi Hillel the Elder in the first century BC, who started the Passover tradition of placing chopped nuts, apples and spices between two pieces of matzo.

Flat blocks of stale bread, known as trenchers, were used instead of plates during the Middle Ages. The bread absorbed the juices from the meat and was then either eaten or, if you were feeling generous, tossed to a waiting peasant. Plates weren't invented until the 15th century.

So in 1762 when John Montagu, fourth Earl of Sandwich, asked for his steak served between two slices of bread so he wouldn't have to leave the gambling table, he wasn't really inventing anything that new. But other members of his club began asking for their steaks 'the same as Sandwich', and the name stuck.

The Earl of Sandwich, incidentally, was a patron of Captain James Cook, who named the Sandwich Islands after him. They're now known as Hawaii. Cheese and pickle hawaii, anyone?

Drink facts

All kids love soft drinks – even if there are those of us who believe that the only appropriate drink in restaurants is tap water. Here are some facts that should help to pass the time before your food arrives.

Coca-Cola

In 1863, a Corsican named Angelo Mariani invented 'cocawine' – a mixture of wine and cocaine. It was copied by Dr John Pemberton in Atlanta, Georgia, who called

it Pemberton's French Wine Coca, using coca leaves as the stimulant. But when Georgia brought in Prohibition (the banning of alcohol) in 1886, Pemberton replaced the wine with a caffeine-based beverage made from cola nuts, and changed the name to Coca-Cola.

In 1903 the company started using 'spent' coca leaves (after the cocaine had been removed). They still use this formula today, and legend has it that only two top executives know the precise details – they're said to have half the formula each.

During the Second World War, the Coca-Cola company guaranteed to make its drink available to US servicemen anywhere they happened to be fighting. Of course, this meant building bottling plants all over the world – with US Army backing. When the war ended, the Coca-Cola company was poised for world domination.

The highest consumption of Coke per person in the world is in Mexico and Chile.

Pepsi

Invented by a chemist called Caleb Bradham in the 1890s, Pepsi was originally called Brad's Drink. He sold it as a cure for stomach pains, or 'dyspepsia' – which could explain the change of name. Bradham initially sold Pepsi as a syrup, which customers would dilute themselves.

Pepsico went bankrupt due to high sugar prices in 1923 and again in 1931. They introduced a 12-ounce bottle in 1934, double the size of the Coca-Cola bottle, under the slogan 'Twice as much for a nickel'. Their slogans have included 'More bounce to the ounce', 'Be sociable, have a Pepsi' and 'Now it's Pepsi for those who think young'. You can see why Coca-Cola have stuck with 'The real thing'.

Other soft drinks

Lemonade was first brewed in Egypt, over 1500 years ago, and was made with lemons and honey. The Compagnie de Limonadiers was formed in Paris in 1676 and had exclusive rights to sell lemonade from street vendors. In 1788, the newly invented 'Geneva Apparatus' allowed artificial mineral water to be created, which meant lemonade could be given its fizz.

7UP is a lemon and lime flavoured fizzy drink first created by Charles Grigg in 1920. No one knows exactly where the name came from; some believe it to refer to the fact that the company had gone bust six times before the drink was invented. Whatever the origin, it's better than Grigg's original name for the drink – 'Bib-Label Lithiated Lemon-Lime Soda'. Catchy, we're sure you agree.

Ginger beer first appeared in England in the 1700s and was made from ginger, sugar, water and 'ginger beer plant' – a slushy, thick white goo containing yeast and a special bacteria, which together cause the fermentation.

Tomato juice is made simply from squeezed tomatoes, and is the official state drink of Ohio. It's mixed with beer in Canada and Mexico, where it's known as a Calgary Red-Eye or Cerveza Preparada; and with vodka, when it's called a Bloody Mary. Tomato juice is popularly believed to be useful in removing the odour left by skunks.

Perrier is the best known of the mineral waters. It comes from a spring in France called Les Bouillens, and was formerly owned by one Louis Perrier. He sold it to the English aristocrat Sir St John Harmsworth, who marketed it in green bottles shaped like Indian clubs. Perrier does come out of the ground fizzy, but not *that* fizzy: carbon dioxide (from the spring) is added later.

Dandelion and burdock has made a recent revival since being sold in cans. But only in bottles can you see the rich dark colour that made it look like cough medicine but tasting so much better. Traditionally, this supposedly detoxifying drink was made from fermenting the roots of burdock plants and dandelions, but it's unlikely these days to contain any element of either. Americans tasting it would think it very similar to their sarsaparilla.

Disgusting food around the world

If your children insist that food set before them is gross or are fractious in a restaurant, it can be handy to remind them of some of the more unusual gastronomic treats savoured in other countries. If you're worried you haven't come out with enough money, it might even suppress their appetites, making it less likely that you'll end up in the kitchen washing dishes. If they're made of tough stuff and claim they'd love giant toasted ants or whatever, call their bluff – a surprising number of these delicacies are now available to buy online.

Japan: Ice cream flavours include squid, octopus, ox tongue, crab, shrimp, eel, raw horseflesh, goat, whale, cactus, shark fin noodle, chicken, seaweed, spinach, garlic, tulip, lettuce and potato and even silk.

Gold is a permitted food additive (E175). In Japan they add gold leaf to tea and use it as a garnish on other dishes.

A poisonous puffer fish, a delicacy known as fugu (right), is 25 times more dangerous than cyanide. The poison is removed before serving; many deaths occur each year through inept preparation.

Watch it, mate – I'm a kung fu-gu

Indonesia: Deep-fried monkey toes are eaten off the bone. Smoked bats are a delicacy.

Thailand: Giant Bug chilli paste is a hot sauce made from water scorpions. Thais also eat rat, which apparently tastes a little like rabbit.

Among a selection of Thai delicacies for purchase on the web are edible roasted giant water bugs (left), bags of roasted scorpions, roasted giant crickets, roasted pregnant crickets, roasted meal worms and a can of smoky barbecue flavour canned scorpions.

South East Asia: Cats, dogs and even monkey brains are part of a well-balanced diet.

China: Duck or pig blood is eaten in the form of a jelly. There's also a restaurant in Hunan province that uses fresh human breast milk in their recipes.

Scorpion toffee (right) is a big lump of amber-coloured toffee with a crunchy scorpion trapped inside. Specially bred to be eaten, they aren't poisonous. Or so the makers would have us believe.

Vietnam: Rats. Often the star ingredient in rat stew.

USA: In the south, cooked squirrel brains are eaten out of the skull. Apparently it's possible to catch mad squirrel disease from this! Several people have died.

Hungary: Freshly killed pig's blood fried up with scrambled eggs.

Ukraine: Pig fat eaten cooked or raw. Now available covered in chocolate.

Sweden: Blood dumplings. Made of flour, reindeer blood and salt and served with bacon, butter and jam.

France: Frogs' legs, snails and horse meat.

Europe: Black pudding (left), also known as blood sausage, *boudin, morcilla de burgos* and *blutwurst*. Whatever the name, it's made from congealed blood, fat and offal.

Spain: *Criadillas,* or bull's testicles (also known as prairie oysters in Canada).

Mexico: *Chahuis* (right) are the worm-like insects that feed on the mesquite tree, and they're commonly found in bottles of tequila. You can also buy them, roasted, to eat as a tasty snack.

Great Britain: Barbecue flavour crispy worm crisps. Also crocodile curry, oven-baked tarantula, chocolate-covered scorpions, giant toasted ants and our favourite: coffee that's been eaten and regurgitated by weasels. Well, OK, these may not be foods that are exactly native to this country, but you can buy them all here through www.lazyboneuk.com. Well worth a visit!

More unusual food facts

Here are some more unusual facts about food that might help pass the time while you're waiting for your waiter to get back from Italy (which is clearly where he's gone to get the pizzas you ordered).

While an apple a day is said to keep the doctor away, apple pips actually contain cyanide, the stuff murderers seem to have elected as the poison of choice, if Agatha Christie is to be believed. Some people seem terrified of apple pips as a result but in fact your digestive system could quite happily cope with the absolutely tiny amount of poison each pip contains. Even a lot wouldn't harm you, particularly as your stomach's acids would have trouble eating through the protective coating. If apple seeds weren't so hardy and were digested in animals' stomachs, there wouldn't be nearly as many apple trees.

Incidentally, peach and cherry stones contain cyanide too, so don't go eating too many of those either. And while we're on dangerous foods, cassava – the root tapioca comes from – is chock-full of the stuff, but it's rendered harmless in the preparation.

Although avocado's a pretty popular fruit these days, don't give any to your pets. All the bits of the avocado, including the flesh we eat, contains persin which, while causing no problems to people, is poisonous to a wide variety of animals, including birds, dogs, fish and rabbits. So no dropping guacamole into the dog's bowl to get out of eating it.

Tarantula spiders are found periodically in boxes of bananas in supermarkets. These so-called banana spiders get transported here despite the bananas being washed, sprayed with fungicide and inspected as they're packed. Creepy crawlies they may be, but they're usually harmless to humans. Very occasionally poisonous black widow or other spiders turn up alive in the veg section of supermarkets, though they're usually killed off by the refrigeration used to keep the fruit and veg from going off.

Makes a change from water spouts

Contrary to the urban myth, the black bits in bananas are not tarantula eggs. They're the remnants of banana seeds, which have been bred out of the fruit to make them more palatable.

15 Sleepover and party games

IF ANYBODY INVENTED the sleepover, they're not owning up to it – probably because they're petrified that countless sleep-deprived parents would want to have a quiet word with them.

Loathe them or hate them, though, sleepovers are now common, particularly among girls. Depending on their age, supplying them with tried and tested games to play can be a good way of keeping down the level and longevity of the inevitable mayhem.

All kids love parties, especially if it's their birthday. But running a successful party involves more than just making sure you've remembered to get the right number of candles for the cake: you need to plan exactly what the little darlings are going to be doing if you want to avoid them rampaging through the house and destroying your prized ornaments.

We've put together a fantastic selection of activities and games that should keep them happy and busy – some involving rushing around expending energy, some more sedentary.

Oh! Where's everybody gone?

The Funky Chicken

This group activity, which works best with large numbers, needs to be initiated by an outgoing child or a Dad utterly lacking in the embarrassment gene. Whoever leads it off starts by shouting out 'Chicken' loudly. Then, imitating panto chickens, they continue by chanting in a sing-song manner:

Chicken with a wing (flapping their elbow like a wing)

Chicken with two wings (flapping both elbows)

Chicken with a leg (lifting and shaking a leg)

Chicken with two legs (doing the same with both legs in quick succession)

Chicken with a head (imitating a chicken's pecking action)

Chicken with a tail (turn and shake your bum)

Chicken chooses YOU.

At that point, they should select somebody else who should come and join in as the chant is repeated, at the end of which the new person picks the next until, before long, you have a massive group imitating chickens. The moment for playing The Funky Chicken needs to be chosen carefully. It can be a little unnerving if the first person goes through all that only to find that nobody else will join in.

Simon's daughter Izzy says she once did The Funky Chicken with a group of bored Girl Guides in Trafalgar Square, dragging hapless tourists into the action. Proof, if any were needed, that while Dads embarrass their children, it works the other way round too.

Little Miss Noisy

The players group themselves in a circle around the person chosen as 'It'. 'It' is blindfolded and counts to ten slowly, allowing the other players to swap positions. 'It' should then point and the player indicated should make noises of any sort but without speaking, trying to keep their identity secret. If 'It' guesses who it is, that person then becomes 'It'. If not, the game continues.

Instead of the blindfold, of course, the game can be played at night with the lights out. What's most important is that this is played in a group where all the players know each other pretty well. If they haven't even been introduced, the game could go on for an awfully long time.

Hide and seek

Children hardly need any instruction on how to play hide and seek. It remains a favourite and, in these days of declining educational standards, parents may even take pride in their child's ability to count up to a hundred. But there's a super variant that works well at sleepovers for younger children as it's confined to just one room, a bedroom being ideal.

Making sure that anything sharp or fragile is safely out of the way, one of the players is blindfolded and then has to tag others in the room. Instead of hiding in the traditional sense, players try to keep out of 'It's way while at the same time teasing them by making noises and tapping their shoulder from behind and so on. If anyone is touched by 'It' they are out and must gather in one place, such as on a bed.

It sounds simple, and it is, but it's also amazingly good fun and can lead to delighted hysterics. On second thoughts, maybe it *isn't* the best game for a sleepover.

Balloon forfeits

Into balloons should be pushed rolled-up slips of paper on which are written assorted forfeits. For younger children, parents might want to make suggestions such as making noises or behaving like particular animals, singing songs, acting out adverts and the like. Older children may prefer to come up with their own devilish ideas.

The balloons should be blown up and then handed out randomly. Players take it in turns to sit on the balloons until they burst and must then carry out the forfeit. An added twist, rather than read out what's on the paper, is to ask the other players to guess what the forfeit says from what is happening.

Sleepover souvenir

The problem with sleepovers is that they're over all too soon – unless you're the sleep-deprived parents of course. It's very easy to conjure a long-lasting memory of the night, though, by getting everyone to sign a message on a light coloured pillowcase. If you're really organised you can tie-dye it first, otherwise simply hand over an indelible marker or two. You can use dedicated laundry markers if you like, but it doesn't really seem to make much difference.

The inscriptions really do last. We've got one or two dating back several years that don't seem to have faded at all and are still in regular use.

Bubble bum

Set out as many chairs as there are players, with a balloon on each chair. The players begin by sitting on the floor, with their legs crossed, a set distance away from the chairs. At your signal, they all rush to the chairs and have to sit on the balloons, trying to burst them.

As the balloons burst, they must rush back to their starting position and sit on the ground again, cross-legged. It's simple, but also great fun to play, if a little boisterous. To make the game rather trickier – and so make it last longer – don't blow the balloons up too much. A partially inflated balloon is far harder to burst!

Touchy feely

For this game, which has similarities to Twister, you need to hand a set of six stickers bearing the numbers from 1 to 6 to each of six players. Each person can choose where they'd like to stick the stickers about their person, be it on clothing or skin.

Everybody is assigned a number and the first person rolls a die to see who they are initially partnered with. If player one rolls a 5, for instance, followed by a 3, then he or she must touch player five's sticker number 3 with some part of their body and maintain contact throughout the rest of the game.

The next player similarly rolls the die twice and ends up in contact with another sticker. It becomes progressively more tangled and difficult for players to keep in contact with the stickers, particularly if everyone starts laughing. Anyone who fails to keep contact should either be taken out of the game or made to perform some embarrassing forfeit.

Once all players have thrown the die once and are attached to each other, put on some music and try to get them to dance. Parents of alarmingly advanced teenagers (is there any other kind?) may prefer to suggest this game only at parties with all girls or all boys.

Murder in the dark

Darkness and murder: two of children's favourite play topics, and a great game for parties, sleepovers and big gatherings. You need as many folded slips of paper as there are players. All but two have 'Suspect' written on them. On the other two, one says 'Detective' and the other 'Murderer'.

The slips are either handed out in secret or are drawn from a bag. After removing anything that might hurt if it's bumped into (as well as the Ming Dynasty vase that you'd rather not have broken), the lights are turned off. The Murderer must wander about the room touching people on the shoulder. All the Suspects he touches should fall to the ground with melodramatic, over-the-top dying noises. This goes on until the Murderer kills the Detective, at which point the Detective says 'The Detective is Dead' and falls to the ground.

On go the lights with all the Suspects playing dead; if he or she chooses, the Murderer can play dead too. The Detective, however, is miraculously reincarnated and should go about the room studying the grisly carnage and trying to work out who they think the Murderer is. They must then make an accusation. If they get it right, they win. Get it wrong and the Murderer has won.

Wink murder

Although outwardly similar to *Murder in the dark*, there's a little more skill in this version. Slips of paper are drawn or distributed. All are blank except for one that bears the title of 'Murderer'.

Trying to avoid being spotted by anyone other than his victims, the Murderer should move about and wink at anyone he wants to 'kill'. Such deaths are usually again accompanied by hammy over-acting.

Accusations as to the Murderer can be made at any point by 'living' players but if somebody gets it wrong, they are immediately killed and out of the game. Some people insist on forfeits being paid as well to cut down on the number of accusations. Get the accusation right, though, and the game is won. The Murderer wins if only one other player is left living.

There are umpteen variants on this. One has a Detective leave the room while the rest of the group, in a circle, decide upon the Murderer. The Detective returns and stands in the middle of the circle as the Murderer begins felling victims with a wink while the Detective tries to guess who the Murderer is. Depending on the numbers playing, he is allowed up to three guesses.

Squeeze murder

Yet another murder game to be played with a decent-sized group in the dark. Players should be in a circle and pick pieces of paper from a hat, all of which are blank bar one bearing an 'M' for 'Murderer'.

When the lights go out, everybody holds hands. The Murderer decides who he or she wants to murder, reckoning up how many places to their left that person is. The Murderer then squeezes the hand of the person to their left that number of times. That person should squeeze the hand of the person to their left one time fewer and so on until somebody feels their hand being squeezed only once. That person should die dramatically and move out of the circle.

There's no investigation here. It's just a bit of fun and continues until everyone is dead, unless of course the Murderer miscalculates and kills his or herself.

Bucket bounty

Rather than simply giving children party bags stuffed with teeth-rotting sweets, tubs of bubbles and cheap knick-knacks, why not make them work for them? Set up several buckets – one might have sweets, the next a particular sort of toy, and so on.

Get the children to throw a tennis ball into the first bucket from a set distance. When they get the ball into the bucket, they can take their prize from it and pop it in their party bag. Those kids who don't succeed the first time can move a little nearer for their second go and nearer still if they don't get a prize that round. Once everyone has a prize from that bucket, you can move on to the second and so on. It helps them appreciate the party bags just that little bit more and has the added advantage that you don't have to stuff the bags yourself.

Party obstacle race

Set up an obstacle race, either timing how long it takes children to go round it or doubling it up with the obstacles in two lines, so that two teams can compete against each other. If there's a garden and the weather's decent, set it up outside.

Among the things you might think of including are:

- A coat to put on backwards

- Having to tie shoelaces or a tie with gloves on

- A row of chairs to crawl through

- A musical instrument on which a sound has to be made

- A skipping rope for a certain number of skips

- Food to eat without the use of hands

- A sheet of paper with a forfeit – sing the highest note you can, cluck like a hen, and so on

- A tarpaulin or sheet to crawl under

Plane madness

Hang on to your scrap paper for months before party time, particularly A4 paper you can't use in your printer. Sort everyone into two teams and set up something to 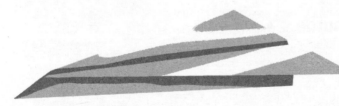 divide the room into two, either a line with a sheet thrown over it or a settee or table on its side.

Each team is given an equal number of sheets of paper and told to make them into darts. Once this is done, give them the signal and they must throw them, only one at a time, into the other team's part of the room, the aim being to see who has the fewest number of planes in their half when time is up. It's noisy but it's great fun, both to take part in and to watch.

Sofa samba

This is one of those rare party games that involves an element of strategy. It makes it marginally more difficult to begin with, but it's well worth it.

Two teams of four is the ideal number, and it's best if one team is all boys and the other all girls. The names of every player should be written on pieces of paper and handed out randomly, the idea being that everyone is not themselves, but the person on the piece of paper in their hand.

Group five chairs in a semi-circle in front of the sofa and have everyone sit down alternately, so there's a boy then a girl and so on, with four people on the sofa and one of the chairs unoccupied. The idea of the game is to get all of your team onto the sofa by getting the other team off it.

The game starts with whoever is sitting to the left of the empty chair. They call out somebody's name and the person with that name on the piece of paper must occupy the empty place, swapping their piece of paper with the person who has just called out. There's now a different empty space, so the person to the left of that should call out a name. Whoever holds it must sit in the empty place, swapping their paper with the caller.

As the game progresses, so the location of more names are steadily revealed. Players must keep track of where they are as they try to manoeuvre the other team off the sofa. The game ends when one team manages to get all their players onto it.

You can play with more people, if the couch will stand the strain, but the game takes correspondingly longer.

Knock knee shuffle

Two teams, two glasses or mugs of water a few yards away and two equal piles of loose change.

Players have to cram as many coins between their legs as possible, shuffle their way across to their glass and drop as many coins into it as they can, all of course without using their hands once the coins are in place. The team with the greater number of coins in the glass wins.

This is a variation on an old drinking game, which tended to involve the coins clenched somewhere a little less visible. The rules are the same, except that it was usually mandatory for the participants to hum the theme to *The Dambusters* while attempting to drop their bombs in the water.

Potato wars

Rather than throwing them out, keep hold of old pairs of tights and they'll come in very handy for party games. Put a couple of potatoes into one leg of the tights and tie the other leg around the player's waist, so that the tights hang down in front: put a balloon in front of each player.

The objective is to swing the 'bat', without using your hands in any way, so that it hits the balloon forward. The game is a race between two people, either to get the balloon to go a certain distance or to hit it into a goal of some sort. Potatoes or oranges work well on hard floors or out of doors but you might not want to risk using either on a beautiful shagpile carpet. You'd be better off substituting apples or ping pong balls.

This is a game that's every bit as entertaining to watch as to play, but if you're playing at a party, you can always turn it into a team game, the 'bat' being removed and tied round the next player's waist. If you have plenty of spare pairs of tights, make the players wear them on their heads and they'll look like old-style bank robbers.

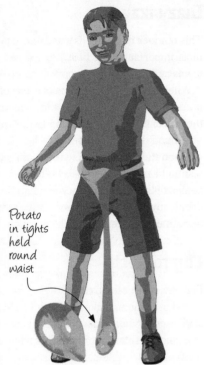

Potato in tights held round waist

The Malteser game

Pop some Maltesers in a bowl and get everyone sitting around it with a straw and a cup. A die gets passed around the circle, with each player rolling to see if they get a six. If not, it is passed to the next person. When somebody does roll a six, they try to get as many Maltesers as they can into their cup by sucking through the straw. They have until the next six is thrown.

It sounds easy, but gets very tricky if people begin laughing, for it then becomes well nigh impossible to keep the sweets on the end of the straw.

Dizzy Izzy

This outdoor game needs six or more people and two broomsticks or similar, the most important thing being that it has a smooth top. Divide everyone into two teams and line them up, placing the two sticks some distance away.

When the game begins, the first player in each team must run to the stick, place it upright with their forehead leaning on it and run around it ten times, keeping their forehead in contact with it, while the other players on the team count as they go around the stick ten times.

When they've finished ten laps of the stick, the players must run back to their team and tag the next person and so on, with the first team whose players all complete the task being the winners. What makes this so much fun is watching the drunkenly dizzy running as the players try to get back to their team. Even staying upright can be tricky.

Egg roulette

For obvious reasons, this is best played outside. If you do have to play it indoors, make sure you've got a tarpaulin or something similar covering the floor. Put as many eggs as there are players into a bowl. All are hard-boiled except for one.

Players have to select an egg from the bowl and hold them on their head. Somebody will be holding a raw egg, but nobody knows who. Each person is allowed to switch their egg once with another player.

When all the switches have been made, everyone must smash their egg against their forehead. Somebody is in for a nasty surprise. To keep the tension high, make them smash the eggs one by one.

Egghead aside: If you have another hard-boiled egg, you can demonstrate how to tell the difference between it and a raw egg without having to smash it open. Simply spin each of the eggs and lightly touch them as they are spinning, taking your finger off again quickly. Both eggs will stop spinning, but the raw egg will begin spinning again when you remove your finger. This is because, although the egg stopped moving, the yolk is still rotating inside the egg.

Another method is to spin them on their apexes. You can only manage this with hard-boiled eggs. To make the test more interesting, do it in a flat frying pan or on a tray with a thin layer of water. As the egg spins, water rises up the egg and starts spraying out like a lawn sprinkler.

Captain Freeze

At a party or other large gathering, one person should be appointed 'Captain Freeze'. Everybody else is told that if Captain Freeze freezes, suddenly being completely still, then everybody else should do the same.

Invariably there'll be one or two who take ages to notice that the room has gone suddenly quiet. The very last one to freeze becomes the new Captain Freeze. If you're playing at a party for youngish children, it makes sense for Captain Freeze only to go into his or her freeze routine at the instigation of an adult. Otherwise the guests are likely to spend a great part of their time motionless.

Hard taskmaster

Split the party up into groups of between four and six players. The Taskmaster calls out different tasks for the teams, who must carry them out as quickly as they can, the leader of a team shouting out 'Team ready for inspection, Taskmaster' when they believe they have completed a task.

At this point, the other teams must remain motionless and quiet, while the Taskmaster, possibly with the assistance of other onlookers, inspect the team to ensure that they have indeed carried out the task properly, giving them a point if they have. If not, the Taskmaster shouts out 'Task on' and the other teams then continue, with the first team penalised for jumping the gun by having to remain stationary.

Among the tasks that might be set are:

- arranging themselves in order of height, foot size or age

- swapping items of clothing

- taking off their shoes and putting them on their hands

- taking their jumpers off and putting them back on inside out

- putting the numbers 1 to 10 in alphabetical order

- pronouncing each of their names backwards with no mistakes

- sitting on the floor with their knees pressed against each other's backs

- eating a cream cracker each with no water

- peeling an apple each.

16 Surf and turf

THERE'S NOTHING SIMON LIKES BETTER than spending a day frolicking on the beach, splashing about in the waves and building sandcastles... or at least lying down watching the kids doing it. For Steve, on the other hand, the beach is seen as the holiday setting from hell: not enough shade, too many over-oiled bodies, nowhere comfortable to sit, and the rest of the evening spent scraping sand out of every orifice.

For those who *do* like to be beside (tiddley-om-pom-pom), here's a collection of games and pastimes, as well as a handy guide to the seashells you might find.

For those who prefer the security of feeling the grass beneath their feet, we've a range of outdoor activities – as well as a guide to how to stay afloat (and ensure that your kids do too) while messing about in boats.

If your love of the Great Outdoors extends to sleeping out under the stars, we've a few ideas for turning a camp fire into a meal to remember (and we're not talking about food poisoning here).

What is sand?

Q: Why is it impossible to be hungry on the beach?
A: Because of all the sand which is there.

It's often difficult for young minds to get their head around the fact that sand is made of tiny pieces of rock which have been weathered over the millennia and washed down rivers or blown into the sea where, along with shell, it's ground up further as currents and waves move it about. The rounder a bit of sand or pebble is, the further it has probably travelled.

Although not all 'beaches' are sandy, those that are have the lighter, sandy bits on top while the bigger bits of rock have sunk lower down. There are people – known as psammophiles – who collect sand. This doesn't usually mean bringing lots of it back from a day trip to Mablethorpe, but finding sand of varying colours, textures and so on. In Hawaii, for instance, there are black, green and red sands.

Sand collectors and others use the 'Wentworth Article Size Classification' under which anything between 0.06mm and 2mm is defined as sand. Anything over 2mm is known as gravel, including granules, pebbles and cobbles, while anything over 256mm is a boulder. Particles below 0.06mm are known as silt – finer than sand but still gritty. Below 0.0004mm is clay or mud, the finest material of all, which, if it gets wet, becomes a sticky ball.

What is quicksand?

It's a mixture of sand and salty water and is actually a liquid, which is why objects that are thrown in have a tendency to sink. Despite the cinematic cliché of quicksand sucking people to their death, it's actually denser than water so that, unless you're wearing heavy equipment, you'll probably float.

Quicksand is often found under leaves and crusts of mud, or near limestone caves where underground springs reach the surface. If you do fall into quicksand, stay calm. Often it won't come any higher than your knees or waist. Even if it is deeper, most people will float once they're waist-deep. The problems come if you wriggle about, because that will pull you down further. With a consistency like treacle, however, it is hard to get out of quicksand.

Keep calm, get rid of anything heavy, like a rucksack, and try to float on your back. Eventually, your legs and feet should come back up to the surface. Make small circular motions with your legs, which will help keep the quicksand at the surface watery, and slowly paddle your way towards more solid ground.

Nekki

This Japanese children's game simply requires the players to try to knock down a stick stuck in the sand with other sticks. You need a reasonably long and stout stick pushed into the sand as the target, or you could use one of those bamboo canes with a fishing net on the end.

You need to find as many smaller but similar sticks to throw at it as there are players. Mark the throwing positions in the sand, handicapping the stronger players by making them throw from further away. The first to knock over the target is the winner of that round.

Beach darts

Draw a series of concentric circles in the sand, assigning increasing points to them the closer they are to the centre. Each player should be sent off to find three similar objects they can throw, such as pebbles or a particular type of shell.

Throw the objects in turn, adding up the score after each round and keeping track by writing in the sand.

Lame Hen

This is a relay race for a sizeable number of people that apparently originates in China, though you could just as easily pretend to your warlike offspring that it's an obstacle course game played by the army. Get them to gather up twenty sticks, which ought to be at least 15 cm long – ideally double that.

Line them up in two rows about 40 cm apart, rather like rungs on a ladder. Organise the players into two equal teams some distance away from the sticks. The first person in each team should hop on one leg over all the sticks, pick the last one, then return to the beginning, putting the stick down so it becomes the new first stick in the 'ladder'.

This is the signal for the next person to set off. The first team to complete the course once wins. If children are too small to hop on one leg, they can always do the bunny hop instead. The Chinese apparently require the hoppers to cluck like hens. We found a marked reluctance on the part of our guinea pigs to do this, on the grounds that it was 'so not cool'.

Boules

If you haven't a Kubb set to hand (see page 162), Boules is the next best game to take to the beach. A set consists of a small jack and eight metal or weighted plastic balls with markings identifying them as pairs. The French take the game very seriously: they call the game Pétanque, and it's boules that they throw. They play on hard terrain like dirt or gravel rather than on the beach. The great advantage of playing on the beach is that you can always run into the sea to cover your annoyance at having been beaten by your children.

Play with two teams of one or two players on each side. You can choose whether to play with two or four boules. With four people, it's two boules each. Don't play in sand that's too soft, or the boules will simply stop where they land, making it a much less skilful game.

Although there are no rules about how boules should be thrown, it's usual to hold the ball in the hand, palm downwards. This way, backspin can be imparted to the boule in an attempt to get it to stop where it lands, rather than overshooting the jack, rolling down the hill and ending up in the sea.

The person who begins draws a line in the sand with their foot and, standing behind it, throws the jack. They should then try to get a boule as close to the jack as possible. Touching it is fine. A player from the second team should try to get

You all right, Jack?

a boule closer to the jack than the first team, if necessary knocking their boule out of the way. Play continues with the team furthest from the jack throwing next. After every player has thrown, points are scored for all the boules a team has that are nearest the jack. If, for instance, a team has three boules closer to the jack than any of the other team, they score three points. The first to 13 points is usually the winner of that game, but you can set any total you wish.

How to determine which ball is nearest the jack

We still remember arguments over boules from childhood family holidays, with hankies brought out to measure the distance of two competing balls from the jack. While amusing as a spectator sport, no two hankies seemed to tell the same story and, these days, who has a hankie handy anyway, particularly if you're wearing swimming trunks?

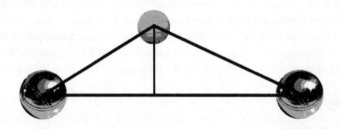

Fortunately, there's a much easier way of determining which boule is closest to the jack. Imagine a triangle formed by the two boules and the jack. Stand behind the jack and visualise a line drawn to meet, at right angles, a line drawn between the two boules. Whichever boule is nearest to that meeting point is the one closest to the jack.

Beach bowling

Damp sand's the perfect stuff for setting up your own bowling alley on the beach. Depending on what sort of ball you plan on using, fill either a bucket or a plastic cup with sand and upend it to make ten 'pins'. Arrange them in a triangle with one in the front row, then two, then three, then four.

A pin is scored not when it is hit, but when no flat surface remains on the top. It's a mite tedious having to reset the pins so either set up two or three lanes to start with or else place two sets of pins opposite each other and have two teams, rolling in turn to see who can demolish all ten pins first. Depending on the skill of the players and the solidity of the ball you're playing with, you might want to give each player two rolls of the ball at a time, rather than just the one.

If you're at Southport and the sea's too far away to dampen the sand, or you want to play when you aren't at the beach, empty plastic water bottles or drinks cans can also be pressed into service as pins.

Castles in the sand

Children find making things from sand well nigh irresistible but they often need a helping hand. That's *our* excuse, at any rate.

It's a great deal easier building castles and other sculptures if you give it some thought before you set off. Making anything substantial with the sort of plastic spade you get at most seaside resorts is hard going. If you're travelling by car, take a garden spade or, even better, a shovel. Yes, it looks completely over the top when you arrive on the beach in the morning. But the sneering of other parents will change to envy when they realise just how quickly you can get the job done and return to reading your suntan-cream-and-sand-covered paperback while watching them struggle to build a castle half the size of yours.

Planning and tools: Have a good hunt round before you set off for things that could be useful. Plastic implements and shapes of the sort bought for young children can be handy, along with old pastry knives, trowels, rulers, plastic containers, skewers, paintbrushes and straws (great for getting rid of loose sand) as well as an assortment of cutlery of the type that tends to lurk at the bottom of drawers. You can actually *buy* sand-sculpting tools, but then you have no excuse if your creation looks any less than brilliant.

If you intend making anything substantial then you need sand that is good and wet. Not all beaches lend themselves to this, but if you can site your construction area around the high-water mark and dig down to water, that's ideal. With the spade or shovel you so sensibly brought with you, mix the sand and water up really well before you begin. Start it too near the sea and you risk having the sea wipe out all your hard work before it's finished.

Starting to build: The traditional Dad and children castle seems to involve plonking a big mound in the middle, making a few turrets using upside-down buckets and then shaping some walls. By all means use the sand you've dug out of the hole as a base, but you can make the construction more impressive by building a tower or two to begin with.

If you can find something to make a cylindrical mould, splendid. Fill the shape with sand, packing it down as you go. If not, then link your hands and scoop out as much sand from the hole as you can, plonking the 'pancake' on top of the mound, holding it while the water drains from it. This will bond the layers of sand and is the secret to making a sandcastle that lasts. Keep on piling 'pancakes' of sand on top, each smaller than the one underneath so the tower doesn't get too top heavy.

Simon hard at work (out of shot) watching his friend Peter build a sandcastle

Making walls: For walls connecting the towers or around a central tower, you need to get the sand into 'brick' shapes, holding your hands parallel and a few inches apart, again letting the water drain. Do one layer of bricks at a time, trying to make them a regular size, then do the same on the next level and so on. The kids could start carving the towers while you are doing this, giving the towers pointy tops, carving recesses for windows and doors, adding balconies and stairs, etching the outline of stones and so on. This is where all those tools you brought with you really come into their own.

The walls will almost certainly need to be castellated, preferably with a walkway in the middle for the troops (no matter where you are in the world, the supermarket is almost certain to sell packs of plastic soldiers to add to your castle). Staircases

Who needs to go to Jordan to see the temple at Petra?

are best made by constructing a ramp and then cutting out the steps. If you're brave enough, try for an arch or two. You can carve away at a wall to create a hole that you shape into an arch. Alternatively, for a truly impressive arch, build two towers close together, bringing them near each other at the top and have someone hold their hand to support sand as you create a bridge between them.

Extra decoration and twiddly bits can be added by getting extremely wet sand and letting it dribble out of your hand where you need it. If the sand is getting dry in places, a spray bottle will restore the sand to a state where you can work with it again.

We have a fondness for building roads that descend into tunnels under our castles. Sometimes they go all the way through and out the other side, but they don't have to. If you've timed it well, now could be a good time to construct a moat, ready to receive the tide as it comes back in.

Bear in mind that most beach sand is nothing like the quality of sand used by those amazing sand sculptors. So don't feel too inadequate if your effort ends up looking more like a ruined burial mound than the Taj Mahal. And if you finish with a flourish, only to discover that the children vanished over an hour earlier, you might have been taking it all a little too seriously.

Sand boats and other creatures

The more impressive a sandcastle is, the less suitable it will be for the kids to play in. They tend to love holes, of course, and it's very easy to oblige if you've brought a decent spade or shovel with you. Don't get carried away, though, by making it too deep. If the sides collapse, it could be dangerous. Don't forget that when the hole no longer seems exciting to them, you can get them to stand in it and bury them up to their waists, packing the sand down so it takes them ages to wriggle their way out.

The other standby is the sand boat, almost invariably something resembling the sort of craft you get on a park lake. You don't need to be quite as particular over the wetness of the sand as you would for a large-scale castle. Build it with a pointy end and a couple of raised seats inside. Use shells for the dials on the dashboard, perhaps using an inverted bucket or flying disk for the steering wheel. A car is only a little more adventurous. Model two-thirds of the wheels against the body, tie sticks together to make a Flintstone-like roof and make use of driftwood, shells, seaweed and the like for decoration, indicators, lights, number plate and so on.

If you're of an artistic bent, then don't stick to man-made objects. Umpteen creatures can be conjured up out of sand, be they dragons, dinosaurs, hippos or snakes.

Sea shells

What visit to the seaside would be complete without returning with a handful of shells? We used to put them in airtight jars, only to watch the water turn green over time. The longer they were left, the more odious was the odour when the water was eventually thrown away. But what *are* the shells we see all the time on the beach? In the absence of an informative 'she' selling seashells by the seashore, here's a guide to some of the more common ones and an explanation of how to tell the age of a shell.

Scallop

The scallop is a bivalve – its shell is in two halves – and was used as the design for the Shell logo. Although the shells are often washed up on beaches, the scallop lives in deep water where predators are fewer. It can actually swim, which it does fairly nippily by opening and shutting its shell, forcing water out on either side of the hinge. They are hermaphrodites, having both male and female sex organs. Scallops are edible. The great scallop, which can be as much as six inches across, often ends up as an ashtray.

Mussel

The mussel is another bivalve. Very tough, it attaches itself to rocks, jetties, piers and the like. Purple or dark blue on the outside, the two halves of the shell are held together by a powerful adductor muscle. They get their food by filtering water but should only be eaten when properly cultivated – usually on ropes – in areas where the cleanliness of the water is guaranteed. If you find a mussel shell with a little round hole drilled in it, this will be from a dog whelk which bores into a mussel then sucks it out!

I've lived here since I was a young shaver

Periwinkle

Common throughout the UK, the best-known periwinkle is the edible variety which can be as much as 5cm long. The conical shells have a spiral ridge though this becomes less pronounced in older winkles. The periwinkle is a gastropod, the marine equivalent of a snail or slug. All gastropods have one large 'foot' for moving around.

Razor shells

The long, thin, discarded shells aren't uncommon, though finding one with both sides in perfect condition, still joined, is rarer. Few of us have actually seen the creatures themselves. Living vertically in sand, they shy away from light and vibration, and can burrow down faster than somebody could dig with a spade.

Limpet

The conical protective shell of the common limpet, one of several limpet varieties in the UK, has probably been taken home in more buckets than any other. Limpets can live for fifteen years. They use their tough watertight seal to cling tenaciously to rocks, feeding off algae by moving slowly and scraping at it with a sort of conveyor belt of teeth. Don't try to prise a live limpet off its rock or you could kill it.

Cockle

This thick, rounded, ridged shell is a bivalve, although it's rare to find both halves still joined. Cockles live in shallow burrows, often exposed after storms. Like most bivalves they don't grow much in winter, so you can tell its age by looking at the number of bands running across the ridges. The dark lines are the winter marks, the lighter bands are where growth has speeded up in the warmer weather.

Messing about in boats

It may be that the smallest boat you've been in since you were a kid is a cross-Channel ferry yet, for some reason, every Dad is supposed to know how to mess about on the water. You may be lucky and find that the only transportation for hire is a pedalo. But if you're being badgered to take your children out in a rowing boat, a punt or a canoe, you'd better have some idea of what to do. Whatever method of transport you end up with, make sure they're wearing flotation devices, even if they are decent swimmers.

Rowing

We aren't talking about trying to get into the Oxford and Cambridge Annual Boat Race here, just being able to handle a rowing boat for a fun trip on a river or lake without making yourself look too ridiculous. It's a good idea to know that the pointy end is the front or bow and that you have to sit with your back to it.

Before you start: Make sure that the oars provided are of the same length, with paddles at the end that are the same size as each other and undamaged. The oars should be roughly double the width of the boat and you should also check that the rowlocks, the circular pivots the oars fit in, are in decent condition and pivot freely. The oars must also have a stop to prevent them slipping through the rowlocks. If anything is amiss, sort it out there and then or you will have a miserable time, made worse when your attempts to shift the blame are not believed.

Technique: Remember that you face away from the direction you're going. Fit the oars in the rowlocks with the full face of the blades facing the stern of the boat. Sitting as comfortably as you are able and with the oar blades out of the water, stretch forwards as far as you can. Dip the blades in the water and pull back, using your weight to help get the oars through the water. If there's something to brace your legs against, so much the better.

Use your legs, then your back and finally your arms to pull. At the end of the stroke, lift the oars so the blades are slightly out of the water, stretching forwards to repeat over again. And over again. And again. Find a stroke that is comfortable over a long period rather than trying to go too fast from the word go – you may be in for the long haul.

It's important to pull with the blades just under the surface of the water so you need to experiment to get the pitch of the blades right. If the angle is too far back, the blades will pull themselves too far under. If it's too far forward, the oars will skip along the surface and you may fall backwards. As you become more confident, you can turn your hands back a little for the return stroke so the oars are 'feathered' and offer less wind resistance.

Steering: To make small changes in direction, pull one oar less strongly than the other. If you need to adjust your heading more drastically, lift one oar clear of the water while still pulling with the other. Some rowing boats have tillers which

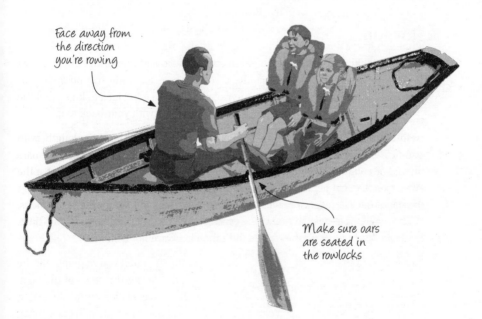

Face away from the direction you're rowing

Make sure oars are seated in the rowlocks

make the rower's job easier, unless the child assigned to tiller duty decides that their favourite way of progressing up the river is in zig-zags. You should probably look behind you from time to time, just in case they think it would be fun to ram another boat.

If you need to change positions at any time, keep as low and near the centre of the boat as you can.

If you row for any length of time and it's not something you're used to, be prepared for some sizeable blisters and aching muscles the next day.

Canoeing

There are essentially two types of canoe. The enclosed kayak type that originated with the Eskimos have double-bladed paddles and are certainly nippy but are generally just for one person. More suitable for family outings is the open, more stable Canadian canoe. They use paddles with only one blade and Dad is usually positioned in the back doing most of the work.

Even if there is somebody in front paddling, it's important to know how to control the canoe on your own as the enthusiasm of your co-paddler may diminish after a while. Sit up as straight as you can (sometimes kneeling is more comfortable). For paddling on the left, hold the top of the paddle with your right hand and have your left much lower down. The paddle should go into the water almost vertically with the blade at 90 degrees to the direction of the canoe.

The J-stroke: If you simply pull the paddle back, you will start heading to the right. So your action must end in a 'J-stroke'. As you near the end of the stroke, use your top hand to twist the paddle 90 degrees so that it's parallel to the canoe and push the blade of the paddle away from the boat a little (from above the whole stroke looks vaguely like the letter 'J'). In this way, the paddle also acts as a rudder turning the canoe back to the left and keeps you on track. The more you push away from the canoe, the more you will turn. For paddling on the right, switch the hands over to the other side of the canoe and carry out a mirror-image stroke.

The J-stroke pushes the rear of the canoe away from the paddle. You should also know the 'draw stroke' which pulls the canoe towards the paddle (and thus helps you head to the right if you're paddling on the left). Stretch out to the side with the blade parallel to the canoe and pull in the paddle, largely using your bottom hand. As the blade nears the canoe turn the paddle and continue the stroke, pushing the blade backwards and keeping the canoe going forwards.

The sweep stroke: For tight steering, you can use the 'sweep stroke'. The paddle is held out to the side with the bottom hand further up the shaft and the blade in the normal orientation. Putting the blade only partly in the water, bring the paddle in an arc towards the rear of the canoe. As the blade isn't fully in the water, it's easy to do several sweep strokes quickly. It will bring the rear of the canoe to the side you're paddling, but you'll get little foward movement.

Don't hold the paddle too tightly for any of the canoe strokes. A slightly loose grip will actually help to keep control and, even more importantly, minimise the aches and pains that are almost certain to come.

Kneeling
may be more
comfortable
than sitting

Give the paddle a twist
at the end for a J-stroke

Two people paddling: When you're canoeing with somebody in front, you must emphasise that the person in the rear is in charge. You should generally paddle on opposite sides of the canoe with the rear canoeist calling out when they want to switch paddles from one side to the other. For much of the time, the person in the front will simply be providing forward motion by pulling their paddle back in the water, lifting it and repeating it ad nauseum. Very minor changes of direction can be accomplished by the rear person making a stronger or weaker stroke.

As with rowing, it's much more satisfying and efficient to use regular, moderate strokes rather than going hell for leather and finding that you're exhausted a mile away from where you started. If you want to teach the person in the front something other than the basic pull, the draw stroke is probably the most useful. This way, you can turn the canoe quickly in case you have to avoid trees, other boats or prehistoric monsters.

Kayaks are usually enclosed and generally, though not always, made for single person use. However, in order to be able to use one safely, it is essential that you know how to roll it and escape from it if it capsizes, something far better taught by a qualified instructor.

Punting

It's a sunny day, you're in Oxford or Cambridge and the bright young things are drifting past effortlessly in lovely flat-bottomed punts. What could be more fun than a family outing on a punt? Be warned. Of all the forms of messing about on water, none offer quite so comprehensive a chance for the novice to look a complete fool – and possibly end up with a ducking.

Although you can rent punts on the Avon, the Thames and elsewhere, the two places most closely associated with punting are the Cherwell and Isis in Oxford, and the Cam in Cambridge. Naturally, Oxford and Cambridge do things differently.

The Cambridge technique: stand at the back of the boat and try not to fall in

Which university was it Daddy didn't go to, Oxford or Cambridge?

The Cambridge technique: Punt from the deck at the back (the 'till'), standing sideways on and a little nearer the side you want to punt on. The pole should be raised, hand over hand, until it is clear of the water. The aim is to have it vertical as you look from back to front, but angled back a little as you'd see it from the side, so that you are able to push with it, though, once the punt is moving, it can be completely vertical.

Open your hands and let the pole drop to the river bed, keeping your hands around it. Grip and push the pole along the bottom, letting your hands 'walk' up the pole as the punt moves forwards. At the end of the stroke, when your hands are near the top of the pole, grip it again, giving it a twist just in case it is stuck in mud. The pole will probably be around 30 degrees from the vertical at this point. The pole, these days usually made of metal, should float behind the boat. At this point, as the punt glides along, the pole becomes a rudder. Pivoting your body, move the pole gently to the left to turn left and to the right to turn right. Then, when you're ready, begin pulling the pole up, hand over hand, getting it ever more vertical until it clears the water and you're ready to let go again.

The Oxford technique: At Oxford and pretty much everywhere else but Cambridge, people punt from inside the boat which, Cambridge people claim, leads to more splashing of the occupants. They also use the punts the other way around, with the till at the front, but you'll be told about this when you hire it.

Whichever punting method you use, it is very important not to get carried away and run out of pole. Don't leave it till the last inch or two before gripping or this will be the moment that the pole gets stuck in mud and either drags you into the water with it or leaves the punt moving forward with the pole still sticking out of the water and receding into the distance. The punt will be provided with a paddle, but having to go back for the pole is likely to invite ribald comment, and not only from your own family. If the bottom is muddy, don't push down vertically with the pole but angle it further backwards, even though it might mean you don't move as quickly.

Resist the temptation to move about as you punt or you may find yourself walking back too far and end up clinging to the pole as the punt continues on. Trying to get past other punts by heading under trees with hidden low branches can also lead to disaster, as Simon can testify, having been knocked off this way recently. Naturally, he claims this was essential research to see how easy it is to climb back into a punt (very easy). Just as naturally, nobody believes him.

I knew I should have left my phone in the car

Touch football, American style

Despite several attempts to get to grips with the rules of American football on trips to the USA, it remains mystifying, though we had no trouble mastering 'tailgating', which essentially entails having boozy, pre-game picnics at college games using the back of a pickup truck as a table.

However, we've had great family fun playing this slimmed down version, which has some of the exhilaration of British Bulldog though it's probably well-nigh unrecognisable to connoisseurs of the game proper. Those bruising tackles that make rugby seem a game for softies are replaced by a simple one- or two-handed touch below the neck. A variant on this is to stuff long socks, scarves or similar into pockets or waistbands and have 'tackling' players grab these instead.

You need a reasonable-sized playing area with two end zones, much like rugby. The ball doesn't have to be oval shaped, although this is better. You need at least three players on each team. Only one team is attacking at any time; the other is defending. The best thrower on the attacking team is chosen as quarterback.

Play begins with a 'scrimmage', in which one player stands at the midpoint of the pitch and passes the ball backwards between their legs to the quarterback. The quarterback has four seconds free of being tackled to throw the ball to one of their team anywhere on the pitch. The aim of this person, the 'receiver', is to run with the ball into the opposition's end zone without being tackled. The ball can only be transferred once in each 'play'.

The quarterback may choose to run with the ball, but if they do they can be tackled and can't throw it to another player. If the player with the ball is touched, play stops and there's another scrimmage. The centre again passes the ball between their legs to the quarterback for another play.

The attackers have four goes to get the ball into the opposing end zone. This counts as a touchdown (though the player doesn't actually have to place the ball on the ground) and scores six points. If the ball goes out of bounds or touches the ground, that play ends and the ball is returned to the site of the previous scrimmage for the next play.

Goal! After a touchdown, two of the defenders form goalposts, holding hands horizontally, while their free arms point upwards. An attacker throws the ball backwards to another player who puts it down for a third person to try to kick

Kick the ball too close to a goalpost and it's likely to run away

it between the posts and over the bar. Despite the difficulty of converting, it only scores one point.

Following the conversion attempt, the attackers return to their end zone and kick the ball upfield for the other team who grab it and now become the attackers. Until they touch the ball, however, it is not in play and the new defenders can't touch it.

From the spot where attackers are first tackled, they begin their four attempts at a touchdown with their first scrimmage. If the attackers fail to score a touchdown with their four plays, play switches direction, with the opposition becoming the attackers at the point where the last tackle was made.

Now they have four plays for a touchdown. If at any point a defender gets hold of the ball in the air or on the ground, their team now has possession and they become the attackers with the first of their four scrimmages starting at that point.

And so it goes on, until everyone is exhausted or a prearranged total is reached. In the real game, there's a good deal of strategy and, without taking so long that the opposing team get bored and look for something else to do, it can be fun to try to devise team gameplans before each play, even if they almost never pan out.

Frisbee® golf

We're not supposed to mention Frisbees® without using that annoying ®, which frankly is a bit of a pain in the ®s. So we're going to call them discs instead, but you know what we're referring to, right?

If you get bored of throwing the disc to and fro, here's a great variation which lends itself well to a beach or a park. If you aren't playing solo, you'll need a disc for each player. First, decide on a course of whatever size you choose. You might assign a tree as the first 'hole'; a deckchair as the second; a lamp post as the third, and so on. As with golf, players have to hit the tree with as few throws as possible, taking each successive throw from the point where the previous one landed. Players compete for that hole and then move on to others.

To our surprise, we learned that there is a Professional Disc Golf Association

which holds world championships. Not only that, it seems that many American parks have disc golf courses, with metal baskets as each 'hole'. There are even special discs for the game, divided into drivers, mid-range and putters.

Given our ability to throw the things unintentionally into the middle of people picnicking fifty yards to one side of us, we'll stick to the simple version.

Kingo

Kingo was one of Simon's favourite games at primary school – that and running up and down the school playground pretending to be a police car and singing the theme tune to *Z-Cars*.

The game, best with a large group, begins with all the players standing in a circle with their legs apart and their feet touching the next person. Somebody bounces a tennis ball in the middle, calling out the letters of 'Kingo', one per bounce, letting it drop to the ground after the last. It will inevitably roll towards one of the players, who have to kick the ball away to someone else if they can, pivoting on their toes like the flippers on a pinball machine.

The player whose legs the ball eventually goes through becomes 'It'. Everyone runs away within the designated playing area and when 'It' grabs the ball, they yell out 'Stop' and all the other players must halt and stay stationary. Depending on the size of the area being played in, 'It' either throws the ball at any other player from there or takes one stride for each letter of 'Kingo', calling out each letter as they go, and then throws the ball, aiming at the legs.

The player hit then becomes 'It' and round and about you go. One variant has the hit players joining 'It' and throwing the ball between them preparatory to nailing a player.

Forfeit catch

Any number of players group themselves in a circle, giving themselves plenty of room. The ball – a tennis ball is ideal – is thrown randomly to other players. Anyone dropping the ball has to work their way through a series of forfeits.

First drop: one hand behind their back.

Second drop: stand on one leg, still keeping their hand behind their back.

Third drop: go down on one knee.

Fourth drop: go down on both knees.

Fifth drop: close one eye.

Sixth drop: out of the game.

If, however, they catch the ball after receiving a forfeit, they progress back through the forfeits, one step at a time.

So somebody down on one knee who catches the ball can now stand, though it must be on one leg. Catch it again and they can stand on both feet, but still with their hand behind their back.

Of course, there's some skill required to throw the ball to another player – especially if the one throwing is on their knees with one eye shut and an arm behind their back. You should be judicious in choosing when to allow the ball to be re-thrown if a catch seems to be impossible.

Raising cane

If you have a bamboo cane lying about that is six feet long or so, here's an activity that will mystify children and – to be honest – us too, until we figured out what was going on.

You need four or more children standing side by side. Hold the cane so that it's balancing on your two outstretched middle fingers, and tell them that you want them, as a team, to lower the stick to the ground, doing so yourself as you explain it.

Have the kids put their arms out with their middle fingers extended (those that can't manage this are allowed to use their index fingers). When they're all roughly in line, lay the cane on their fingers and tell them to lower it to the floor, *without any of them letting the cane slip off their fingers.*

Bizarrely, instead of going down, the cane will invariably rise upwards instead: they'll be so anxious to maintain finger contact with the cane that they'll tend to push it up rather than risk it falling off.

You can always dress this up as a magic trick. As you command them to try to lower it, stare with wide eyes, mutter some mumbo-jumbo and lift your arms, palms upwards, as if commanding the stick to rise. Be warned, though, that the 'magic' will quickly fade as they do work out how to lower it, so don't do it more than once or twice.

If you have two canes and eight children or more to hand, arrange them so they're facing each other in two lines and turn it into a competition to see who can lower their cane first. The desire to win will make it even harder to get the cane to the ground.

Torch tag

This is a great night-time game if you're with a group of people when camping, providing you have an area to play it that you know is perfectly safe. But it will work equally well in a large garden.

It is a variant of tag with 'It' using a torch instead of having to touch people. Players should wear dark clothing, the better to hide themselves. They may even blacken their faces with camo cream or burnt cork, providing Dad's happy to oblige by first opening a bottle of wine with an old-fashioned cork. A base is set up, ideally in the centre of the playing area, from which everyone scatters. While 'It' counts to the agreed number, players should hide, though they must keep within the agreed playing area.

'It' then goes hunting with the torch. If they shine the light on somebody and call out their name then that person is caught and must return to the base. Those who are caught can be rescued. If a player gets to the base they can release the first of the players who's been caught there; they then have 30 free seconds to hide themselves again.

If 'It' fails to call out a name or gets a name wrong, the person they've tried to tag must yell out that they've made a mistake and has 30 seconds free to hide themselves. They can't use that time for rescuing another player.

'It's task is to get all the players into the base, though you might want to set a time limit. If the group is particularly large and you have a plentiful supply of torches and batteries, two or more people can be 'It' to even up the chances.

We'll be safe here,
I've hidden the
batteries

One-and-a-half-a-side football

Playing football is great if you have plenty of kids – but if there are only three of you, it can be tricky to divide the sides up equally. Solomon had one answer to this conundrum, but we don't recommend slicing your offspring in half.

We find the best method is to have one player in goal, leaving two out on the field. One of these is the attacker, one the defender. If the defender manages to tackle the attacker and gain possession of the ball, then he becomes the attacker and the attacker becomes the defender.

Once someone scores, they go in goal, and the former goalie comes out to be the attacker. It's a neat solution to an otherwise tricky problem.

Swimming pool games

These days you're not allowed to do anything in public swimming pools that might possibly constitute fun, for 'health and safety' reasons. (Much as we'd like to, this isn't the place to go into a rant about *that* subject.) But if you're on holiday, perhaps staying in a villa with a pool, then you're going to spend a lot of time in it with your kids: here are a couple of ideas to increase the fun.

Pool basketball is a game we've enjoyed over the years, and has the great advantage that it doesn't require a basket. You'll need a soft ball, slightly larger than a tennis ball: sports shops sell small rugby balls, about 20cm long, that are ideal for this purpose (although if you can't find one, then a tennis ball will do).

Divide the players into two teams, and give the ball to one of them. The rules are simple: you have to throw the ball between players on the same team, and the other team has to intercept it and then throw it between themselves. It's a family-friendly game in which everyone can join in, since Dad can always make sure the ball gets passed to the smallest players frequently.

Underwater football is another good pool game. You'll need an old, punctured football: fill it with water by holding it underwater and expelling all the air. If you leave it for half an hour or so, it should fill with water by itself, regaining something approaching its original shape. Now play football with it, *in slow motion*: all the fun of an action replay, without any of the irritating commentary.

Acrobatic backflips are easy and fun, as long as your kids are small enough. They face you, with their arms around your neck and their legs bent, resting their feet on your hands. On the count of three, you lift upwards as they straighten their legs and throw themselves back: with a bit of practice, they can achieve quite spectacular somersaults in the air. Do make sure there's no one directly behind them when you do this, of course.

Football balancing involves a football for each player. They have to push it down so they're sitting on it – this can be quite tricky, as the ball will be very buoyant and will try to push itself up past them. Once they've managed this, their next task is to push the ball down so they're standing on it. It takes skill and delicate balancing: one advantage is that the smaller the child, the less deep the ball has to go, and so the easier it becomes.

Next time can I fly first class, Daddy?

Is it a bird? No, it's a plane

Lie on your back and, holding their hands to keep them steady, let your child lie on your upturned feet. Your feet should rest on their abdomen, their centre of gravity. Hold their hands or wrists as they climb on, until they feel comfortable. Once they're balanced, get them to put their legs out straight behind them and let go of your hands, holding their arms outwards. Hurrah! They're flying! As they become more confident, you can move your legs from side to side and extend them so they fly high up the air – at least it will seem so to them.

This is one for relatively young children. Once they're coming round for Sunday lunch with your grandchildren in tow, you might want to consider giving it up.

Camping food

Kids seem to love camping. The hard, lumpy ground, the hours spent watching Dad struggling with a tent whose assembly instructions have been imperfectly translated from the original Korean, the sensation of having your extremities nibbled by hitherto undiscovered species of venomous insect in the middle of the night, and above all the cold when the anaesthetic campfire beers finally wear off at three o'clock in the morning. Don't you just love it?

There's always the recourse to food, to make the pain a little more bearable. Here are a few of our tried and tested campfire recipes. You *can* cook them over a barbecue; but a real campfire is more fun for everyone.

Chocolate bananas

Keeping the skin on, slit a banana most of the way through along its length. Break chocolate up into pieces and push them into the slit. It doesn't matter if they are sticking out a little.

Wrap the banana completely in foil and place it on your fire, Trangia or Primus and leave it there until the foil is completely black. Open up the foil and spoon out the disgustingly mushy, but yummily delicious choconana mix inside.

Izzy's chocolate digestive marshmallows

The bigger the better when it comes to toasting marshmallows around a campfire. Rather than use any utensils you've brought with you, it's much better to get the children to use twigs. Try to ensure, though, that they're not too long dead. If there's no green left inside, you'll suddenly find that the whole twig is ablaze and gets dropped into the fire. A waste of a good marshmallow.

Izzy's preferred way of toasting marshmallows is to shove it completely into the fire. That way, it gets covered in ash. When it's nicely melted, pull it out, blow or scrape off the ash and put the gooey marshmallow between two chocolate digestive biscuits. Naturally, when you get home, you should tell their mum that they've eaten nothing but salad and protein the entire time.

Camp doughnuts

This is an international favourite with Scouts and Guides around the world, no doubt because they know it's the sort of thing that would give health-conscious parents palpitations. They are unquestionably delicious, though, and if the children *are* getting plenty of fresh air and exercise, why not give them a whirl – they're bound to need a blood sugar boost at some point.

There might be campers keen enough to make the pancake batter mix needed from scratch with flour, milk and eggs, but it's far easier to use the packet stuff. Make up jam sandwiches (using white bread, naturally). Dunk them in the pancake batter then fry them in oil until they're golden. Whip them out, dip them in white sugar and serve them to appreciative, hungry campers. You might even consider adding these to your barbecue recipe list as a treat for the kids.

If you are cooking in a pan on an open fire, it's worth knowing that if you rub washing-up liquid on the underneath of the pan first, it will be a great deal easier to clean later.

Dampers

This perennial camping favourite is a simple form of bread, originating in the Australian outback. Mix up ten parts of self-raising flour with three parts of water, a sprinkle of salt and a little sugar, kneading the dough.

Roll the dough into long fingers. Find some strong sticks and twist the dough around them in a spiral, cooking over an open fire if you have one, but again a barbecue is also fine. Try not to make the snakes too thick or the outside will burn before the inside is cooked.

Fun though this is, bear in mind that the dough is relatively tasteless, so you might want to try some variations. Cook a sausage on a stick, for instance, wrap dough around it and bake it in the fire. Or put some chocolate spread in the snake of dough before you twist it around the stick. Wrapped in foil, loaves or patties can be cooked in the embers of a fire.

Campfire songs

For some reason, the very act of being out in the open at night, huddled up to a roaring fire, seems to bring out the community spirit and the desire to burst into song in even the most reserved of families. Just in case this should happen to you, it helps to know the words to at least a few songs.

The Quartermaster's Stores

This, one of the most popular of all campfire songs, probably originated in the services, but it doesn't *have* to be ribald. The best thing about it is that it's easy even for children to make up new lines in the middle of the song. Give them a bit of warning and they should be able to come up with lines about the other members of the group ('There was Steve, Steve, bogeys on his sleeve', etc.).

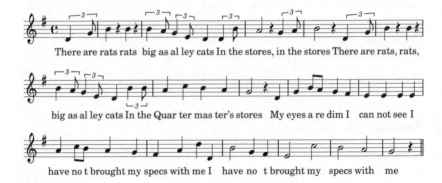

There are rats, rats, big as alley cats
In the stores, in the stores.
There are rats, rats, big as alley cats
In the Quartermaster's stores.

Chorus:
My eyes are dim, I cannot see
I have not brought my specs with me
I have not brought my specs with me

Continue with the following verses, repeating the same 'eyes are dim' chorus each time:

There are mice, mice, running through the rice...

There are snakes, snakes, as big as garden rakes....

There is cheese, cheese, that brings you to your knees...

There is gravy, gravy, enough to float the navy...

There are cakes, cakes, that give us tummy aches...

There is butter, butter, running in the gutter...

There is bread, bread, with great big lumps like lead...

There are bees, bees, with little knobby knees...

There are apes, apes, eating all the grapes...

There are turtles, turtles, wearing rubber girdles...

There are bears, bears, with curlers in their hair...

There are buffaloes, buffaloes, with hair between their toes...

There are foxes, foxes, stuffed in little boxes...

There is Coke, Coke, enough to make you choke...

There are flies, flies, swarming round the pies...

There are fishes, fishes, washing all the dishes...

Head, Shoulders, Knees and Toes

Songs with actions are a great way of keeping warm when the flames begin to die out. Here's an old classic that's still fun to sing.

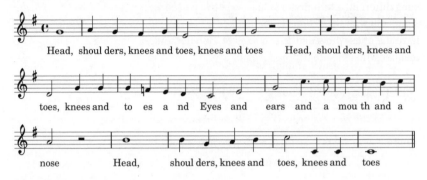

Head, shoulders, knees and toes, knees and toes.
Head, shoulders, knees and toes, knees and toes and
Eyes and ears, and a mouth and a nose.
Head, shoulders, knees and toes, knees and toes.

It looks delightfully ridiculous when everyone touches the body part mentioned. It gets still better if, with each successive singing, one more body part is omitted, though still touched. The penultimate time around, only the word 'and' is heard. The final time, it should be sung in full but incredibly quickly.

Forty Years on an Iceberg

The fun in this song comes from everyone doing the actions together. In a similar way to 'Head, Shoulders, Knees and Toes', sometimes the subsequent verses are sung differently, with first one line, then two and so on hummed rather than being sung, still with the actions being made. Or you could split the group into two and have the ones who sing the two lines of 'Buh duh duh da da da' continuing in like manner while the other group sings.

Forty years on an iceberg *(make the number 10 four times with your hands)*
Over the ocean wide *(make waves with your hands)*
Nothing to wear but pyjamas *(pull up the shoulders of whatever you're wearing)*
Nothing to do but slide…WEEEEEE! *(pretend to dive)*
The wind was cold and blustery *(shiver with your arms crossed)*
The frost began to bite! *(pinch a neighbour)*
I had to hug my polar bear *(hug your neighbour)*
To keep me warm at night, Oh!
Buh duh duh da da da
Buh duh duh da da da

If I Were Not Upon the Stage

If you're prepared to put in a little effort, working up a version of this song with your children and perhaps a few of their friends could be one of the most hilarious things you'll ever do. The song is popular on cruise liners as 'If I Were Not Upon the Seas', as well as with Boy Scouts and Girl Guides singing what they'd do if they weren't. The tune is academic and often seems to be more chanted than sung.

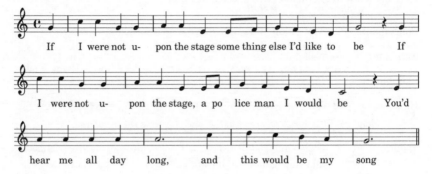

If I were not upon the stage something else I'd like to be.
If I were not upon the stage, a (*profession*) I would be.
You'd hear me all day long, and this would be my song.

At this point, the singer has not only to yell out the cry of their chosen profession for two bars, but also to act it out. The trick is to come up with professions that involve daft gesticulations and cries as well as spreading over into the space of the person next to them.

So a policeman, for instance, might direct traffic with 'Move along now, move along now. Passing to the right', putting out their right hand as they do the 'Passing to the right'. This would hit their neighbour, were the neighbour not perhaps a carpenter. They might 'Nail it up here, nail it down there, nail it to the floor', bending over to hit an imaginary nail into the floor just as the policeman extends their hand.

As more professions are introduced, you might have someone who doesn't get out of the way of the person next to them. A window cleaner with a sponge might wash the face or glasses of the person next to them, who could be a referee removing their glasses the better to stare myopically at the ball. Adult versions of this can tend towards the bawdy. You need to establish if you want any of this. You might all think that someone inadvertently goosing their neighbour as they bend down is fine. It's up to you.

The new profession is introduced alone each time. Then, after they've done their cry once, they continue it as the previous person joins in, followed by the one before them, and so on, until everybody does it together, at which point a new person comes on 'stage'. The kids should enjoy coming up with ideas of their own. Here are a few to get the creative juices flowing.

Policeman: 'Move along now, move along now. Passing to the right.'

Carpenter: 'Nail it up here, nail it down there, nail it to the floor.'

Plumber: 'Plunge it. Flush it. Look out down below.'

Hippy: 'Love and peace. Joy to the world. Cool, man. Far out. Wow.' (making peace signs)

Tailor: 'Chest thirty-two. Waist forty-six. Cutting it to size.' (making snip snip actions to the side)

Shop assistant: 'Four ninety-nine. Here's your change. Have a nice day, sir.' (holding out the change at the end)

Banker: 'Charging for this, charging for that. Banking's really interesting.' (It's fun if the banker reaches out to take the money from the shop assistant. Or have a politician instead of a banker.)

Lifeguard: 'Save yourself, man, I'm a busy guy. I'm working on my tan.'

Painter: 'Open the tin, stir the paint. Slap it on the wall.'

Fireman: 'Jump, lady, jump. We'll catch you. Whoops. Splat.' (looking up and then, rapidly, down, pulling away an imaginary net)

Aerobics teacher: 'Arms up, arms down. Hips left, hips right.' (knocking their hips into the neighbour on one side, then the other)

Teacher: 'Sit down. Shut up. Throw away your gum.'

Airline steward: 'Stay in your seat. Do up your belt. Here's your sick bag. BLEH!'

Electrician: 'Neutral's blue. Brown is live. So what's this one here do? Argghh.' (miming being electrocuted)

Ging Gang Gooley

Legend has it that this perennial but nonsensical Scout and Guide song was conjured up by Robert Baden-Powell himself for the first World Scout Jamboree in 1920 so that Scouts, whatever their native tongue, could sing it. For the jamboree, the exhibition hall at Olympia was filled with earth a foot thick which was then turfed, enabling the Scouts to put up their tents in the glass-roofed hall.

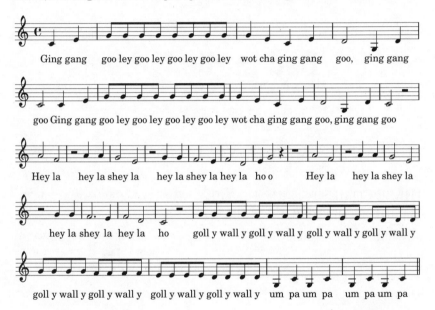

Ging gang   goo ley goo ley goo ley goo ley   wot cha ging gang   goo,   ging gang

goo Ging gang goo ley goo ley goo ley goo ley wot cha ging gang goo, ging gang goo

Hey la   hey la shey la   hey la shey la hey la   ho o   Hey la   hey la shey la

hey la shey la hey la   ho   goll y wall y goll y wall y goll y wall y goll y wall y

goll y wall y goll y wall y   goll y wall y goll y wall y   um pa um pa   um pa um pa

Ging gang gooley, gooley, gooley, gooley, watcha
Ging gang goo, ging gang goo.
Ging gang gooley, gooley, gooley, gooley, watcha
Ging gang goo, ging gang goo.
Heyla, heyla sheyla, heyla shey-la, heyla ho
Heyla, heyla sheyla, heyla shey-la, heyla ho
Golly wally, golly wally, golly wally, golly wally
Golly wally, golly wally, golly wally, golly wally
Um-pa, Um-pa, Um-pa, Um-pa.

17 Dad in the kitchen

THERE COMES A TIME IN EVERY DAD'S LIFE when he has to venture into the kitchen. (It's that room at the end of the corridor, which often has delicious smells emanating from it. If you still can't find it, ask your kids.)

We're not suggesting that all Dads are incompetent cooks, by any means. But it's a sad fact that many of us are less adept at the culinary arts than we (or our partners) would like.

Next time you have the kids to yourself for a time, rather than cracking open a six-pack of ready meals, try cooking something using raw ingredients. We've a selection of easy but tasty recipes that will fill them up a treat, while restoring your reputation as the Dad who really *can* do everything.

There's more fun to be had in the kitchen than just making food, of course. So we've also thrown in a selection of experiments, activities and assorted nonsense that you can do using everyday foodstuffs.

The recipes

For those occasions when Dad is left to feed the family, here are some easy and tasty ideas to keep the wolf from the door (and the kids from the biscuit tin).

GRILLED FISH SNACKS

Frozen fish fillets	*Tomatoes*	*Butter*
Dry cider	*Cheddar cheese*	*Salt*

Although those Dads who don't fancy themselves as budding Jamie Olivers think of fish as being fiddly to cook, this tasty recipe can be whipped up in next to no time with little preparation. Next time you're in a supermarket (making sure to have your phone with you, of course, so you can call your partner to ask where things are), grab some skinned fish fillets. White fish like cod, haddock or halibut is what you're after. Forget the fresh-fish counter and instead pick up ungarnished, unbattered frozen blocks and shove them in your freezer.

Get out as many as there are mouths to feed. The only other preparation needed is to slice a tomato or two thinly, doing the same with some Cheddar cheese. You could grate the cheese, but that means cleaning a cheese grater afterwards. Do you really want to bother? Have a bottle of dry cider ready – you may as well pour yourself a glass while you're at it.

Proper cooks will butter the grill pan to stop the fish sticking (take the rack off). Dads who loathe washing up should shove foil in it instead, making sure it curves up on all sides to keep the juices in. Rub a knob of butter over the foil, leaving it in the grill pan at medium heat to melt while you defrost the fish in the microwave.

Salt the defrosted fish then shove it into the grill pan, spooning the melted butter over it. Cook it on one side for three minutes or so, then turn it over and spoon the juices over it. Pour one tablespoon of cider over each fillet and cook for another three minutes. Don't worry, the alcohol will burn off.

Add the slices of tomato and cheese and keep cooking until the cheese has melted, probably another three or four minutes. Then serve. As long as the foil hasn't torn, you can simply dispose of it, happy that there's no necessity to wash the grill pan.

FRENCH TOAST

Eggs	*Vegetable oil or butter*
Milk	*Cinnamon sugar*
Sliced bread	*Maple syrup or fruit*

This recipe is also commonly known as 'eggy bread'. But how much more exotic and delicious it sounds when given a continental flavour. In the United States, they tried to change the name to 'freedom toast'.

For each five pieces of French toast, you need three medium-sized eggs. Beat the eggs, adding enough milk to swell the mixture by about 25 per cent. Locate a big shallow dish and pour in the mixture. Get your bread ready. The white, sliced stuff we're told isn't good for us seems to make the best French toast. Indeed bread that's too stale for toast or sandwiches is perfectly fine, just so long as it isn't actually mouldy. We keep the slices intact, others prefer to half or quarter them, enabling you to get more in the frying pan.

Add vegetable oil or butter (our preference) to a frying pan at medium heat until it's melted and the whole pan is greased. Using a fork, dip a piece of bread into the mixture so that it soaks it up, turning the bread over if the mixture isn't deep enough to do both sides at once.

Put this, and as many similarly treated others as you can fit, into the frying pan. Turn them over after a couple of minutes. You're aiming for a golden brown colour. If they're burnt, you've gone a bit too far and know to pull the next batch out more quickly.

Put the cooked French toast on to sheets of kitchen roll to cut down on their greasiness. Continue frying with more bread until the mixture is all used up. Keep adding enough butter or oil to the pan to prevent burning but not so much that the bread drowns in it.

Eggy bread is particularly nice served with cinnamon sugar (mix powdered cinnamon with sugar if you haven't any), maple syrup or even fruit such as strawberries or tinned peach slices.

FRIED MATZO

7 matzo sheets	*Milk*
4 eggs	*Vegetable oil or butter*

Matzo, or unleavened bread, was apparently invented when the Jews got fed up with building pyramids for the Egyptians and fled the country with the army in hot pursuit. They were in such a rush that they didn't have time to let their bread rise and so discovered they'd made a crunchy, thin cracker. Matzo is now promoted as a healthy snack, being 98 per cent fat free and with no added salt. But it's a doddle to negate such health benefits with this delicious teatime treat.

Matzo is available in most supermarkets and many convenience stores, usually among the crackers. It's best to use the rectangular matzos in the big box. If you can't find any, try water biscuits instead.

For three to four people with healthy appetites use the seven sealed sheets that make up half the box's contents. Break them up in a colander until they're in bite-size pieces. Do this in a sink as there will be lots of crumbs. Soak the matzo with hot running water for two or three minutes until it's soft but not completely squishy, then shake it around to help the excess water drain off.

Break four eggs into a mixing bowl along with a small amount of milk and beat the mixture. Mix in the well-drained matzo so that it absorbs the eggs.

Add butter (or vegetable oil) to a hot, non-stick frying pan and spoon in the gooey matzo, spreading it around the pan. Stir it fairly often, occasionally adding

more butter to stop it sticking and burning. Fry until golden brown and just going crispy at the edges.

We serve it with added salt to taste. Others season it with cinnamon sugar, syrup, fruit or jam and we've also heard of people cooking it with bananas, grating cheese over it towards the end of cooking and even adding mushrooms, peppers and the like and treating it as a stir-fry.

Fried matzo is a doddle to make, though cleaning all the matzo mess from the colander afterwards isn't our favourite chore.

EGG IN A CUP

| 2 eggs | 1 slice of bread |
| Butter | Salt and pepper |

This is a great favourite, especially when our kids are feeling unwell and need a comfort snack in bed. It's dead easy to make and goes down a treat with kids of all ages.

Boil the eggs so they're still soft inside (three minutes from boiling!). Butter the bread and cut into small squares. Then mix the whole lot together in a large teacup (remembering to scoop the egg out of the shells first), adding a little salt and pepper to taste.

ANCHOVY SPAGHETTI

| 1 tin anchovies | Spaghetti |

There aren't many recipes whose title contains all the ingredients, but cooking doesn't get much simpler than this. It really helps if your kids like anchovies, of course, and we realise that many don't.

First, boil up some spaghetti. It takes about 12 minutes. Tip the anchovies out of the tin and into a small frying pan. No need to add oil as they're already swimming in it. Cook until the anchovies dissolve into a brownish paste, then pour into the spaghetti and mix well. It tastes a lot better than it sounds!

STEVE'S SUPER SLIPPERY SLURPY SOUP SHOP SPECIAL

3 peeled carrots	2 pints water	1 tsp vegetable oil
1 peeled onion	1 tbsp powdered chicken soup mix	
4 slices of ham	Half packet rice noodles	

Thinly slice the carrots and the onion, and fry them in a little oil a large saucepan until the onion goes soft. Add shredded ham, all the water, and the chicken soup mix. When the water boils, add the rice noodles. Stir for about five minutes until the noodles soften. Absolutely delicious.

The surprising world of tomato ketchup

Derived from the Chinese *ke-tsiap*, ketchup would originally have tasted very different, being a savoury pickled fish sauce akin to the likes of Worcestershire or soy sauce. It was brought to Europe in the 17th century by sailors but early ingredients might have included mushrooms, oysters, lobsters or anchovies. The word 'ketchup' first appeared in 1711 but other spellings like catsup or catchup were common too.

Early ketchups in colonial America were savoury but the Americans' sweet teeth were indulged in the mid-19th century with various sweetened tomato ketchups. In 1876, H. J. Heinz added one to his product line and never looked back.

The Americans have regulations governing the flow of ketchup, which must ooze between 3 and 7 centimetres in 30 seconds. If it doesn't, it can't call itself 'ketchup'.

Ketchup has recently been discovered to be healthy as it – along with other processed tomato products – contains lycopene, which apparently helps in fighting some cancers. Organic ketchup, of course, is the healthiest of all. Mind you, it does contain both sugar and salt.

In 2000, Heinz started making coloured ketchups in the hope of appealing to children. But kids didn't take to green, purple, pink, orange, blue or teal ketchup (only green was available in the UK), so they were abandoned.

The world's largest ketchup bottle is a water tower built in the shape of a sauce bottle at a former ketchup bottling plant in 1949 in Illinois. It stands 170 feet tall. Incidentally, ketchup is also great for cleaning copper! Smear it on and leave it to do its magic for ten minutes before rinsing off.

Getting ketchup out of the bottle

Everyone knows how difficult it is to get ketchup out of a glass bottle. The new squeezy bottles, particularly those designed to be stored upside-down, take all the fun out of the process. Luckily many restaurants still serve it in bottles, giving Dad a chance to show off. Ketchup, of course, is very viscous and tends to stick to the inside of the bottle, a property scientists call thixotropic.

The standard way of trying to get ketchup out involves hitting the inverted bottom of the bottle but the restaurant trade has long known a better way. It

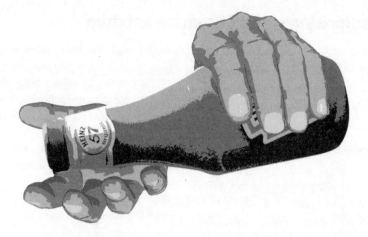

involves tapping the neck of the bottle, held only slightly downwards (as you would when you pour any other liquid), onto a fist or open hand. If it's Heinz, the 57 circle on the neck is exactly the right spot.

This method not only helps air get into the bottle to free the ketchup but also gives it some downward impetus when the bottle stops on striking the hand. The correct way of getting ketchup out of the bottle, it seems, is all down to G-forces.

Why is an ice cream with a Flake in called a 99?

Cadbury's introduced the Flake in 1920 (presumably using only the crumbliest, flakiest chocolate). In 1928, one of their sales managers saw some Italian ice-cream makers cutting them in half to sell with ice cream. So Cadbury's produced a shorter Flake in 1930, specifically intended to be shoved into an ice-cream cone at a jaunty 45-degree angle. By the mid-1930s, this combination was known as a 99.

Nobody, though, seems to know exactly why it's called 99. In Roman numerals, IC (Ice Cream) can be 99, though it's more usual as XCIX. The boxes of Flakes for the ice-cream trade cost six shillings and sixpence, written as 6/6 which, upside down, would look like 99. Others have suggested that there were 99 mini-Flakes in each box or that the cornets of the time were stamped with '99'.

There may be no definitive answer, so just enjoy them. For chocoholics, even better than one Flake is two, known for rather obvious reasons as 'Bunny Ears'. When Simon was growing up, you normally asked for a '99 with monkey blood', which meant you wanted loads of raspberry syrup on it too.

Music in the kitchen

Right, that's the recipes and food facts out of the way – now let's get on to the fun stuff. To the resourceful Dad, a kitchen is a toolbox of ideas: more fun can be had in here (with your kids) than just about any other room in the house. Our first few examples are all about making music with everyday kitchen items.

Bottle blowing

Still too high – better drink some more

Bottles are wonderful music-makers. If you have enough filled with different levels of liquid, you can play them by blowing across their open tops: hold them against your lips and blow straight across. The bigger the bottle, the deeper the pitch.

If you want to fine-tune the pitch, add a little water to the empty bottle to make it sound a little higher. Give a differently pitched bottle to each child, and you've got yourself an orchestra.

A wine bottle makes a splendidly bass-like accompaniment, though the less full the bottle, and the more you've drunk of it, the better the music seems to sound.

The straw oboe

We show on page 14 how to make the noise of a duck with a straw. But you can use straws in other ways, particularly the fat kind you tend to get in fast-food joints. Instead of making a V-cut, flatten the straw at one end. You can do this in your mouth by biting it around an inch of the way in, and then pulling it out of your mouth while flattening it with your teeth. Cut half an inch or so along the fold on each side of the straw.

Put it in your mouth, pressing the two halves together with your lips, and blow. This is effectively a double reed, as used for playing oboes and bassoons and these are notoriously tricky to get a good note from, as the parents of any budding oboeist will tell you. So a bit of experimentation is needed. If you can't get it to work, stick the straw further into your mouth and blow, and you get something curiously similar to the duck-call maker.

Penny whistle on the cheap

A whole penny? What a waste! Here's a whistle you can make for almost nothing, again using a simple drinking straw.

Wrap one end of the straw around your finger once or twice, pinching it with the thumb so that you have a firm grip on it. With the straw pointing upwards, blow across it as you would a bottle. Squeeze the straw with the thumb and index finger of your free hand and, by sliding it up and down, you can make a sound like a Swanee whistle, though it's much easier to go up in pitch than to go down again.

HOW DOES IT WORK?

Both the bottle and the penny whistle work in much the same way as a flute. By blowing, the mouth causes the column of air in them to vibrate. These vibrations are perceived by our ears as a note. The longer the column of vibrating air, the lower the note.

If you experiment with the level of liquid in eight bottles, you can produce a scale over a full octave. Perceptive children will notice that the more liquid and the less air a bottle contains, the higher the note.

Following in Mozart's footsteps

If you have a set of wine glasses, you can make them sing with your finger. Holding the base of the glass with one hand, moisten the index or middle finger of your other hand and rub it around the rim of the glass at a constant speed. Vary the pressure and speed until a note sounds. The better the quality of the glass, the easier it usually is to produce a note and the purer the sound. Crystal, they say, is particularly good but you may think twice about letting your kids loose on your best wedding presents.

The diameter of the bowl matters, too. Flute-style glasses, despite the promising

name, are well-nigh useless. The easiest glasses to get a sound from are those old-fashioned and unstylish ones with the hemispherical bowls. If the glass has traces of slippery washing-up liquid, it will be much harder to play.

Adding water to the wine glass will raise the pitch, and you can tune your glasses to play a recognisable scale.

With some glasses you can actually see the surface of the liquid rotating in the same direction as your finger. Dropping something small that floats will demonstrate this. With certain glasses, moving your finger at a slower rate while pressing harder can create spectacular wave patterns on the surface of the water.

People have been making music with glass for centuries. It became something of a craze in the 18th century. The noted American inventor Benjamin Franklin devised a mechanical glass harmonica with a revolving spindle that did much of the work in 1762 (pictured bottom left) while, in 1791, Mozart composed an adagio for glass harmonica.

People noticed that musicians who specialised in making music with tuned glass often went mad. It wasn't the ethereal music that sent them potty, but the lead with which the rims of the glass were painted. Over time they absorbed the poison through their fingers, just as the Romans had done internally and rather dramatically from their lead plumbing.

HOW DOES IT WORK?

Every object has a natural frequency. The friction created by your finger slipping and sticking hundreds of times a second causes the molecules of the glass to vibrate at its natural, or resonant, frequency.

Although your finger can't impart any more energy than this, a singer hitting the glass's resonant frequency can, which is how some singers can shatter glasses with their voice. Noises that coincide with natural frequencies explain why heavy vehicles driving past a house can make the windows rattle.

Resonance can be a problem for suspension bridges. In 1940, shortly after it was opened, winds caused the Tacoma Narrows Bridge in America to begin to vibrate. The vibrations grew bigger until the roadway began buckling, oscillating up and down and from side to side. The bridge literally tore itself to pieces, huge sections falling into the river below. There are amazing videos of this easily locatable on the web.

For this reason, some bridges carry signs warning troops that they must 'break step' when they are crossing. It is the reason that the Millennium Footbridge across the Thames in London had to be closed in 2000 for a time. People walking across were feeling queasy at the way the bridge swayed and the vibrations had to be damped down.

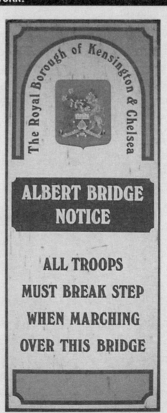

The Royal Borough of Kensington & Chelsea

ALBERT BRIDGE NOTICE

ALL TROOPS MUST BREAK STEP WHEN MARCHING OVER THIS BRIDGE

How to play the spoons

It is one of the sadder facts about Simon that, having been taught to play the spoons as a teenager, he now carries a pair of spoons around with him in case he gets a chance to show off this so-called talent. It seems only fitting that he should pass on this skill so that others may also experience the 'pleasure' of listening to two bits of cutlery being banged together.

Although teaspoons and serving spoons can be used, it's best to learn on dessert spoons (the kind you use for cereal). Assuming you intend playing them right-handed, with the fingers of your hand curled towards your palm, push the

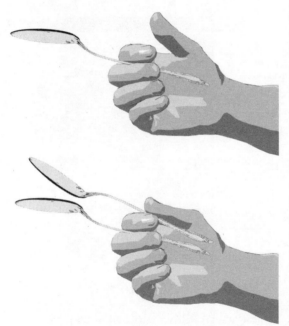

handle of one of the spoons, bowl downwards, between your index and middle fingers. It should be positioned above the first joint of the middle finger with the finger curling back to hold the spoon against your palm.

The other spoon, bowl upwards, should sit on your index finger with the finger curling back to hold the spoon in place. Your thumb should rest along the handle of the spoon, helping to keep it in position. (Those with smaller hands may need to rest the lower spoon on the ring finger rather than the middle.)

With your index finger as a fulcrum, squeeze the ends of the spoons with your palm so that there is a gap of half an inch or so between the bowls of the spoons. Seated, strike the spoons against your leg and they should sound a note. If you're holding the spoons correctly, they should spring apart again. Once you're able to do this, hold your free hand – palm down – above the spoons. Bring them up to strike it, then back down on your leg and so on. You should soon be able to make very fast beats between your hand and your leg,

changing where you accent the notes and occasionally beating twice on your palm to each downstroke. Loosening your grip a little, riffle the spoons down the spread fingers of your hand.

Don't use your best spoons for this. Over time, the bowls of the lovely spoons you were given as a wedding present will gradually get flattened. In any case, lightweight, tinny spoons actually give better 'notes' than heavier spoons. Simon prefers to use two different types of spoon, a heavier one on the bottom and a lighter one on top. He was also once told by Martin Ash, aka Sam Spoons of the Bonzo Dog Doo-Dah Band, that wrapping old-style plasters around the handles stops them slipping if your hands get sweaty.

Teach your kids how to play the spoons and they have another invaluable life skill. Who knows how much university will cost by the time they're old enough to go? Now they won't have to serve burgers to help pay for it. They can busk instead, an activity that can be done outdoors, thus ensuring they get plenty of fresh air.

Oi! Keep the noise down out there!

The noisy kitchen

To the average toddler, a kitchen is a percussionist's paradise. Forget buying expensive plastic drum sets that make plastic noises: give them a couple of wooden spoons and a set of saucepans instead. You can even tie a string around a saucepan lid and suspend it from a table to make a passable cymbal. This is the point where kitchen roll comes in handy: wad it up into small pieces, and stuff it in your ears to muffle the noise.

Bog roll kazoo

Even if your children don't learn any conventional instruments, that's no reason why you can't have musical fun together with the likes of Swanee whistles and kazoos. Swanee whistles are perhaps a little tricky to make yourself but while kazoos are pretty inexpensive to buy, they're also incredibly easy to make, even if they aren't the prettiest-looking of objects.

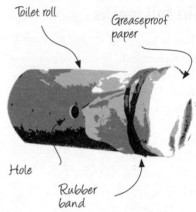

Toilet roll

Greaseproof paper

Hole

Rubber band

Get hold of some some waxed or greaseproof paper. There's probably some lying around in a drawer in the kitchen somewhere. That most uncomfortable household item, Izal toilet paper, will also do if you still encounter it anywhere (see, progress *is* a wonderful thing).

Wrap it around the end of an empty loo roll, or half of the inner tube from a kitchen paper or tin foil roll. Fasten the paper in place with a rubber band, ensuring that the paper is tight enough to vibrate. Using something like a pencil, make a hole in the side of the tube for the air to escape and that's it, your kazoo is ready.

The best way of getting a note is not to hum, as people oddly seem to recommend for kazoos, but to sing 'Ahh' into it.

Cornflour magic

Cornflour is weird stuff: when mixed with water, it has the bizarre property of being both gloopy and solid at the same time.

Mix together two cups of cornflour and one cup of water. Place a teaspoon in the glass, and ask your kids to stir the mixture slowly. They'll have no problem, as the consistency will be similar to custard. Then, tell them to stir it quickly, and they'll find they won't be able to: when they try rapid movements, the cornflour mixture will suddenly go solid, preventing the spoon from moving.

Pour some into your hands and, moving fast, roll it into a ball between your palms. As long as you keep rolling, it will form what appears to be a solid ball. Pass it to your children, though, and it will revert to its slushy form, slipping straight through their fingers.

Tin foil masks

There's bound to be a roll of tin foil (aluminium foil) around somewhere. This is a far more interesting use than just cooking with it.

Take a sheet about 30cm square. Sit your child down and carefully mould it to the shape of their head. It'll get crumpled as you scrunch it into position, but this isn't a bad thing: the more crumpled it is, the better it will mould to the shape of their face, and the stronger it will be.

You don't want to push too hard around the eyes, obviously, and it can be a good idea to make sure they're still breathing occasionally. Use your fingers to press it around the nose and cheekbones: it can help if they open their mouth slightly and grab the foil with their lips, which will help to hold it in place. Pretty soon it should form a shape that approximates their head. You should be able to lift it off without it distorting too much, and you'll end up with a mask that – in profile, at least – looks exactly like your child.

Make your own play dough

Long before Play-Doh was available in little plastic pots, parents were mixing the stuff up for themselves. It's easy to make and you don't have to worry if your kids accidentally swallow some.

Into a mixing bowl, pour two cups of plain flour, a cup of water, a cup of salt and two tablespoons of cooking oil. You can add a few drops of food colouring if you have any. Mix all the ingredients together with a fork – or with your fingers – and you'll have enough play dough to keep small kids happy for an afternoon. Cut it with cookie cutters, or simply roll it around and mould it into shapes.

The submarine diver

This is a surprisingly good experiment, which shows how small changes in pressure can produce a strong effect. This was sent in to us by *Dad Stuff* reader (and obviously Great Dad) Mark Grant.

Bubble of cling film

Tied off with cotton

Blu-tack

To do this trick you'll need an empty mineral water or fizzy drink bottle, some cling film, a piece of cotton and a blob of Blu-tack. Try to avoid forcing your kids to drink all the Coke in one go, or you'll have a hard time explaining the burp overdose in Casualty.

Start by cutting a piece of cling film about six inches square, and sucking the middle of it into your mouth (best not to let your kids do this!) to form a bubble of the stuff somewhere between the size of a pea and a walnut. Tie it off with a piece of cotton to make an airtight bulge.

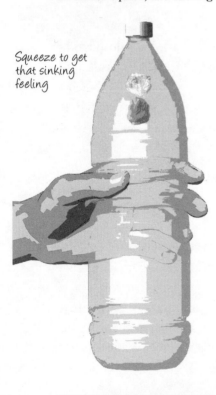

Squeeze to get that sinking feeling

The other end of the cling film will splay out into a sort of fan: this is where you stick the Blu-tack. Have a glass of water handy, and place the assembly into the water. It should just about float, so that a tap on the top will send it under only to bob back up: keep adjusting the amount of Blu-tack until this works. It's worth taking the time to get the buoyancy right now, as it's hard to extract it from the bottle later.

When the assembly is complete, fill the bottle with water, drop the diver assembly in and screw the lid on tightly. The diver will, of course, float to the top. But here's the clever part: squeeze the bottle, and the diver will sink to the bottom. By varying the pressure with your hand, you can make the diver rise and fall at will: you can even make it float at any position within the bottle. Amazing!

18 The behaviour thing

AS WELL AS ALL THE FUN TIMES to be had, kids do have to learn to do what their parents ask of them. The days of 'Wait until your father gets home' are, thankfully, largely behind us, but it's often the case that one parent, more than the other, is responsible for enforcing the dreaded D-word: discipline. And, more often than not, that parent is Dad.

It's an evolution thing. The male of the species has an Adam's apple so he can roar louder, and bigger muscles so he can fend off challenges from young stags. It isn't always Dad who enforces discipline, of course; but, whichever parent the task falls to, we'll give you some useful tips on how to do it with less pain.

The key lies in respecting your children, in recognising that they're not your possessions but people who live with you. Their problems and anxieties are real ones, no matter how trivial owning the newest PlayStation game may seem in comparison with your need to pay the mortgage. Treat them with respect, and they're more likely to respect you in turn.

Keep it simple, part one

Kids love to play games, and one of the best games of all is seeing how far Dad can be pushed before he snaps. If your children dangle your wedding ring over an open drain, or hold a bottle of milk as if they're going to upend it on the carpet, the chances are they're only fooling with you.

Try to resist flying into a sudden rage. It may be what your instinct tells you to do, but it's not necessarily the best solution. Yelling is likely to shock a child into dropping the ring, or spilling the milk, which may well prove your point – but at a cost.

You may regard their actions as irritating, provocative, or just downright idiotic. But unless what they're doing is immediately life-threatening, start with the smallest reaction that will achieve your goal.

Step 1: The eyebrow trick. A comically raised eyebrow is often enough to stop kids in their tracks. It shows them that you've seen what they're up to, and it signifies that their behaviour is inappropriate. The fact that no words have been spoken makes it easier for the child to understand the gesture, and a clear sign is often far more powerful than a barrage of instructions.

Step 2: The head shake. If the eyebrow trick doesn't work, then try simply speaking your child's name. Once you've got their attention, your best course of action is to stay non-verbal as long as you can. A slow shake of the head is a clear, unambiguous statement that every child will understand.

Step 3: Keep their attention. If the actions don't stop after these two interventions, try saying just their name again, with increasing firmness in your voice. And then shake your head again. They know they're doing something they shouldn't, and really don't need you to spell it out for them. Launching into a rant will only confuse them.

Step 4: Explain yourself. Once they've stopped doing whatever it was that started the whole thing off, don't continue to chide them. Instead, explain in as few words as possible why their actions were dangerous or antisocial – and then just leave it at that.

Step 5: Teach them the method. Even if the eyebrow and head shake don't work the first time you try it, it's worth using these two steps each time a minor misdemeanour is in progress. The more you use these techniques, the quicker your child will learn them – and the easier it will be next time.

Keep it simple, part two

If you talk to an adult and they don't understand what you're saying, the usual procedure is to say the same thing in a different way. And to keep on trying different formulations of speech until they get the point.

It doesn't work that way with kids. Mainly because the problem here isn't one of comprehension at all. They know exactly what you want them to do, but they just aren't doing it. This may simply be because it takes longer for them to process the instruction, or because they're doing something else. By constantly changing what you're asking of them, you only add to the confusion.

Here's a typical Dad–child interchange:

Dad: Put your coat on, we're going out.
Child: (ignores the instruction)
Dad: Put your coat on, it's cold outside.

Child: (no response)

Dad: Come on, your Mum and I both have our coats on.

Child: (no response)

Dad: If you don't put your coat on, you'll catch a cold.

Child: (no response)

Dad: Put your coat on or you won't get to go to the park.

Child: (no response)

Dad: Granny bought you this coat for Christmas, she'd love to know you're wearing it.

Child: She didn't get it for me for Christmas, she got it for my birthday.

Dad: I'm going to get cross if you don't put your coat on right this minute.

See what's happening? Each time you ask your child to put the coat on, you're giving a different reason. You're constantly searching for new ways of saying the same thing, and in doing so you're leading yourself into a trap: your child is all too likely to pick up on a single flaw to defeat your whole argument, which will tend to make you more cross. The less ammunition you give them to use against you, the more success you'll have. Stay consistent: there's only one reason you want them to put their coat on, and that's because it's cold outside.

Of course, knowing this doesn't help you to get them to actually put their coat on; you still need to repeat the instruction. But here's the trick: use fewer words, rather than more. Begin with the instruction, then explain it if necessary; but after that, reduce the number of words you use rather than increasing it.

Here's a better way of holding this rather one-sided exchange:

Dad: Put your coat on.

Child: (no response)

Dad: Put your coat on, it's cold outside.

Child: (no response)

Dad: Put your coat on.

Child: (no response)

Dad: Coat.

Child: (no response)

Dad: Coat.

Eventually, your child will be so ground down that they'll comply with the instruction. They know exactly what you want them to do. All you have to do is to stay as calm as you can!

Don't tell them: show them

Parents often get worked up about table manners, especially when the family's in public or visiting a grandparent. In *Keep it simple*, on the previous pages, we looked at using gestures to get your point across: the same principle can be applied here.

Nothing's worse for a child than to be humiliated in front of others. So rather than telling them to keep their mouth closed when they chew, instead mime using a finger and thumb to close your own lips. If they're talking with their mouths open, mime dragging a finger down your throat to indicate to them that they should swallow. If they're interrupting an adult conversation, mime putting your finger to your lips and then to your ear, to show that they should listen rather than talk.

It's like a private code between you and your child. It's discreet, easy to understand, and looks like you're reminding them, rather than nagging them. And grandparents will certainly be impressed at how well behaved they are – without having to be reminded!

Swallow first

Mouth closed

Don't talk...

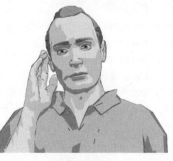

...listen!

Yes, no and maybe

Kids ask for things all the time: an ice cream, a trip to Disneyland, a new bike, one more go on the dodgems. They may not appreciate the difference between one that costs a few pence and one that may cost hundreds of pounds.

Before you shoot off a reply, take a beat to consider your answer. 'Yes' always goes down well, but make sure you listen to the question carefully before using this one. 'Maybe' is that old favourite of parents, and it's one of the most useful standbys there is: it gives you time to defer the real answer until you've had time to give it some more thought.

The trouble with saying no straight away is that once you've said it, you really, really do have to stick to it. Otherwise you're likely to end up with this sort of situation:

Child: Can we got to McDonald's?
Dad: No.
Child: I really want to go to McDonald's!
Dad: No, we're going to the pizza place.
Child: I hate pizza. I want a McDonald's.
Dad: No, I've made up my mind.
Child: Please! I really really really want to go to McDonald's!
Dad: No.
Child: If we go to McDonald's, I promise I'll tidy my room when we get home.
Dad: No, we're going for pizza.
Child: Please, Dad, please.
Dad: No, sorry.
Child: Please, please, please, Dad. I love you, Daddy.
Dad: Oh… all right then.

And there, right there, is the single most dangerous phrase a parent can ever use. It slips out so easily, and looks so innocuous, but does all the damage in the world: 'Oh, all right then.'

Once you've used it, your child has won. Worse still, they'll have learned how to win. It may have taken ten minutes to get there, but they beat you down eventually.

So what will happen next time? Exactly the same thing. Except that this time it may take fifteen minutes, or half an hour, or a couple of days. It makes no difference to kids, who have an endless capacity to nag. Once they know that you'll give in eventually, they'll never let up. It may take a little longer each time, but it's worth it: there's an ice cream or a trip to the toyshop at the end of that particular rainbow, and they'll use all the cunning they can muster to get there.

If your child is old enough to understand, then try 'Let me think about it' as a first response. Don't be rushed into saying no and then feeling you have to defend your position, unless you're absolutely sure. So be careful before you say no. Because you really do have to mean it.

When you mean no, say so

Many childcare books will tell you that saying no to a child is a negative response, and that you should find other ways to express your intention. Well, try that if you like, but we reckon you're just letting yourself in for an awful lot of bother.

Earlier in this chapter, we looked at why repetition of the same reason is always better than coming up with a different reason each time. The same technique should be used when you want to stop your child playing with a football or skipping in the house, for instance. Again, parents will typically come up with a variety of reasons why indoor football is inappropriate: 'You might break something.' 'You'll burst the ball.' 'You'll get the carpet all muddy.' 'Wayne Rooney doesn't play football indoors, and you shouldn't either.'

If your child wants something they really can't have, or shouldn't do, then we recommend saying no first, with a single reason; then repeat that reason; then just stick with no:

Dad: No, you can't play football indoors, you'll break something.
Child: (continues to play)
Dad: No, you'll break something.
Child: (continues to play)
Dad: No.
Child: (continues to play)
Dad: No.

Repetition alone should be enough for your child to stop. Eventually.

Tantrum time

All kids have tantrums. Small kids do it by throwing themselves on the floor and thrashing about, big kids do it by going to their bedrooms and slamming the door. It's the same behaviour, but expressed in different ways.

How you deal with it depends largely on your personal tolerance for humiliation in public places. Certainly, nothing makes the task of dealing with a screaming toddler in a supermarket more difficult than the disapproval of total strangers. Try to ignore their grimaces as much as possible: concentrate on helping your child to deal with the situation.

There are a number of methods for dealing with tantrums. Yelling at them, telling them to snap out of it and shaking your fist in their face is usually counter-productive: and if you've ever seen a grown man yelling at a two-year-old in a pushchair you'll know how absurd it looks.

Here are some of our tried and trusted methods:

Turn them upside down. It's a great mood breaker for under fives, and can usually get them giggling through their tears. Tell them you're going to tip them upside down so that all the anger can fall out, then gently lift them by their waist and turn them over. Ask them, 'Has the anger fallen out yet?' Usually, you'll get a giggly 'Yes'.

Get down to their level and talk quietly. If your child is rolling around on the floor and you're looming over them, then anything you say is just likely to frighten them into further tantrum behaviour. Kneel, crouch or even lie on the ground with them, stroking their head if they'll let you, and talk quietly. Reassuring words, such as 'Shh, OK, don't worry, everything is all right' will help them to calm down. A hug is far better medicine than shouting at them.

Change the subject. For younger kids especially, distraction is often the best solution. They'll usually be glad of an excuse to get out of their tantrum; becoming interested in an external event allows them to save face, and put the tantrum behind them. Point out an interesting bird in the garden, for example: 'Oh, look, there's a magpie. Over there, on the bush. You can tell it's a magpie, because it's all black and white. Magpies often take shiny things to decorate their nests, you know, so we'd better make sure Mummy's jewellery is locked away…' and so on. Keep on in this vein, and the chances are their interest will be captured. If you can get them to help out – going upstairs to make sure the bedroom window is closed so the magpie can't get the jewellery, for instance – then you'll have achieved your goal.

Be firm, but in control. If the tantrum continues, this could be your signal to move up a gear. 'OK, that'll do now', spoken in a firm tone of voice, is a clear indication that it's time for the display to come to an end. Depending on the age of the child, you can say phrases like 'Stop this, that's enough, we can talk about this' – but be sure to keep an even temper. Don't make it sound as if you're cross, or it will only make things worse. Make it clear you're in control, both of your own emotions and of the situation. Give them a rock to cling to, as it were: the implication is that however bad the situation may be, Dad can deal with it.

Count to three. We don't know why this works, but it frequently does. If a child's in the middle of a tantrum, or about to start on one, say 'one' in a firm, no-nonsense voice, and pause for a couple of seconds. Follow it with 'two', and pause again. On 'three', get up and walk over towards your child. They won't know what's going to happen next, and generally nothing will – except that they'll snap out of the behaviour. It won't work for all children, but it's certainly worth a try.

Ask them what's wrong. It sounds obvious, but it's not a technique most parents even consider. If your child is rolling around on the ground and bashing their fists on the floor, the chances are that something's bothering them. Rather than just telling them to snap out of it, see if they're able to explain what the problem is. A lot of tantrums are caused by children's inability to express their feelings: if you can help them to put their emotions into words, you'll give them a valuable tool with which to deal with them. If they're too young to express themselves coherently, ask them to draw a picture showing how they feel. You may lose a couple of crayons, but it's a small price to pay.

Leave them to it. Removing the audience is a method that's recommended in most textbooks on childcare: 'They're only attention-seeking', runs the advice, 'so withdraw the attention.' It's a solution that works to some extent within the security of your own home, but not one that we've had a lot of success with. When your child is emotionally overwrought, they need your help. Turning your back may work for some parents, but it's not an option we'd recommend.

Be ridiculous

Kids love seeing adults making fools of themselves. It's a technique that can often be used effectively to get them out of a tantrum: placing a saucepan on your head, or taking your socks and shoes off and putting them on your hands, will get most young children laughing – and they'll find it hard to laugh and scream at the same time. Once they start to giggle, you're on a winning streak.

Let's say your child has crawled under the table and is refusing to come out. You could just stand there insisting, but it probably won't do any good. Instead, sit under the table with them, and try conversation along these lines:

Dad: What do you think these table legs are made of?

Child: (no response)

Dad: Are they made of glass?

Child: (no response – but an absurd suggestion is going to grab their attention)

Dad: Maybe they're made of water. Do you think they're water?

Child: No.

Dad: So what are they made of? Paper?

Child: No.

Dad: What do you think they're made of?

Child: Wood.

Dad: Hmm. Wood, eh? Could be. Let's have a look at the top, and see if that's made of wood as well.

(Dad comes out from under the table, and examines the top)

Dad: No, I think the top's made of fur.

Child: No, it's wood, silly.

Dad: Really? It looks like fur to me.

At this point, your child should come out from under the table to look at the surface. The absurd suggestions have provided enough distraction to bring the tantrum to an end, and you can get on with your lives.

Making ridiculous comments is also a good way to stop kids from damaging household objects – something they're only doing to show how much, at that moment, they want to hurt you. Let's say your child has got hold of a pair of scissors, and is preparing to cut a hole in the carpet.

Here's an exchange that can defuse the situation:

Dad: Oh, dear. That's not going to be good. I'd better call a carpet repair man.

Child: (no response)

Dad: Looks like it's going to be too serious for that. I think I should call an ambulance instead.

Child: (pauses for a moment, wondering what's going on)

Dad: Or a lion tamer. Yes, on second thoughts I think a lion tamer is the best solution.

The more absurd you are, the more chance you have of turning the situation around. Use your imagination!

Give them a choice

Young children have very little control over their own lives. They don't decide when to go to bed, where to go on holiday, which school to go to, or even which clothes are bought for them. As they get older, they take on more responsibility and are allowed to make more decisions: but it's still nowhere near enough. It's no wonder kids rebel against direct instructions so often: saying no is about the only option they have.

One way of making them feel better about themselves – and of getting them to do what you want – is to give them a choice of two different courses of action. So rather than saying, for instance, 'There are your clothes – now get dressed', let them become part of the decision process. Don't insist they wear the shirt you've laid out, but give them a choice between two different ones. It's a small inconvenience for you, but it can be very empowering for the child.

Once they've got used to the idea of making choices, you can turn the situation to your advantage. So instead of 'Go and tidy your room', offer them a couple of options. Tell them they can either tidy their room, or do the washing-up. Neither is all that palatable, but at least they'll have made the decision themselves.

Keep the choices direct and simple. And give them the opportunity to make choices whenever possible: it will help them to feel they've been consulted, and that not all of life's decisions have been taken out of their hands.

Kiss and make up

However good a parent you are, however calm and in control, there are times when you'll simply fly off the handle and start yelling. Fair enough: Dads are people too. We can also be hurt and upset.

If you yell, you can certainly expect them to yell back. It's not necessarily a bad thing, and can help to clear the air: getting out all your frustrations and pent-up anger every now and again can make for a more healthy relationship.

The important thing is not to let it linger. Sulking is a bad habit to get into. If one or other of you has stormed out of the room, leave it ten minutes and then go and apologise. It really doesn't matter if you don't think the argument was your fault: apologise anyway. Not for whatever the cause of the problem was, but for yelling.

We'd strongly recommend a hug at this stage. If it seems appropriate, when things have calmed down you can then go on to explain just what it was that made you so cross in the first place: but be sure to listen to the other side of the argument as well.

Invent code words

If you've followed the advice in 'Kiss and make up' and found it works for you, then there's a valuable extra step you can take to avoid exactly the same argument cropping up again, and that's to recall the situation with a code word.

Let's say you've been arguing over whether or not your child should try the Thai curry you've so lovingly prepared. (It sounds trivial, but it's exactly this sort of mundane occurrence that leads to the biggest bust-ups.) You've both yelled, stormed out and slammed the door, and now calmed down. A couple of hugs later, you've discussed the situation and come to a reasonable conclusion: that you, as a Dad, promise not to force your child to eat food they really find disgusting; in return, they'll try at least a mouthful of new foods with an open mind, just in case they find they like it.

So you invent the code words 'Thai curry'. The next time you feel a similar disagreement coming on – which may be about going to see a movie with no car chases in it, or visiting a museum, or reading a book that you enjoyed when you were their age – just say 'Thai curry'. With any luck, both of you will be able to recall the earlier situation, and act accordingly.

Of course, the code words work both ways. So if your child really hates *Swallows and Amazons* you must be prepared to accept the Thai curry argument as well.

Give positive attention

Kids do many things that annoy us. They also do a lot of stuff that's calculated specifically to annoy us – or so it seems. In reality, they're just trying to get our attention. Celebrities will tell you that all publicity is good publicity, and so it is with kids: any attention is often better than none at all.

So if your child is irritating you by, say, constantly tapping their fingers, telling them to stop tapping is feeding their need. A better method is to reward them for *not* tapping, by giving them the attention instead. Rather than saying 'Stop tapping', try saying 'Be still' instead – placing your hand gently on theirs to hold it. When they stop, reward them with 'Good', and a smile of encouragement.

Then, of course, you have to address why they were so desperate to get your attention in the first place. Chances are, they were being missed out of the conversation: so instead of immediately resuming your discussion about the relative merits of a variety of broadband suppliers, take a moment to discuss something of relevance to them.

Reward good behaviour

One way of recognising – and so rewarding – good behaviour is to set up a Star Chart system. Exactly how it works is up to you, but here's a method that we found successful.

We made a set of stars about two inches across, cut out of blue cardboard. Half of them were sprayed gold. A hole was punched in each one, and a peg board made

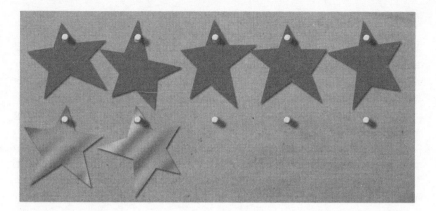

that would hold the stars. Then we hung it on the kitchen wall, and explained the rules to our kids.

They would get a blue star every time they did something exceptional – such as doing the washing-up, or remembering to clean their teeth, or behaving well when Grandma came for tea. When they had five blue stars, they'd get a gold star, and a small prize: this was often a Kinder egg in our case. When they had five gold stars, they'd then get a big prize – perhaps a sum of money to spend on a toy of their choice. The prizes and amounts depend, of course, on the age of the children.

We found this system enormously effective, and it lasted from the age of about three until verging on teens.

Let reasoned argument succeed

It may sound obvious, but if your kids have a reasonable point, it's worth listening. Say you tell them it's time for bed while they're watching *The Simpsons*. They'll point out that it's halfway through, and it will only be another fifteen minutes – can't they watch till the end? They promise to go to bed the moment it ends.

It's a fair request, which won't seriously upset their night-time routine. Rather than insisting they stop what they're doing and comply with your instructions immediately, let yourself be won over by their reasoning, and let them *see* that this is what's happened. Apart from making for an evening devoid of yelling, it will show them that you're a reasonable person, and that you respect their views. All of which will make life easier in the future!

One at a time

When a child of any age is behaving badly, or needs to be told off for any reason, it's often the cue for all the adults in the vicinity to jump in and start telling them off as well.

It's a disastrous approach, of course. Not only will the child feel – perhaps rightly – that everyone's against them, they'll also simply block out all the noise and ignore the instructions.

One adult should be in charge at any one time, and only one. It's clearer for the children, and it's easier for all the other adults concerned. Plus, of course, there's the significant bonus that those who are not on duty can relax without having to worry about enforcing discipline.

Lighten up!

If this chapter makes the whole childcare thing sound like a nightmare, it needn't be so. Kids have a sense of humour, and they'll enjoy joking with you and playing jokes on you. Enjoy their company, recognise when they're being silly for the sake of it, and join in the fun.

19 Teach your child how to think

ALL CHILDREN LIKE PUZZLES. They're great for stimulating the brain: they get the little grey cells working overtime, stimulating the parts that TV and video games cannot reach.

But kids often need help working through a complex puzzle. You can't just tell them the question and leave them to get on with it: they'll frequently give up in despair, without having the foggiest idea where to begin to solve a difficult conundrum.

In this chapter, we'll give you some ideas on how to help your child to work the puzzles out for themselves, with a little guidance from you. It's not giving the game away, merely steering them in the right direction. What seems an impossible task at first sight can be nibbled away at, piece by piece, until the truth is revealed.

As well as working out puzzles designed specifically for that purpose, you can also encourage your children to treat everyday problems as puzzles that need to be solved. In this way, you'll be encouraging them to think laterally, to bring their solving skills to a wider range of issues – and so become more effective thinkers.

Puzzle 1: The Queen's mustard pot

An easy one to start off with. No historical knowledge required – just a small amount of common sense.

The puzzle: *While browsing in an antique shop, you come across a tarnished silver mustard pot. Inscribed on the front is the legend 'Presented to our most loyal subject by Queen Elizabeth I, in the year of Our Lord 1597'. The owner of the shop assures you that the piece is genuine, hence the high price tag. You, however, suspect it to be a forgery. How can you tell?*

Your child may first make all kinds of suppositions: that Queen Elizabeth's reign ended before 1597 (it didn't), that mustard hadn't reached England by that date (it had), that the spelling is too good to be 16th century (it isn't).

They don't need to know anything about Elizabethan history to solve this one. If they're really stuck, ask them what the inscription would have said if the mustard pot had been presented by Queen Victoria. They'll probably come up with a reasonable version of the wording, perhaps even dredging up enough school history to hazard a guess as to a date within Queen Victoria's reign.

What they won't say, of course, is 'presented by Queen Victoria I'. Because she won't be Victoria I until there's been a Victoria II. It's just the same with Elizabeth: it wasn't until the coronation of Queen Elizabeth II that she was referred to as Queen Elizabeth I. In the three and a half centuries before that, she was plain Queen Elizabeth.

Prefented to our
moft loyal subject
by
Queen Elizabeth I,
in the year of Our Lord
1597

Puzzle 2: The helmet problem

This is a tricky one to solve by yourself. There just doesn't seem to be enough to go on. But, as with all the best puzzles, the solution lies in the wording of the question.

The puzzle: *At the beginning of the First World War, soldiers fought in cloth caps or berets. Naturally, there were heavy losses, so they were soon issued with tin helmets instead. However, in the weeks after helmets began to be worn, the field hospitals reported treating a far higher number of casualties with head injuries. Why was this the case?*

Children often approach this puzzle by assuming that there must be a fault with the equipment. Perhaps the helmets weren't as strong as they thought, so they were shot when they put their heads up over the parapet. Perhaps they wore their chin straps too loose, so the helmets were blown off the back of their heads and the straps strangled them.

They have to be assured, at this point, that the helmets were in no way faulty, and that they were being worn and used correctly. They don't need any specialist knowledge of wartime conditions. And no, the soldiers didn't become reckless and foolhardy as a result of wearing what they assumed was adequate protection.

So why were there so many more head injuries?

There weren't. And that's a key point to get across when your child starts to run out of ideas: there were no more head injuries after the helmets were issued than there were before.

Let them stew on this for a while, since it may well be enough to get them thinking along the right lines.

When they get stuck – and they probably will – try repeating the key phrase in the puzzle again: 'Field hospitals reported *treating* a far higher number of casualties with head injuries.' It's the fourth word that gives the game away. Before the helmets were issued, soldiers with head injuries didn't get as far as the hospital.

Puzzle 3: The burning fuses

This one appears baffling at first sight. But it's a straightforward enough problem, and one that most children ought to be able to solve with a little assistance.

The puzzle: *You have two string fuses, of the kind you see attached to round black bombs in cartoons. Each one burns for exactly one hour. They're not of uniform thickness, so may not burn at a constant rate. How can you use these fuses to measure exactly 45 minutes?*

Kids will try to cheat at this one. They'll suggest measuring three-quarters of the way along a fuse, so you must point out that they don't burn in a uniform way. They'll suggest cutting the fuses in half, but the same rule applies.

Eventually, they should realise that if you light one of the fuses at both ends, it will last exactly half an hour. But how does this help? You could try lighting one at both ends to get half an hour, then lighting the other at both ends for another half an hour – but this gets us back to an hour, and we want 45 minutes. So we want the second fuse to last for a shorter time.

Let's say we light the first fuse at both ends, and the other at one end. When the first fuse is completely burnt, half an hour has elapsed. Now what?

The second fuse is now exactly half gone, which means it has half an hour's worth of burning left in it. How can we make this one burn for just 15 minutes? We've already cracked the problem of making a fuse burn twice as fast, so we can apply that solution here. As soon as the first fuse is extinguished, light the second one at the other end as well. The remaining half an hour's worth of fuse will be used up in half the time – 15 minutes. So, in all, we've managed to time 45 minutes.

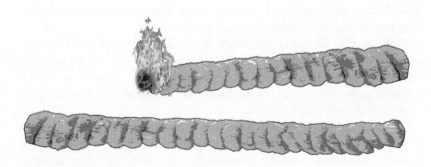

Puzzle 4: The seven trees

This is a puzzle that almost all children fail to get right first time. And they'll continue to make the same mistake each time the puzzle is repeated using different wording – until they finally grasp the point. It's something to do with the way their brains are wired!

The puzzle: *Seven trees are planted in a single line. Each tree is exactly 10 metres from the next. What's the distance between the first tree and the last?*

Most children will immediately answer '70 metres'. Rather than giving them the right answer, simply tell them that their solution is wrong. They'll think about it, multiply seven by ten once more, and come up with the same answer, assuming *you've* got it wrong and can't do basic maths.

It may be helpful, for younger children at least, to draw seven dots in a line on a piece of paper, and get them to count the gaps. Of course, seven trees make six gaps: so the answer is 60 metres, not 70.

Once they get the point, give them the puzzle again over the next few days or weeks, using perhaps ten stones on a beach, or five fence posts, or eleven footballers in a line-up. You'll be surprised at how often they'll get it wrong before they fully grasp the principle!

Puzzle 5: The 100 trees

This is a good puzzle to follow *The Seven Trees*, as it looks at first sight as if you're simply repeating one they already know. But this is a different case entirely!

The puzzle: *100 trees are planted in a straight line. The distance from the first to the second is 1 metre; from the second to the third is 2 metres; from the third to the fourth is 4 metres, from the fourth to the fifth 8 metres, and so on. The gap between each pair of trees is double the previous one. If you walk from the first tree to the last, which tree are you nearest when you've walked exactly half the total distance?*

Your child may begin here by assuming it's a mathematical task of monstrous proportions, and start adding together 1, 2, 4, 8, 16 and so on. They'll quickly realise that it would take an age to add up all the numbers needed, so reassure them that no such complex maths is necessary. As with all the best puzzles, this one comes down to common sense.

The fact that there are so many trees appears to make this one unmanageable, so ease them into the solution by starting with a smaller number of trees. Let's say there are just five in a row, following the same doubling rule. How far is the total distance between the first and the last? You may need to draw this on paper to help them out.

Once again, they may begin by adding 1, 2, 4, 8 and 16 – the first five multiples. Except, of course, five trees means only four gaps. So all they need to add is the first four numbers, which makes a completely manageable 15. When they're halfway, they've walked 7.5 metres. The gaps between the first four trees (the first three gaps) comes to 7 metres, so they're nearest to the fourth tree.

At this point, they may have that flash of insight that helps them to solve the original puzzle. If not, ask what happens if there are six trees in a row. The total distance is now 31 metres; half that is 15.5 metres; the distance between the first and the fifth is 15 metres, so they're nearest to the fifth tree.

So if halfway between the first and the fifth tree is the fourth, and halfway between the first and the sixth tree is the fifth, what's halfway between the first and the 100th? The answer, of course, is the 99th tree. They'll be seriously impressed with themselves when they figure it out!

Puzzle 6: The chiming clock

Just when they think they've got the hang of *The Seven Trees* puzzle, it's a good time to give them this one. It looks completely different, but it's exactly the same puzzle.

The puzzle: *A clock takes 5 seconds to chime six o'clock. How long will it take to chime twelve o'clock?*

The immediate response is to double the length of time, giving 10 seconds. That, of course, is the wrong answer: what we're looking for is the time between the first strike and the last. Just like *The Seven Trees* puzzle, it's a question of counting the gaps. If it takes 5 seconds to chime six o'clock, then that's five gaps – one chime per second. So, of course, it takes 11 seconds to chime twelve o'clock.

Puzzle 7: Three cats eating

When maths is involved in a puzzle, it's important to use logic as well as arithmetic to get the right answer. This one baffles most children, despite being fairly straightforward.

The puzzle: *If three cats eat three bowls of food in three days, how much food does one cat eat in one day?*

The first response is generally to divide everything by three, and to come up with the answer: one bowl. But there are too many terms here to be able to do this division so simply; more thought is required. Your first piece of assistance should be to ask them how many bowls of food one cat will eat in three days, which should be enough to get them thinking along the right lines.

If there are three cats, and they eat three bowls in three days, then that's one bowl per cat; so one cat will eat one bowl in the same three days. Which means that one cat will eat one-third of a bowl of food in a single day.

Puzzle 8: Two men walking

Most of the puzzles involve some kind of calculation or logic in order to solve them. But it takes a different kind of logic to realise when a puzzle is, itself, the puzzle. This is a good one to follow the *Three Cats Eating* puzzle.

The puzzle: *It takes one man three hours to walk to London. How long does it take two men to walk to London?*

If they say either six hours or one and a half hours, then they're good at mental arithmetic – but not so good at spotting when they're being fooled. It's still three hours, of course.

Wouldn't it be easier to work this out on paper?

LONDON

Puzzle 9: Three fruit boxes

A very straightforward puzzle, but one that can be hard to visualise. It helps if you have a pen and paper handy to draw a diagram!

The puzzle: *Three boxes of fruit are labelled A (apples), B (bananas) and C (cherries). All the labels on the boxes are wrong. How many boxes do you have to open in order to label them all correctly?*

Rather than simply accepting their initial guess of 'one', 'two' or 'three', get them to explain their reasoning. Having a drawing of three boxes labelled A, B and C in front of you will make it much easier for them to show what they're thinking.

Let's say you open box A, and it has bananas in it. What does that tell us about the contents of box B? Well, it could contain either apples or cherries. But if it had apples in, then box C must contain the cherries, right? Wrong. It can't contain cherries, since all the boxes are labelled incorrectly; so box C must contain the apples, which means the cherries must be in box B.

You can repeat the process with each of the boxes in turn, if you like, but it's probably not necessary since the logic is the same with each box. You only ever have to open one box to be able to label them all correctly.

Puzzle 10: Three coin boxes

This is a good one to follow on from the *Three Fruit Boxes* puzzle, as it takes the problem one step further. It appears to be the same puzzle, but there's an added twist.

The puzzle: *Three boxes of coins are labelled 'Gold', 'Silver', and 'Gold or Silver'. All the labels are wrong: the boxes actually contain gold, silver and bronze coins. How many boxes do you need to open in order to put all the labels right?*

Let's say we open the box labelled Gold, and it contains... no, wait, we don't need to do that. There's a better way of approaching this puzzle, which is to step back and think about it before y§ou start lifting the lids.

Start with the box labelled Gold or Silver. What do we know about that one? Well, obviously, if the label is incorrect, it can't contain either gold or silver coins. So without even opening it, we know that this one must contain the bronze coins.

That should be enough to get them to work out the rest of the problem. Having figured out where the bronze coins are stored, we're left with only the silver and the gold. So what goes where? Clearly, the gold can't be in the box labelled Gold, so it must be in the one labelled Silver. And so the silver has to be in the box labelled Gold.

And so we come to the rather surprising solution: we don't have to open any of the boxes in order to put all the labels right.

Puzzle 11: The violinist's dilemma

This is one of those puzzles that seems, at first sight, to be impossible. But the explanation is perfectly rational – although a slight knowledge of Pythagoras certainly helps.

The puzzle: *A violinist is going to perform a concert in a foreign country. He's stopped at the airport check-in desk, and told that he can't board the plane. 'The violin is OK,' says the attendant, 'since it's 40cm long. But that's the maximum dimension of item you're allowed to take on the plane, and your bow is 50cm long. Sorry, you can't take it with you.' The violinist is in despair – he can't play the concert without his bow, and doesn't want to risk putting it in the baggage hold. Eventually, he works out a way to carry it onto the plane legitimately. How's it done?*

It doesn't involve breaking the bow in half, or sliding it down his trouser leg, or any of a dozen ruses the quick-witted child might come up with. So how is it possible?

The Pythagoras solution, mentioned above, is the answer. You'll dimly remember from school maths lessons that if a right-angle triangle has two sides of lengths 3 and 4 units, then the hypotenuse will be 5 units long (since $3^2 + 4^2 = 5^2$). So all the violinist has to do is find a box 30cm by 40cm, and place the bow in it diagonally. Amazing!

Puzzle 12: The age of children

This is the trickiest puzzle in the book, and one which will take some real thought to figure out – for adults as much as for children. Is there enough information to get the solution?

The puzzle: *A man is going from house to house doing market research. He knocks on a door and a woman answers. 'Good morning,' says the man. 'I wonder if you can tell me how many children you have?' 'Three,' answers the woman. 'And how old are they?' The woman, being rather mischievous, tells him: 'The product of their ages is 36.' [That is, you get 36 if you multiply all their ages together.] 'That doesn't give me* *the answer,' says the man. The woman replies: 'The sum of their ages [that is, if you add them all together] is the same as the number of the house next door.' The man goes to look at the neighbour's house, then comes back with a despondent look on his face. 'That still doesn't tell me,' he says. The woman gives him one final clue: 'The oldest plays the piano.' Now the researcher can work out the children's ages exactly. How does he know?*

At first glance, it looks as if we don't have anything like enough information here. For one thing, the researcher may know the number of the house next door, but we don't. And what possible difference can it make if the oldest plays the piano?

The only solution is to take each piece of information in turn. We know that the product of the children's ages is 36; so we can begin by working out all the permutations of three children that multiply together to make 36. Write them in columns:

36	18	12	9	9	6	6	4
1	2	3	4	2	6	3	3
1	1	1	1	2	1	2	3

Next, we know that the sum of the ages is equal to the number on the house next door. Well, we don't know that number, but let's add up all the sums:

36	18	12	9	9	6	6	4
1	2	3	4	2	6	3	3
1	1	1	1	2	1	2	3
38	21	16	14	13	13	11	10

We know that, even knowing the sum of the ages, this information wasn't enough to give the researcher the ages of the children. In order for there still to be some doubt, this means that the number on the house next door must be 13, as there are two possible solutions with this sum. So the ages of the children is either 9, 2 and 2, or 6, 6 and 1.

And the final piece of information? The eldest plays the piano. If they were 6, 6 and 2, there would be two older twins: but 'the oldest' indicates a single person. So the children have to be aged 9, 2 and 2.

Simple? Far from it. But you'll look most impressive to your kids when you show them how it's worked out!

Puzzle 13: The hungry bookworm

This one seems, at first sight, like a straightforward problem of addition. And so it is: but you need to use a little logic before you begin adding.

The puzzle: *Three volumes of an encyclopaedia are arranged in order on a shelf. The pages of each book are each 30mm thick, and each hard cover is 5mm thick. A bookworm eats its way from the first page of volume 1 to the last page of volume 3. How far does it travel?*

Simple, your child thinks. Each book is 30mm for the pages, plus 5mm for each cover. Add them up, and you get a thickness of 40mm for each book. There are three books, so that makes 120mm in total. No, hang on: the worm doesn't go through the first cover, or the last. So it's 110mm.

Except that it isn't. Tell them they've got the answer wrong, and that they should go and look at a book on a shelf to see why.

The encyclopaedias are arranged in order. Where's the first page of volume 1? On the *right*-hand side of the book as you look at the spine. And the last page of volume 3 is on the *left*-hand side of the book.

So to eat from the first page of volume 1 to the last page of volume 3, the bookworm only has to eat through one cover of volume one (5mm); then the whole of volume 2 (40mm); then one cover of volume 3 (5mm). Which makes 50mm in all.

Puzzle 14: Manhole covers

With all the made-up puzzles, it's good to pose some questions that relate to real life every now and again. This one's a good example.

The puzzle: *Why are manhole covers usually round?*

You'll get all sorts of answers to this one: you should point out that there's a distinct advantage in them being round, rather than rectangular, or triangular, or any other shape. Try to get them to think about the special properties of round things.

The answer, of course, is that a round cover can never fall down the hole from which it has been lifted. Just about every other shape can.

Puzzle 15: The tennis tournament

Even kids who are a whiz at mental arithmetic will find this one daunting on first sight. But you have to reassure them that maths really has nothing to do with it: all you need is a bit of logic.

The puzzle: *128 people take part in a knockout tennis tournament. Each player drops out as soon as they lose a match. How many matches are played in total?*

Well, this shouldn't be too complicated. 128 is double 64, which is double 32, which is double 16, which is double 8, and so on, so all we have to work out is two multiplied by itself enough times to make…

No, stop right there. As we said, there's really no mathematics involved. Look at it from a logical point of view. How many outright winners are there? Just the one. So how many losers? Well, it has to be 127. And since each player can lose only one match, that means there must have been 127 matches in all. Easy when you think about it!

Puzzle 16: Bags of gold

Another puzzle that looks more complicated than it really is. There's a neat solution here that may take a while to arrive at.

The puzzle: *You have five bags full of gold coins (lucky you!). Although they look identical, the coins in four of the bags weigh 10 grams each, while those in one of the bags weigh 11 grams. You also have an accurate set of scales that shows the weight placed upon it. How do you work out which bag holds the heavier coins?*

The first thing to explain here is that you only need one weighing in order to find which bag holds the heavy coins. So how is it done?

Here's the solution: tell your kids to take one coin from bag 1, two from bag 2, three from bag 3, and so on. We'll have 15 coins altogether (1+2+3+4+5). But how does this help?

If they all weighed 10 grams, the total weight would be 150 grams. Of course, because of the heavier coins, the total will be slightly more than that. How much more, exactly?

And this will give us the answer. If the total is 2 grams heavier, then there must be two oversized coins – which means bag 2 contains them. If it's 4 grams overweight, then bag 4 holds the heavier coins. Simple, when you know how!

Puzzle 17: Not enough time

There's a bit of maths involved in this one. Not a lot, but enough to get them thinking. The answer, however, owes more to logic than mathematics.

The puzzle: *James insists that he does not have enough time to go to school more than 17 days a year. He comes to this conclusion based on the following list that he put together.*

Activity	Number of days per year
Sleep (8 hours a day)	122
Meals (2 hours a day)	31
Weekends	104
School holidays	60
TV & play time (2 hours a day)	31
Total	348

Inspired by the list, James claims he has only 17 days left in the year for school. What's wrong with his thinking?

Get a calculator out, if you like, to check James's sums – but you'll find they're all correct. So where has he gone wrong? It all appears to make sense!

The problem is that James's categories overlap. For example, he's counted 60 days for holidays, during which time he will both eat and sleep, activities that he has already counted separately. These 60 days also include weekends, another category that he has already counted separately. He should not count the same periods of time more than once. Similarly, his weekend counting includes sleeping time, and so on.

Puzzle 18: Running the race

The puzzle: *You're running a race to a distant landmark and back. On the way there, you run at 10 miles per hour. On the way back, you're tired, so only run at 5 miles per hour. What's your average speed over the whole race?*

You might be tempted to say 7.5 miles per hour, which seems logical. But it's not the right answer. Let's imagine this is a 20 mile race. The first 10 miles take one hour; the second ten miles take two hours.

So you've run 20 miles in three hours in all, which makes an average speed of $6\frac{2}{3}$ miles per hour – irrespective of the length of the race.

Quickfire puzzles

Quickfire 1: *What's wrong with these sentences?*

1. No one goes to that restaurant these days because it's too crowded.
2. If you can't read this sign, ask for help.
3. Stay away from the water until you've learned how to swim.

Answers: 1. If no one goes, how can it be crowded? 2. If you can't read, how do you know what it tells you to do? 3. You can't learn how to swim unless you go in the water.

Quickfire 2: *Where would you be if, when you move forward it is summer, backwards and it's winter, right and it's July 1st, left and it's July 2nd?*

Answer: Where the equator meets the International Dateline, facing north.

Quickfire 3: *What are the most northerly, southerly, westerly and easterly states of the USA?*

Answer: Alaska, Hawaii, Alaska and... Alaska. That's right. The Aleutian Islands, part of the state of Alaska, cross the International Dateline and so are both the furthest west *and* east you can go in the United States.

Quickfire 4: *If a friend tells you he's hidden a twenty pound note in a boring dictionary between pages 813 and 814, would you believe him?*

Answer: No, because odd page numbers are on the right hand side of every book and even on the left, which means there is nothing between 813 and 814. They are two sides of the same piece of paper.

Quickfire 5: *What's the only fruit to have its seeds on the outside?*

Answer: A strawberry.

Quickfire 6: *A sundial is the timepiece with the fewest number of moving parts. What is the timepiece with the greatest number of moving parts?*

Answer: An hourglass, which has thousands of moving grains of sand.

The chequerboard illusion

Here's our Dad devising a new board game. All the squares except two have counters on them. The two squares that *don't* contain counters are exactly the same colour. Don't believe us? Punch a couple of holes in a sheet of paper and place it on top, so you can see only those two squares through the holes. It's amazing how the eye is deceived!

That's the last time I buy a cube from IKEA

The impossible cube

This wooden cube has got into a tangle, and Dad's trying to sort it out. Is it possible, do you think? Or is our valiant would-be fixer fighting a losing battle?

20 Stuff and nonsense

THERE ARE MANY THINGS that mark out a great Dad. The ability to fix things, to entertain kids, to play football in the park – these are all essential skills, as we'd be the first to admit. But a Dad is also expected to know stuff that no one else does: not just general information, but stuff so obscure your kids will wonder how you ever came to know it all.

What's the chance of being struck by lightning? What colour is a polar bear? When were tea bags invented? All facts a Dad needs at his fingertips. The opportunities for showing off your intricate knowledge of the bizarre, the wonderful and the downright homely are endless. Whether in a restaurant, on a car journey, in the home or out and about on a shopping trip, you should be able to amaze and entertain your kids with a wealth of information.

Not everything you tell your kids needs to be informative, or even true. So we've added a selection of really, *really* silly jokes and riddles to keep you going.

Fascinating facts

Information is power, we're told. That may or may not be the case with these tasty morsels: but as far as our researches can tell, they're all 100 per cent true.

Babies are born without kneecaps. The knees don't show up on X-rays, as they're made of cartilage; they only turn into bone at the age of around three in girls and five in boys.

Pigs can't look at the sky. They just aren't physically able to bend their necks back far enough. Oh, and they can't fly, either.

Branwell Bronte died standing up. The brother (left) of novelists Charlotte, Emily and Anne contracted tuberculosis, and met his untimely end standing up while leaning against a mantelpiece, simply in order to prove that it could be done.

The Mona Lisa once hung on the wall of Napoleon's bedroom. When it was stolen from the Louvre in 1911, the artist Pablo Picasso was taken for questioning by the police. It turned out to have been stolen by a thief who commissioned a well-known forger to make several copies that he could sell to collectors.

The average lifespan of a rat is 18 months. But they breed so quickly that in that time they could have over a million descendants.

Tsar Nicholas's finger was chopped off in 2001. Legend has it that when the Tsar sketched the route of the Trans-Siberian Railway from Moscow to St Petersburg, he drew a straight line with a ruler on the map – but his finger got in the way, which produced a kink in the line. The engineers faithfully followed his instructions, constructing a 17 kilometre detour near the town of Novgorod. 150 years later, the 'kink' was removed and the line put straight.

Dolphins sleep with one eye open. Sharks, on the other hand, don't find fish by looking for them: they listen for their heartbeats.

The first couple to be shown in bed together on American TV were Fred and Wilma Flintstone.

The average Frenchman eats 500 snails a year. Snails themselves, however, can sleep for three years without eating. The world's largest exporter of frogs' legs is Japan.

The most popular pizza topping in the United States is pepperoni – served on over half of all pizzas sold. In India, favourite toppings include pickled ginger and minced mutton.

If you shave a tiger, the skin underneath will be striped. Best not to try this at home, though.

Jesus Christ is the 13th greatest American of all time, according to a recent poll. Ronald Reagan came first. Another poll revealed that 12 per cent of Americans think Joan of Arc was married to Noah.

Australian banknotes are made of plastic. The first polypropylene polymer note was made in Australia in 1988, and contained a transparent window in which an image of Captain James Cook appeared. And if you'd like to see what one looks like, they'll be introduced into the UK from 2016.

Venus is the only planet which rotates clockwise. All the other planets in the solar system rotate anticlockwise, relative to the Sun, except Uranus, which has tilted so far on its axis that it rolls on its side.

Polar bears are actually black. At least, that's the colour of their skin, since it absorbs more heat that way. Their fur, however, isn't white. It's transparent.

There is no ozone at the seaside. The smell, which happens to be similar to that of ozone, is actually rotting seaweed.

The .tv domain name is owned by Tuvalu. The tiny island in the Pacific has an area of just ten square miles, and a population of under 12,000. No point on the island is more than five metres above sea level and they're seriously worried about global warming.

Every cubic mile of seawater contains about 25 tons of gold. The trouble is, no one has yet found a cost-effective way of extracting it. So don't add a filtration plant to your seaside kit just yet. A cubic mile is actually an awful lot of water – the equivalent of over one and a half million Olympic-sized swimming pools.

The Hawaiian alphabet has only 13 letters – A, E, I, O, U, H, K, L, M, N, P, W and a type of apostrophe, called 'okina'. Chinese script, on the other hand, has more than 40,000 characters.

Planespotting

So many summer afternoons are ruined – or enhanced, depending on your point of view – by the constant drone of planes flying overhead. Rather than simply cursing them for spoiling your peace and quiet, here's your chance to show your limitless knowledge by pointing out exactly what they are.

These are the planes you'll most often see flying over Britain.

Airbus A320

ATR 42

BAE 146

BAE Jetstream

Ilyushin 86

BN Trislander

Boeing 737

Are we there yet?

BN Islander

Boeing 747

Boeing 767

DC9

DC10

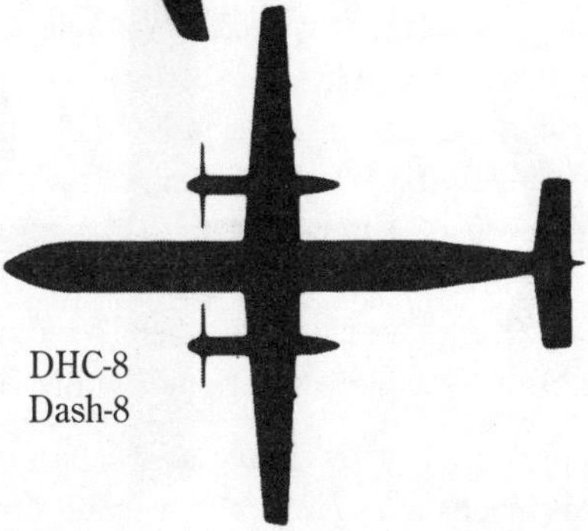

DHC-8
Dash-8

Embraer
ERJ-145

Names of the trade

We're all familiar with the household names of the products we use every day. But where did these names – and the products themselves – come from? A great opportunity to show off to your kids every time one crops up!

Rolls-Royce had a succession of cars with airy-fairy names such as Silver Ghost, Silver Wraith and Silver Phantom. Then they came up with 'Silver Mist', which seemed fine, until somebody pointed out that 'Mist' is the German name for 'manure'. The car became the 'Silver Shadow' instead.

The name **Frisbee** comes from the pie-tins that people discovered had aerodynamic properties when they were thrown. These came from the Frisbie Bakery in Connecticut, North America. The first Frisbee as such came out in 1957, made by the Wham-O Manufacturing Company in California.

Hoover: Compact electric vacuum cleaners were invented not by a Mr Hoover but by J. Murray Spangler, a department store caretaker who thought that the carpet sweeper he was told to use was making his asthma worse. William Henry Hoover was the businessman who bought the rights from him.

The principle behind it, though, had been adopted earlier by the British engineer H. Cecil Booth. He first demonstrated the idea by putting a handkerchief on a chair and sucking it, noting the dirt that collected on the other side. However, his devices were drawn by horses and originally oil-fired, and pipes had to be run into the building to be cleaned – not the most practical of methods.

Jelly Babies: Initially produced by Bassett's in Sheffield in 1919, they were originally called 'Peace Babies', as the First World War had just ended. They were known by that name right up to 1953 when they became Jelly Babies. The white stuff on the outside is edible starch, which was originally used to stop the sweets sticking in the old wooden moulds. It's still added because customers grew to like it.

Black Jelly Babies are made from leftover bits of all the other colours. More than a billion are produced every year, and they have names: Brilliant is red, Bubbles is yellow, Bonny is pink, Bigheart is black, Boofuls is green and Bumper is orange.

WD-40: The great lubricating spray that has so many uses, stands for 'Water Displacement, 40th Attempt'. It was invented as a way of preventing corrosion by keeping water at bay and was first used on the outside of Atlas missiles to stop them rusting.

On sale since 1958 and produced by what was then called The Rocket Chemical Company, it has many unconventional uses, such as removing chewing gum from shoes, getting rid of spray snow after Christmas, spraying on fishing bait to cover up the smell of human hands and, perhaps most useful of all, freeing a tongue that has become stuck to metal in freezing weather. And, of course, it's great for getting rusty bicycles running again.

Mr Kipling's Cakes: There never was a Mr Kipling. His name was conjured up in the 1960s as a supposed 'master baker', simply because it sounded mellifluous and traditional.

Subbuteo: Peter Adolph, who invented this football game in 1947, wanted to call it 'The Hobby', after the breed of falcon. But he wasn't allowed to copyright such an all-embracing name, so instead he named it after the falcon's Latin name *Falco subbuteo subbuteo*.

Crisps: The invention of crisps was a complete accident. In 1853 George Crum, a Native American chef at Moon's Lake House in Saratoga Springs in New York became irritated by a fussy diner who claimed that the chips he made were too thick and not salty enough.

After he sent them back a second time, Crum wanted to teach the customer a lesson. So he made the chips as thin as he possibly could and poured oodles of salt over them, reckoning the guy would never be able to eat them with a fork and would hate the taste. Instead, the diner loved them. And so the crisp was born.

Post-it Notes: The adhesive on Post-it Notes, just sticky enough but not so sticky it damages whatever it's attached to, was invented at 3M back in 1959 by Dr Spence Silver. Unfortunately, Dr Silver had been trying to produce a strong adhesive, so his formula was forgotten about.

Twenty-one years later another 3M employee, Art Fry, was trying to find a bookmark that would keep his place in his hymn book when he sang with his church choir. He experimented with Dr Silver's formula and came up with the Post-it Note. Initially, his bosses couldn't see the point. So Fry gave some secretaries at the company the first trial blocks of Post-it Notes to see what they'd use them for. They proved so popular that the order was given to manufacture what has since become one of the most popular stationery products ever, with a billion sold. As an employee of 3M, however, Art Fry didn't become rich as a result.

How loud is it?

Scientists will tell you that it means nothing to describe a noise as being so many decibels (named in honour of Alexander Graham Bell, inventor of the telephone). But then scientists say it isn't possible to travel faster than the speed of light and that we'll never have transporter beams, so they're just spoilsports.

Technically, a decibel is a unit of comparison rather than an absolute measure. But decibels are almost always related to the quietest sound that somebody with normal hearing can detect.

Decibels are measured on a logarithmic scale so that 20db, for instance, isn't double 10db but 10 times as loud, while 30db is 100 times as loud. It's also interesting to point out that 0db isn't absolute silence: it's just the point below which people can't hear.

Bizarrely, a nuclear submarine has audio detection equipment so sensitive that it can detect prawns chewing on food from 100 metres away, a sound level that is apparently –80db. By way of comparison, somebody talking 20 miles away would be –30db.

0db	20db	40db	60db	70db	75db	90db
Lowest level of human audibility	A soft whisper, rustling leaves	Suburban street with no traffic	Background music in a restaurant, normal conversation	Busy traffic, a noisy restaurant, noise inside a jet plane	Vacuum cleaner	Orchestra playing at its loudest heard from front row

If anybody says it's quiet enough to hear a pin drop, you can tell them that would measure 15db, assuming it was a metre away falling from a height of one centimetre (and not onto a cushion).

Sudden loud noises may startle but our ears are sensitive instruments, and if noise is continuous our hearing can be permanently damaged. Noise above 85db 8 hours a day will eventually harm hearing as will 15 minutes at 115db and 2 minutes at 130. MP3 players can often play above 115db, and while iPods are limited in Europe to 100db, that can still cause permanent problems if listened to at full volume for extended periods, particularly as the earbud style of headphones that intrude into the ear are noisier than the conventional sort. If you listen while travelling and turn the music up to drown out the noise of a busy street or a train, it can be difficult to tell just how loud the sound really is.

Experts recommend a 60/60 rule, listening for no more than an hour at a time at 60 per cent of maximum volume. Perhaps it's better to endure loud music coming from your kids' rooms than have them saying, 'Pardon, Dad', every time you try talking to them in ten years' time.

100db	110db	130db	150db	180db	280db	310db
Pneumatic drill, outboard motor	Heavy rock band giving it welly	Gunshot heard at close range	Balloon popping by your ear	Russian Soyuz rocket on take-off	57 megaton hydrogen bomb	Eruption of Krakatoa in 1883*

*heard 3,000 miles away, shattered concrete 30 centimetres thick 300 miles away

When did they start eating...

Popcorn, 3–2000 BC

Ancient popping corn was discovered in New Mexico during an archaeological dig in in 1948.

Chewing gum, 1869
William Semple filed the first patent on chewing gum, though the Ancient Greeks chewed resin from the mastic tree.

Corn flakes, 1894
Dr John Harvey Kellogg, a Seventh-Day Adventist who ran the Battle Creek Sanitarium, insisted on a vegetarian regimen that forbade booze, caffeine, tobacco and sex. Corn flakes, invented by accident, were thought to lower the sex drive and were served with milk and marshmallows.

Baked beans, 1890s

In Britain, where baked beans were introduced in 1904, beans are usually associated with Heinz, and Henry J. Heinz first came up with his baked beans in tomato sauce in Pittsburgh in 1895. However, the top baked bean producer in America is actually Bush's and even Heinz beans in the US are very different to the UK, being darker, mushier and much more sugary. In some places beans are sweetened with maple syrup or have mustard added.

Instant coffee, 1890
Although invented by invented and patented in 1890, by David Strang of New Zealand, instant coffee wasn't actually available commercially until Nescafé was launched by Nestlé in Switzerland, in 1938.

Ice-cream cone, 1904

The cone first came to the public's attention at the St Louis Fair of 1904, where it's said that a pastry maker helped out an ice-cream salesman who had run out of dishes. But there are several rival claims.

Tea bag, 1904
The first tea bags, made from hand-sewn muslin bags, appeared in 1904 and were sold by Thomas Sullivan of New York. Tea connoisseurs despise tea bags for containing low-grade, dusty tea, known as 'floor sweepings', that make the tea taste harsher than using leaves in a pot.

Frozen food, 1925
On a trip to the Arctic, Clarence Birdseye (his real name!) noticed that fish that froze quickly still tasted fresh when it was defrosted months later. In 1925 he developed a commercial freezer, which kick-started the frozen foods industry.

Sliced bread, 1928

If something's 'the best thing since sliced bread' then that really means since 7 July 1928, which is when the Chillicothe Baking Company of Missouri first produced 'Kleen Maid Sliced Bread' from their new slicing machine. It took a little while, though, to work out how to wrap the loaves and it wasn't until 1930 that pre-sliced 'Wonder Bread' was sold throughout the USA and in the UK.

Campbell's tomato soup, 1932

Although brands of tomato soup existed before this, it was in 1932 that Campbell's first produced their tomato soup, made even more famous by Andy Warhol.

Shopping trolley, 1937

Apparently basing it on the traditional design of a folding wooden chair, Sylvan Goldman came up with the first trolley. It looked like a folding chair on wheels with one basket where the seat would be and another higher up and further back. A year later, they added a holder for young children as customers were simply putting their kids in the baskets, which was dangerous as the early trolleys had a tendency to fold up unexpectedly.

Initially customers wouldn't use them. Men thought others would think they were too weak to carry baskets while they reminded women of pushing baby carriages. He had to employ fake customers to push them around before they took off.

Fish fingers, 1946

Frozen 'fish sticks' were apparently first conjured up by Edward Piszek of Philadelphia, although the American firm Gorton's claim they were there first. In the UK, however, the introduction of 'fish fingers' was an error.

They were originally made of herring, a fish the British didn't really like and called 'herring savouries'. To show just how tasty they were, bland cod sticks were made to compare them with but the British, being suitably perverse, preferred the cod version.

Chicken nugget, 1950s

Contrary to popular opinion, it wasn't McDonald's that came up with Jamie Oliver's least favourite food, it was food science professor Robert Baker of Cornell University. He worked out how to form chicken bits (comprising skin, muscle tissue and reconstituted meat) into any shape before being coated with breadcrumbs before cooking. Sadly for him, he didn't patent his findings.

What's the chance of...

Dying from a plane falling on you . . . . 1 in 25,000,000*

Dying from a lightning strike . . . . 1 in 18,700,000*

Dying from motorcycle racing. . . . . 1 in 1,100**

Dying from mountain climbing . . . . 1 in 1,750**

Dying from smoking 10 cigarettes a day . . . . 1 in 200**

Dying from having a meteorite fall on you. . . . . 1 in 1,000,000,000,000*

Dying from a road accident . . . . 1 in 16,800*

Dying from playing football . . . . 1 in 50,000**

Dying in a rail accident. . . . . 1 in 1,000,000*

Dying from a nuclear power accident. . . . . 1 in 10,000,000*

Being killed by a tree in a public space . . . . 1 in 20,000,000*

Drowning in the bath . . . . 1 in 685,000*

Being murdered . . . . 1 in 100,000*

Dying on a fairground ride. . . . . 1 in 834,000,000 rides

Dying while scuba diving. . . . . 1 in 200,000 dives

Dying while rock climbing. . . . . 1 in 320,000 climbs

Dying while hang-gliding. . . . . 1 in 116,000 flights

Having a serious fire at home . . . . 1 in 160*

Seriously injuring yourself using exercise equipment . . . . 1 in 400**

Having an accident on a fairground ride . . . . 1 in 2,326,000 rides

Finding that the next person you meet
is born on exactly the same day as you . . . . 1 in 25,000

Getting three balls in the National Lottery . . . . 1 in 11

Winning the National Lottery jackpot . . . . 1 in 14,000,000

*   per year
**but only if you race motorcycles, climb mountains, smoke, play football or use
    exercise equipment

Sources: Royal Society of Chemistry, HSE, National Statistics

The cloudspotter's guide

Sometimes they're fluffy and look like elephants or floating castles. Seen from above in glorious sunshine from a plane window, they look like beautifully lit cotton wool. But you might need to know a little more about clouds if you are to head off inquisitive questions, particularly as the beasties are so important to our weather.

All clouds are made up of billions of tiny droplets of ice or water, each droplet so tiny (1/100 of a millimetre) and light that they float on air. Every cubic metre of air contains 100 million droplets. If a child wants to know what it is like being in a cloud, take them out next time it is foggy, for fog is, in fact, simply cloud that is touching the ground.

A cloud is formed when the water vapour in the air cools and condenses into visible water droplets or ice crystals. It is the same process that results in condensation on windows and usually happens when warm air rises. Air might be forced to rise up over hills or mountains. It might rise because the ground has been heated by the Sun, creating thermals that birds and gliders like to ride. Or a body of warm air might meet a mass of cold, denser air and be forced up, which is called a 'front'.

What are contrails?

A shortening of 'condensation trails', these are composed of water vapour produced by the engines of high-flying jets that have condensed in the atmosphere where it is 30 degrees below zero. Although they aren't really clouds, these trails of ice crystals may be visible for some time and in some cases can spread and become the basis of cirrus clouds.

Identifying clouds

Although it can be fun trying to find shapes or faces in clouds, scientists prefer to be a little more precise. Back in 1803, Luke Howard, a chemist of the 'something for the weekend?' variety and a keen amateur meteorologist, came up with the system still used today. Using Latin for his definitions, he said that all clouds were either cumulus – heaped up and fluffy, stratus – in a layer, cirrus – wispy like threads or filaments or nimbus – Latin for 'get out your brolly'.

There are ten main cloud types, divided into three layers of height, depending on where the base of the cloud is. See the following pages for a full description of each one.

Low-level clouds – below 1 mile

Cumulus
The white, fluffy cloud kids love drawing. May bring showers but most often associated with sunny spells.

Cumulonimbus
White on top with a dark underside, like a cumulus which goes much higher and becomes less distinct, sometimes with an anvil shape at the top. This towering storm cloud produces heavy showers at the least and perhaps hail and thunder.

Stratocumulus
Fluffy cloud which resembles stretched-out cumulus and might be in layers or patches. Common in the UK in the colder months, it may produce light rain or snow but is more likely indicative of dry and dull weather.

Stratus
A low-level, grey layer of cloud. If there's nothing above it, you might just be able to see the Sun through it but don't bet on it. On higher ground it's known as hill fog. At lower levels, ordinary fog that lifts may turn into stratus. Stratus might produce drizzle.

Medium-level clouds – 1 to 3 miles

Altocumulus
White or grey with shading, like patches or sheets of medium-height cumulus. Might produce a shower but sunny periods are more likely.

Altostratus
A sheet of grey or bluish cloud without texture covering much of the sky. Altostratus will probably produce light rain or snow.

Nimbostratus
A thick, dark grey, layered rain cloud covering most or all of the sky and obscuring the Sun. Will make rain or snow, possibly heavy.

High-level clouds – over 3 miles

Cirrus
High, wispy, white cloud composed of ice crystals in long streaks or filaments, often described as 'mares' tails'. Cirrus is an indication of bad weather on the way.

Cirrocumulus
Often called a 'mackerel sky', these high-level clouds are made of ice crystals. The individual clusters will appear the width of your finger at arm's length. Indicative of unsettled weather.

Cirrostratus
Layered white cloud made of ice crystals, thin enough for the Sun to cast shadows. Will sometimes produce haloes around the Sun or the Moon. Showers or rain could be on the way.

Timeline of inventions

When did they think of that? Not an exhaustive list, but it includes many of the inventions your kids are likely to ask you about.

1590 **Microscope**
Zacharias Janssen

1593 **Water thermometer**
Galileo

1608 **Telescope**
Hans Lippershey

1643 **Barometer**
Evangelista Torricelli

1656 **Pendulum clock**
Christiaan Huygens

1668 **Reflecting telescope**
Isaac Newton

1700 **Piano**
Bartolomeo Cristofori

1705 **Steam engine**
Thomas Newcomen

1714 **Mercury thermometer**
Daniel Fahrenheit

1764 **Bifocal lens**
Benjamin Franklin

1783 **Hot Air Balloon**
The Montgolfier brothers

1800 **Electric battery**
Alessandro Volta

1816 **Stethoscope**
René-Théophile-Hyacinthe Laënnec

1821 **Electric motor**
Michael Faraday

1827 **Friction match**
John Walker

1830 **Sewing machine**
Barthélemy Thimonnier

1831 **Dynamo**
Michael Faraday

1835 **Pistol**
Samuel Colt

1839 **Electric telegraph**
Cooke & Wheatstone

1840 **Postage stamps**
Rowland Hill

1840 **Calculator**
Charles Babbage

1844 **Safety matches**
Gustaf Pasch

1849 **Safety pin**

Walter Hunt

1852 **Safety lift**
Elisha Otis

1853 **Hypodermic syringe**
Alexander Wood

1861 **Machine gun**
Richard Gatling

1862 **Pedal bicycle**
Pierre Lallement

1867 **Dynamite**
Alfred Nobel

1876 **Telephone**
Alexander Graham Bell & E. Gray

| 1876 | **Microphone** Emile Berliner |
| 1877 | **Phonograph** Thomas Edison |

I've had a great idea

1879	**Electric light** Joseph Swan
1885	**Automobile** Karl Benz
1887	**Pneumatic tyre** J. B. Dunlop
1887	**Gramophone**

Emile Berliner

1888	**Roll film camera** George Eastman
1891	**Glider** Otto Lilienthal
1892	**Vacuum flask** James Dewar
1893	**Motion pictures** Thomas Edison
1895	**X-ray** Wilhelm Röntgen

1896	**Radio** Marchese Marconi
1903	**Aeroplane** Wright brothers
1913	**Zip fastener** Gideon Sundback
1926	**Television** John Logie Baird
1928	**Penicillin** Sir Alexander Fleming
1930	**Jet engine** Sir Frank Whittle
1934	**Cats' eyes** Percy Shaw
1935	**Radar** Sir Robert Watson-Watt
1936	**Helicopter** Heinrich Focke
1938	**Photocopier** Chester Carlson
1938	**Ballpoint pen** László Bíró

1945	**Microwave oven** Percy Spencer
1951	**Superglue** Harry Coover
1954	**Solar battery** Bell Laboratory

| 1955 | **Hovercraft** Christopher Cockerell |

1956	**Videotape** Charles Ginsberg & Ray Dolby
1959	**Integrated circuit** Jack Kilby
1960	**Laser** Theodore Maiman
1964	**Computer mouse**

Douglas Engelbart

1968	**LCD display** George Heilmeier
1971	**Pocket calculator** Sharp
1971	**Microprocessor** Hoff & Faggin
1977	**Home computer** Jobs & Wozniak
1979	**Walkman stereo** Akio Morita
1982	**Compact disc** Philips & Sony
1990	**World Wide Web** Tim Berners-Lee
2007	**iPhone** Apple

Doctors, bars and other jokes

'Doctor, Doctor, I swallowed a bone.'
'Are you choking?'
'No, I really did.'

'Doctor, Doctor, I've got wind! Can you give me something?'
'Of course. Here's a kite.'

'Doctor, Doctor, I think I'm suffering from déjà vu!'
'Didn't I see you yesterday?'

'Doctor, Doctor, my son has swallowed my pen. What should I do?'
'Use a pencil.'

'Doctor, Doctor, I think I'm a bell.'
'Take these, and if it doesn't help give me a ring.'

'Doctor, Doctor, I get a pain in my eye every time I drink coffee.'
'Try taking the teaspoon out.'

'Doctor, Doctor, I've lost my memory.'
'When did this happen?'
'When did what happen?'

'Doctor, Doctor, I feel like a pair of curtains.'
'Pull yourself together.'

Why did the banana go to the doctors?
Because he wasn't pealing well.

A man walks into a bar. 'Ouch!'

William Shakespeare walks into a bar.
'Out!' orders the barman. 'You're bard.'

A white horse walks into a pub. The barman says, 'That's funny, this pub is named after you.'
The white horse says, 'What? William?'

A skeleton walks into a bar and orders a beer and a mop.

A sandwich walks into a bar and asks for a drink. The barman says, 'I'm sorry, but we don't serve food in here.'

A man walks into a bar, with a newt on his shoulder and says, 'A beer for me and an orange juice for Tiny here.'
'Why do you call him Tiny?'
'Because he's my newt.'

An Englishman, an Irishman and a Scotsman walk into a bar. 'What is this?' asks the barman, 'some sort of joke?'

'Mummy, Mummy can we have a dog for Christmas?'
'No, we'll have turkey like everyone else!'

Did you hear about the magic tractor?
It turned into a field.

'What a terrible day. I got pneumonia, then appendicitis, then tonsillitis.'
'You poor thing.'
'Yup, it's the hardest spelling test ever.'

A policeman stops a car packed full of penguins. The driver says he found them running around by the side of the road. 'You should take them to the zoo,' says the policeman.
The following day, at the same spot, he sees the same guy driving by with his car full of penguins again. He orders the man to stop. 'I thought I told you to take them to the zoo.'
'I did,' says the man. 'They had so much fun we're going to the beach today.'

What did Tarzan say when he saw a herd of elephants coming over a hill?
'Here come the elephants.'

What did Tarzan say when he saw a herd of elephants coming over the hill wearing sunglasses? Nothing. He didn't recognise them.

How do you tell when you are sharing your bed with an elephant? He has 'E' embroidered on his pyjamas.

Do you want me to tell you the joke about butter? I'd better not. You'd only spread it.

Do you want to hear a joke about the bed? I haven't made it up yet.

Did you hear about the man who drowned in a bowl of muesli? He was pulled under by a strong currant.

Did you hear about the three eggs? Two bad.

Have I told you the joke about the pencil? I'd better not, you won't get the point.

Knock, knock.
Donkheap.
Donkheap who?

Knock, knock
Who's there?
Biggish.
Biggish who?
No thanks, I just bought one.

A three-year-old put his shoes on by himself. His mother looked and said, 'Your shoes are on the wrong feet.'
'Don't be silly, Mum. They're the only feet I've got.'

The commander of a firing squad asks a man about to be shot for his last request. 'I'd like to sing a song,' he says. His request is granted. 'A million green bottles, standing on the wall...'

'Oh Mum, don't make me go to school today. I hate it.'
'You have to, son. For a start, you're 45. Secondly, you're the headmaster.'

Silly riddles

Two men jump into a lake but only one gets wet hair. How come?
One of them was bald.

Where do you find a dog with no legs?
Exactly where you left it.

What has a bottom at the top?
Your legs.

What part of the fish weighs the most?
The scales.

What's the difference between roast beef and pea soup?
Anyone can roast beef.

What do you call an elephant in space?
Lost.

What's green and wears oven gloves?
A cooking apple.

What did the dragon say when he saw St George in his armour?
'Oh no, not tinned food again.'

If Isambard Kingdom Brunel were alive today, what would he be most famous for?
Being the oldest person alive.

What has four wheels and flies?
A dustbin lorry.

Why did the hedgehog cross the road?
To see his flat mate.

How do you cook toast in the jungle?
Under the gorilla.

Why do the French like snails?
Because they don't like fast food.

What goes up, but never comes down?
Your age.

Why does Peter Pan always fly?
Because he can 'Neverland'.

What gets wetter as it dries?
A towel.

What is the similarity between a monkey and a bicycle?
They both have wheels, except for the monkey.

What's the best way to see flying saucers?
Insult the waiter.

How many Spaniards does it take to change a lightbulb?
Just Juan.

What's green, is fuzzy, has four legs and could kill you if it fell from a tree?
A snooker table.

Where do lions like to shop?
At a jungle sale.

What goes 'Oooohhhhh. Oooohhhh'?
A cow with no lips.

What goes 'Aaaa. Aaaa'?
A sheep with no lips.

Why did the dinosaur cross the road?
Because chickens hadn't yet been invented.

What's slow and sad?
Depressed treacle.

What's red and smells like blue paint?
Red paint.

What do you call a donkey with three legs?
Wonky.

What's green and has wheels?
Grass. I was joking about the wheels.

What's yellow and fills the field with music?
Popcorn.

What do you call a piece of wood with nothing to do?
Board.

What do you call a dinosaur with one eye?
Doyouthinkhesaurus.

Why did the teacher take a ruler to bed with him?
To see how long he could sleep.

Why did the girl take the pencil to bed?
To draw the curtains.

What's the difference between a soldier and a fireman?
You can't dip a fireman in your egg.

What do you call a man who plays with leaves?
Russell.

What do you call a man with a seagull on his head?
Cliff.

What do you call a man who comes through your letterbox?
Bill.

What do you call a man with a spade in his hand?
Doug.

What do you call a man without a spade in his hand?
Douglas.

What's the world's fastest cake?
Scone.

What's black, white and red all over?
A zebra wearing too much lipstick.

Bizarre Olympic sports

The 2008 Olympic Games, in Beijing, were the first to include BMX biking as a recognised sport. This isn't the same as mountain biking, which has been an official sport since way back in 1996. So how often are new sports added?

Fairly frequently, it turns out. The triathlon only made it onto the list in 2000, four years after softball and 16 years after synchronised swimming. The International Olympic Committee will consider any sport that is both geographically widespread and popular enough.

Once a sport is on the list, though, it isn't guaranteed a permanent place. Sports which have fallen from favour include croquet and cricket (both last placed in 1900), polo (1936), golf (1904) and the tug of war (1920).

The 1904 tug of war finals (pictured above), staged in the United States, were won by the United States. The silver medal went to the United States, and the bronze medal to, er, the United States. Clearly, knowledge of the terrain is the key to success in this sport: at the following Olympic Games, held in London in 1908, the gold medal went to Great Britain (City of London Police), the silver to Great Britain (Liverpool Police) and the bronze to Great Britain (Metropolitan Police K Division). The IOC decided the whole thing was too dodgy for its own good.

The 1904 Olympics were quite bizarre. In order to include 'primitive' tribes – Patagonians, Pygmies and so on – events included mud fighting, rock and spear throwing, and greasy pole climbing. It was such an embarrassment that these sports were immediately dropped from the competition.

There were two spare slots for the 2016 Olympic Games, and interested parties put forward a number of sports – including baseball, karate and squash. In the end, 7-a-side rugby and golf became the new sports to be included.

21 Let me explain...

WHICH CAME FIRST, the chicken or the egg? It's a puzzle that has baffled some of the brightest brains on the planet. Well, okay, it's a puzzle that has baffled some of the brightest *kids* on the planet.

But that's the whole point. No question is so daft that it won't have children endlessly puzzling over the answer. They're immersed in a complex world they barely understand; and when they get stuck, naturally they turn to Dad for help.

Unless you happen to be a science teacher, the chances are you'll be stuck on some of the trickier problems. So here are the solutions to some of the common questions kids might ask, as well as a few useful facts to spice up the conversation.

If you *do* know how something works, then be sure to steer the conversation in that direction so that your apparently bottomless fund of fascinating information can get an outing. You should aim to give your kids the impression that the explanations you've learned in this chapter are just the tip of the vast iceberg of your knowledge: they need to come to believe that you know just about everything.

Why can't people be twice the size?

It's a staple of science fiction movies: spiders the size of elephants, people twelve feet tall, horses shrunk to the size of mice. But is it possible?

In a word, no. There's a good reason why spiders have thin spindly legs, while elephants have great thick chunky ones. It's all to do with how length, area and volume get bigger at different rates.

Imagine you have a square Lego brick, with four bobbles on top, that's approximately a centimetre on each side.

Now let's make a brick that's twice as big as this one. That is, it's twice as high, twice as wide, and twice as deep. We end up with an assembly like the one shown on the left.

The height is double the size of the single brick. Look at the top face: that's four times the size of the single brick. Count the number of bricks we've used, and you'll see that doubling all the dimensions has given us a volume that's *eight times* what we started out with.

Now imagine a ball hanging from a thread, so that the thread is just strong enough to support it. If the ball were any heavier, the thread would break. Let's double the size of the ball and the thread.

As we've seen, if the ball's twice as big, its volume will be eight times as much, so it will weigh eight times as much. And what of the thread? It will be twice as wide, twice as deep and twice as long.

Except that being twice as long doesn't make it any stronger; in fact, the thread will only be four times as thick, just as the top surface of the Lego assembly is four times the area of the original brick. So the thread will break.

So it is with people. If we were double the size, we'd be eight times the weight, but our muscles would only be four times as strong. And if a spider were, say, a hundred times the size, it would weigh a million times more (100 × 100 × 100), but its legs could carry only ten thousand times as much (100 × 100). Like super-sized people, it would simply collapse under its own weight.

Why haven't we been visited by aliens?

It's a good question. After all, the Universe is vast, and the chance of there being some intelligent life out there can't be all that small. So why have none of them made it here yet?

There's a good explanation, and it goes like this. First, ask your child to think how fast a supercharged alien rocket could travel. A thousand miles an hour? A hundred thousand miles an hour? OK, let's assume our alien rocket is so advanced it can travel at a *million* miles an hour. That's pretty fast.

But it's not fast enough. The nearest star to us is Proxima Centauri, which is also the nearest place there could possibly be planets that might support life. And it's 4.2 light years away. Which, put another way, is rather over 24 trillion miles (that's 24,000,000,000,000). So even if our aliens travelled at a million miles an hour, it would still take them nearly three thousand years to get here.

Even for aliens that's an awfully long journey, just on the off chance that we happened to be in when they called.

Why don't people have four arms?

Kids should ask questions: it's a sign of an active and enquiring mind. Sometimes, though, they'll ask a question that has no answer – because the questioner is starting from an impossible situation.

Typical questions might be: 'If people could breathe underwater, would we have gills instead of nostrils?'; 'If they managed to invent a camera that could photograph things that hadn't happened yet, would that mean you couldn't stop the things from happening?' – and so on. And on.

We have a standard response to this sort of question. It takes the form of another question: 'If dolphins had wings, would they speak Swahili?' Usually, this is enough to indicate that their original question is unanswerable.

How do seatbelts work?

We use them every day, and at some point it crosses most children's minds that their behaviour is actually rather odd. When you move slowly, they wind in and out freely; but when you move fast, they lock up. How is this achieved?

They're called 'inertial seatbelts' and they work on the principle of centrifugal force. The precise mechanism varies between designs, but here's the basic idea.

Imagine an arm, pivoted at the middle, which spins as you pull the seatbelt. On each end of the arm are weights, held into the centre by springs; there are teeth around the outside:

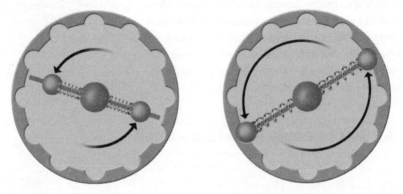

When the belt is pulled slowly (left), the weights stay near the centre – they're pulled there by the springs. But when the belt is pulled quickly (right), centrifugal force makes the weights fly to the outside. They lock into the teeth, preventing the hub from turning, and so preventing the seatbelt from pulling any further.

How do dimmer switches work?

Dimmer switches used to work by passing the current through a variable resistor, which would reduce the amount actually reaching the bulb. The trouble is, all that power had to go somewhere – and it went into heating up the resistor. Which meant that not only did the switch itself get very hot, which was pretty dangerous, it also cost you the same as keeping the bulb on full brightness.

These days, dimmer switches work by turning the bulb on and off, many times a second. The longer the bulb is off, the dimmer it is. Simple, but brilliant – or dim, if that's the setting you prefer.

How do fridges work?

When a liquid evaporates, it loses heat. That's why you feel cold when you get out of a swimming pool, even on a summer's day: the water evaporating from your skin cools you down.

Fridges use this process using a gas which liquifies at a very low temperature. This flows in a zigzag tube through the fridge; you can see the ripples in the back and roof. The cold gas flows through the fridge, absorbing heat; it then goes through a compressor, which turns it into a liquid as it goes through a similar zigzag tube on the outside of the fridge, at the back. A fan blows through this tube, blowing the absorbed heat away; the liquid then goes through an expansion gate, which turns it back into a gas, cooling it down so it can absorb more heat.

In the early days, ammonia was the gas of choice. But it's toxic, and after a number of fatal accidents manufacturers switched to chlorofluorocarbons (CFCs). Then they discovered those damaged the ozone layer, and have switched to hydrofluorocarbons (HFCs). If you know anything bad about HFCs, keep it to yourself.

How do electric toothbrushes work?

When you recharge your phone, your iPod or your digital camera, you can see the metal contacts that join the device to the charger. Rechargeable toothbrushes, however, don't have any visible contacts: bare metal, with current flowing through it, would be far too dangerous to keep in a bathroom.

Instead, the transformer that provides the power to the batteries in the toothbrush is split into two halves. One coil and a metal rod are in the charger, the other coil is inside the toothbrush itself. Since transformers work using magnetic forces, the two coils don't need to be touching, as long as they're close to each other. When you place the toothbrush into the charger, it completes the transformer, so charging can take place.

Which came first, the chicken or the egg?

It's an old problem. The chicken had to come from an egg; but the egg had to come from a chicken. Or did it?

Chickens evolved, just as people evolved. So there must have been a first chicken, before which it was a Jurassic chickenosaurus, or some such pseudo scientific nonsense.

But there were eggs long before there were chickens. Dinosaurs hatched from eggs. So our very first proto-chicken must have come from an egg; but the egg itself came from the immediate ancestor of the chicken. Problem solved!

How does Google work?

Google is such an advanced search engine that it's just about beaten all the rest into submission. It can be startlingly accurate. But how does it locate pages so quickly, among the many millions out there?

Google uses a network of thousands of ordinary PCs, constantly scanning the web and cataloguing each page it comes across. But the really clever part is how it judges how significant each page is.

Let's say you set up your own home page. Google will find it eventually, and catalogue every word on it. But why does a reference on your page come so far down the list, compared with references to the same word on better known sites? The answer is that Google ranks the 'value' of your page depending on how many other pages link to it. Not just that, but more significant pages linking to yours will have a higher ranking: so if your page is mentioned in your friend's blog, it won't score very highly; if it's referred to on *The Guardian* website, it will up your ranking significantly.

Yes, but how do Google make any money out of it?

Let's say you search for 'digital cameras'. Down the right of the results page you'll see half a dozen links to digital camera sites. These links are bid for by people wanting to advertise: Google doesn't set the rates, it's simply the highest bidders who get a listing here. Each time you click on one of those links, the advertiser will pay Google a dollar or so for the privilege of getting your attention.

It's come down to a fine art. Buying adwords for 'digital camera' searches will cost around a dollar: Adwords for 'digital cameras' searches cost double that. Someone, somewhere, has worked out that people searching for 'digital cameras' end up buying one. It's a fine art, advertising.

How fast do things fall?

Acceleration due to gravity, as we learned at school, is 9.8 metres per second squared. Come again? Well, there's a simple way to work out how many seconds it takes a dropped object to hit the ground: double the height in metres, divide by 9.8 and then take the square root. Easier if you have a calculator to hand!

Of course, there are minor things like air resistance to take into account, so this formula won't work for very big distances, or very light objects. But here's a visual guide to some useful distances:

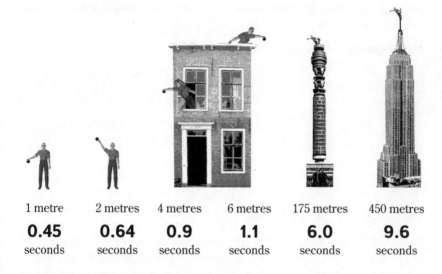

1 metre	2 metres	4 metres	6 metres	175 metres	450 metres
0.45	**0.64**	**0.9**	**1.1**	**6.0**	**9.6**
seconds	seconds	seconds	seconds	seconds	seconds

Why doesn't the Moon crash into the Earth?

In fact, the Moon *is* constantly falling towards the Earth. But the surface of the Earth, being curved, falls away from the Moon at exactly the same rate. If the Moon moved slower, or faster, it would either crash into us or fly off into space.

It's the same as the reason why satellites don't fall down. They're pushed at exactly the right speed to keep them at a uniform distance above the Earth. If the satellite is positioned at exactly 26,240 miles above the Earth, it will stay precisely above the same spot on the Earth's surface: these satellites are in what's called geosynchronous orbit, which is how we can pick up satellite TV without having to keep moving the dish.

Why Fahrenheit and Celsius?

In 1724, Gabriel Fahrenheit measured the lowest temperature he could achieve, and called that 0°. He decided there should be 180° between the freezing point and the boiling point of water, perhaps to mimic the 180° in a semicircle: and so ended up with 32° for the freezing point, and 212° for the boiling point.

In 1742 Anders Celsius decided this was a stupid system, and devised a better one based purely around water. In his system, water boiled at 0° and froze at 100°. Yes, that's right. It wasn't until someone pointed out the supreme idiocy of this approach that it was changed to water freezing at 0° and boiling at 100°. Originally called centigrade, the scale was renamed Celsius to commemorate him.

So what's absolute zero, then?

In 1848, scientist Lord Kelvin decided to see at what temperature the molecules in various gases would stop moving. To his surprise, they all stopped at the same temperature: minus 273°C. He figured out that this was a complete absence of heat: absolute zero, the lowest temperature there is.

A famous piece of music by the American composer John Cage, called 4'33", consists of total silence that lasts for that period of time. 4 minutes 33 seconds is, of course, 273 seconds.

How do 3D glasses work?

The first 3D film was *The Power of Love*, made in 1922. Sadly, the film dropped out of circulation and there are no known copies still in existence. But film makers have been churning out 3D movies, with varying degrees of success, ever since. The 3D effect depends on our ability to see different images with each eye.

Red and green lenses: There are two main ways of making 3D images and films. The simplest uses red and green lenses, one for each eye. When looking through the red lens, everything looks red – so anything that actually *is* red will be invisible. Anything that's green, on the other hand, will appear black, because green is the 'opposite' colour to red; the same works, in reverse, with the other lens.

You can simulate the effect using the red and green transparent wrappers from Quality Street chocolates. Draw a face on a sheet of paper using a red felt pen or crayon; draw an identical face about a centimetre away, so the two overlap, using a green pen. When you hold the wrappers over your eyes, each one will filter out that colour, and you'll see a face that appears to hover above the page.

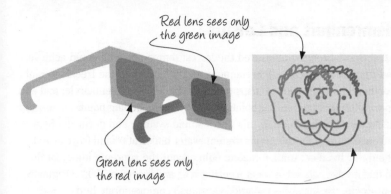

Red lens sees only the green image

Green lens sees only the red image

Polarized lenses: The trouble with red and green lenses is that you can only see things in black and white. For full colour, you need to split an image so that each eye sees a completely different image. Polarized lenses, of the sort used in sunglasses, are made with imperceptible straight lines on them. If the lines are vertical, and you look at an image made of vertical lines, you won't see anything – but you will see an image made of horizontal lines, and vice versa. So colour movies place two images on top of each other, one made of vertical lines, one of horizontal, and the glasses filter out each image.

You can show how this works by taking two pairs of sunglasses and placing them together so you're looking through both lenses at once. When they're arranged so the lines are at right angles to each other, you'll be able to see through them; but rotate one pair by 90° so they line up and they'll go totally opaque, as the lines coincide to cut out all the light.

Look through two pairs of polarized sunglasses. When the lenses are lined up, you won't be able to see through them; rotate one pair by 90 degrees and they'll become clear (but still dark)

How are cranes put up?

Although a common sight in most cities, you rarely see the multiplicity of cranes that tower hundreds of feet up in the air actually being put up. They just seem to appear overnight. How does it happen? Do you need a bigger crane to put a smaller crane up and an even bigger one to get that one up? In that case, how did the world's biggest crane go up?

Cranes on building sites are usually tower cranes. Tower cranes usually *are* initially built by smaller, weaker cranes, either mobile cranes or telescopic tower types. But once the main crane outgrows them, they have to put themselves up. A cradle encircling the tower hydraulically jacks up the crane, enabling the crane to winch up the next section of the mast, which is fitted into position and bolted into place. Then it does it again, and again, each time the cab and jib (or arm) getting further and further from the ground.

A standalone tower crane is usually no higher than 80 metres (265 feet) and can lift a maximum of 20 tonnes (the same as three African elephants), though this decreases the further out along the arm the load goes. However, cranes can go higher and lift more if they are fastened onto the buildings they are helping to erect, often being situated in what will eventually be the lift shaft. The world's largest tower cranes, the Danish K10000, stand 120 metres high (almost three

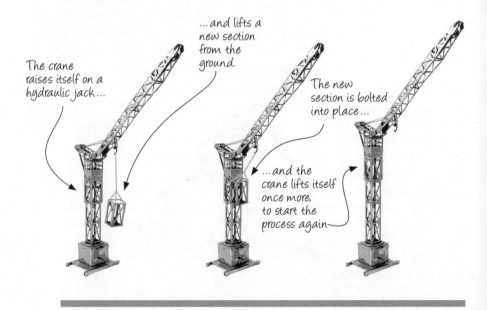

The crane raises itself on a hydraulic jack...

...and lifts a new section from the ground.

The new section is bolted into place...

...and the crane lifts itself once more, to start the process again times the height of the Statue of Liberty). The jib is 100 metres, it has a service crane all of its own on top, can lift a maximum of 360 tonnes and even has a lift for those who have to go up it.

Children often wonder why cranes don't topple over, particularly in high winds. They are anchored with massive bolts to concrete which has been poured into the ground and there are heavy counterweights on the rear of the jib. If the wind rises to more than 40 or 50 miles an hour, cranes have to stop working and they are left to 'weathervane', swinging with the wind so that the jib points in the same direction as the wind is blowing. Cranes in Europe are supposed to be able to survive winds of 100 miles an hour.

Incredibly large mobile cranes also exist. The UK has two of the largest currently made, the Terex Demag AC 700. This telescopic crane can rise to 133 metres when fully extended and can lift a staggering 700 tonnes.

Tunnels are boring? Not!

Tunnels such as the Channel Tunnel are constructed by giant tunnel boring machines (TBMs) which have giant circular cutting wheels at the front. They use the same principle as earthworms to progress, expanding to grip the tunnel and dig its way forward, and then withdrawing the sides so the rear of the TBM can advance.

It took seven years to dig the Channel Tunnel using 11 TBMs. It's 30 miles long with 24 miles actually under the sea. After the two pairs of TBMs met in the middle in 1991 (with an error of only 2cm), the British machines turned off course and buried themselves in the sea bed, where they were concreted in. They're still there, waiting to be discovered like space age dinosaurs. The French decided to dismantle theirs but Chunnel folklore has it that the process was so time-consuming and difficult that it cost more than the new machines would have done.

The first underwater tunnel was constructed under the Thames by the amazingly innovative Victorian engineer Isambard Kingdom Brunel. Several workers were killed and he was badly injured when the tunnel flooded during construction. However the tunnel, finished in 1843, is still in use today by the London Underground East London Line.

Why is the sky black at night?

It's not as daft a question as it might sound. There's no Sun to light it up – but there are billions of suns out there, all shining away. So why isn't the sky dazzling white? The further away the stars are, the more their light diminishes before reaching us; but then the further the distance, the more stars there are around us. This is known as Olbers' Paradox, after the mathematician who was first puzzled by it.

The answer is surprising. If the Universe were infinitely old, then all the light in it would have had time to reach everywhere and the night sky would be bright. But the Universe isn't infinitely old, so a lot of the light is still on its way. Come back in a couple of zillion years and ask the question again.

What's so clever about ballpoint pens?

We use them every day, and lose them every other day. They've become so much part of the furniture that we tend to forget how ingenious they really are.

Before they were invented, people wrote with fountain pens. The problem was that if the ink was wet enough not to dry up as it flowed down the nib, it remained wet on the paper – which is the main reason why people owned blotters. (The other reason was to provide clues for Hercule Poirot.)

László Bíró was a journalist who saw a newspaper being printed with ink that dried as soon as it hit the paper, and determined to devise a method for using a similar quick-drying ink in pen form. But printing ink is too thick to flow through a regular pen. His ingenious solution was a ball that held the ink in its tube, which fitted just well enough to allow a thin film of the ink to roll on to the paper when the pen was used. The mechanism is the same as that used in roll-on deodorants, and in fact their invention was inspired by the biro.

László and his brother Georg took out a patent on the device in 1943; the patent was bought by the British government, so they could supply pilots in the RAF with pens that didn't leak ink at high altitude. The only problem was, they were extremely expensive to make.

In 1945, the Frenchman Marcel Bich invented a manufacturing process to enable him to make ballpoint pens cheaply. He named them Bic, after himself. They were a phenomenal success: in 2005, the company he founded sold its *hundred billionth* ballpoint pen. That's more than 15 pens for each man, woman and child on the planet.

So where the hell are they all, then?

22 Language stuff

FROM THE MOMENT THEY BEGIN to talk, kids start to learn to argue. It's a sad fact of life that we wait years for them to be old enough to hold an intelligent conversation, then spend the rest of our lives waiting for them to shut up.

Kids have an insatiable appetite for new words, continually questioning our speech and asking for definitions of new concepts. But language is much more than a means of everyday conversation: words can be endlessly fascinating, and kids have the ability to latch on to the more obscure words simply because they like the sound they make.

Our language is riddled with peculiar and odd words, from the longest word in English to the longest domain name, from the names for collectors of beermats to the name of the fear of getting peanut butter stuck to the roof of your mouth.

Here's a selection of the interesting, the factual, the absurd and the downright idiotic to keep them amused. We've also thrown in a few nonsense verses which are fun to learn and make useful alternatives to bedtime stories.

A for 'orses

This comic rendering of the alphabet has been around, in one form or another, for a century or more. We've put together the best of the variations and added a few of our own when the originals have seemed a little long in the tooth.

If you don't get what's going on here, try saying them aloud. If you *still* don't get what's going on, ask your kids to help you out.

A for 'orses
B for Veggie burgers
C for Miles
D for Rent
E for Ning All
F for Vescent
G for Police
H for Retirement
I for Knock knock joke for you
J for Cakes
K for Teria
L for Leather
M for Sis
N for Lope
O for the Rainbow
P for Ming Seals
Q for a Bus
R for Mo
S for You
T for Two
U for Mystic
V for La France
W for Quits
X for Breakfast
Y for Runts
Z for a Doctor, I got a code in me dose

A, I'm adorable.
B, I'm beautiful...

Nonsense verse

There's no point whatsoever to these little ditties. Except, of course, that they're fun to say to your kids.

One day next week at break of night
I met a dog whose wings were white.
He bit my tail, I pinched his fins
We fought right through the darkest light.

I shot him with my rubber sword
He opened wide his ears and roared.
He looked me squarely in the nose
And strangled me with a piano chord.

'Why are we fighting?' I whispered loud,
As snow rained from the mushroom cloud.
He answered that he could not speak –
The rule is clear: 'No dogs aloud.'

I laughed a sneer, my blood ran red:
He raised his gun and sliced off my head.
I ate him then, his feathers and all
And we lay there panting, both stone dead.

One day next week as the sun grew dark
I fought like a dog, he sang like a shark.
And when at last the fight was done
I killed him with my question mark.

Algy met a bear.
The bear met Algy.
The bear was bulgy.
The bulge was Algy.

The elephant is a bonnie bird,
It flits from bough to bough,
It makes its nest in the rhubarb tree,
And whistles like a cow.

Trade names

It used to be common practice to refer to vacuum cleaners as Hoovers. Which was immensely annoying for Hoover, who go to great lengths to correct anyone who misuses their trademarked name in print.

All the words below are now so much part of the language that you'd be forgiven for thinking they were generic terms. In fact the only people who probably won't forgive you are the lawyers of the companies who own them:

Astro Turf	*Band-Aid*	*Breathalyzer*	*Brillo Pads*	*Dumpster*
Frisbee	*Hoover*	*Hula-Hoop*	*Jacuzzi*	*Jeep*
Kleenex	*Laundromat*	*Magic Marker*	*Muzak*	*Novocaine*
Ping-Pong	*Play-Doh*	*Post-it Note*	*Q-Tip*	*Rollerblade*
Scotch Tape	*Scrabble*	*Sellotape*	*Styrofoam*	*Super Glue*
Technicolor	*Teflon*	*TelePrompter*	*Vaseline*	*Velcro*
Walkman	*Xerox*			

Sometimes common sense wins out over legal argument. The following words all *used* to be trademarks, but have now been ruled part of the language:

aspirin	*bikini*	*brassiere*	*cellophane*	*dry ice*
escalator	*gramophone*	*gunk*	*kiwi fruit*	*linoleum*
petrol	*pilates*	*plasterboard*	*shredded wheat*	*tabloid*
thermos	*touch-tone*	*trampoline*	*yo-yo*	*zip*

Q here

Are there are any English words where a 'u' doesn't follow a 'q'? Yes, though you aren't likely to be using them every day. *Qadi* is a Muslim judge; *qigong* is a Chinese system of physical exercises; *qin*, a Chinese musical instrument; *qintar*, money in Albania, worth $\frac{1}{100}$ of a lek; *qwerty*, the layout of typewriter and computer keyboards; and *suq*, an Arab marketplace.

What comes after 'once', 'twice' and 'thrice'?

Sadly, there's nothing after that. Quince is a fruit you can make into marmalade but it has nothing to do with five.

Got a fear? Get a phobia

This selection of phobias includes several that bright children could carefully employ instead of claiming that 'the dog ate my homework'.

Ablutophobia . . . . Fear of washing or bathing
Achluophobia . . . . Fear of darkness
Acousticophobia . . . . Fear of noise
Agliophobia . . . . Fear of pain
Ambulophobia . . . . Fear of walking
Apiphobia . . . . Fear of bees
Arachibutyrophobia . . . . . Fear of peanut butter sticking to the roof of the mouth
Autodysomophobia . . . . . . Fear of someone who has a vile odour
Bibliophobia . . . . Fear of books
Chronomentrophobia . . . . Fear of clocks
Cibophobia . . . . Fear of food (also called Sitophobia and Sitiophobia)
Clinophobia . . . . Fear of going to bed
Decidophobia . . . . Fear of making decisions
Deipnophobia . . . . Fear of dining or dinner conversations
Dentophobia . . . . Fear of dentists
Didaskaleinophobia . . . . . Fear of going to school
Entomophobia . . . . Fear of insects
Eosophobia . . . . Fear of dawn or daylight
Ephebiphobia . . . . Fear of teenagers
Epistemophobia . . . . Fear of knowledge
Ergophobia . . . . Fear of work
Gnosiophobia . . . . Fear of knowledge
Hypnophobia . . . . Fear of sleep (or of being hypnotised)
Iatrophobia . . . . Fear of going to the doctor
Ichthyophobia . . . . Fear of fish
Kathisophobia . . . . Fear of sitting down
Logophobia . . . . Fear of words
Numerophobia . . . . Fear of numbers
Odontophobia . . . . Fear of teeth or dental surgery
Poinephobia . . . . Fear of punishment
Ponophobia . . . . Fear of overworking or of pain
Sophophobia . . . . Fear of learning

Tongue-twisters

Almost every language has combinations of sounds that can be hard to say, though tongue-twisters are often so nonsensical there would normally be no reason to say them except as a challenge. In English, the most difficult tongue-twister is said to be 'The sixth sick sheikh's sixth sheep's sick' – which we finally mastered, only to discover that some sadist has since added 'so six slick sheiks sold six sick sheep six silk sheets'.

But that's not to say we don't enjoy tongue-twisters and competing with our kids to see who can say them best. Here are some of our favourites. The shorter ones need to be repeated several times, if indeed that is possible.

Sixish
Big boat
Toy whip
Truly rural
Greek grapes
Ed had edited it
Irish wristwatch
Unique New York
Three free throws
Cheap sheep soup
Preshrunk silk shirts
Three boys felt smart
Aluminium ambulance
Shredded Swiss cheese
Quick kiss, quicker kiss
The myth of Miss Muffet
Plague-bearing prairie dogs
Mrs Smith's Fish Sauce Shop
The soldier's shoulder surely hurts
Plain bun, plum bun, bun without plum
A box of biscuits, a batch of mixed biscuits
Fred fed Ted bread, and Ted fed Fred bread
What time does the wristwatch strap shop shut?
Give papa a proper cup of coffee in a proper coffee cup
Betty and Bob brought back blue balloons from the big bazaar

We find selling seashells and picking pecks of pickled peppers tedious, so we're only including one longer one. As it offers such practical advice, you may want to master it, ready for the day when you can finally usefully use it.

> You've no need to light a night-light
> On a light night like tonight.
> For a night-light's light's a slight light
> And tonight's a night that's light.
> When a night's light, like tonight's light,
> It is really not quite right
> To light night-lights with their slight lights,
> On a light night like tonight.

Of all the French tongue-twisters we looked at, dictionary in hand, this was about the only one we could understand: 'Dans ta tente ta tante t'attend' which means 'In your tent, your aunt is waiting for you'.

In German, which we found tricky enough when we had to study it at school, this is one of the most popular tongue-twisters: 'Brautkleid bleibt Brautkleid und Blaukraut bleibt Blaukraut'. It's pretty nonsensical, meaning 'A wedding dress will be a wedding dress and red cabbage will be red cabbage'.

Musical words

Any number of words can be made using the letters A to G used in musical notation: everyday words such as ACE, DEAF, BED, BAG and so on may sound awkward when played, but it's possible to construct a reasonable tune. There are even some seven letter words, including BAGGAGE, DEFACED and FEEDBAG. Of course, the best word to play is DAD, we're sure you'll agree.

If you have musically inclined kids, here's a little puzzle you can show them – or even play to them, should they happen to have perfect pitch. Can they decipher the words?

All dogs go woof

Or do they? Not according to Professor Catherine Ball, who has collected the sounds made by dogs in different languages around the world. For more animal sounds from cuckoos to crocodiles, visit the University of Adelaide's School of Electrical and Electronic Engineering site at bit.ly/OFitjT.

Afrikaans	woef	Hindi	bho-bho
Albanian	ham ham	Hungarian	vau-vau
Arabic	haw haw	Icelandic	voff
Bengali	ghaue-ghaue	Indonesian	gonggong
Catalan	bup, bup	Italian	bau bau
Chinese	wang wang	Japanese	kyankyan
Croatian	vau-vau	Korean	mung-mung
Danish	vov	Norwegian	vov-vov
Dutch	woef	Polish	hau hau
English	woof woof	Portuguese	au-au
Old English	Hund byrcð	Russian	gav-gav
Esperanto	boj	Slovene	hov-hov
Estonian	auh	Spanish	guau guau
Finnish	hau hau	Swedish	vov vov
French	ouah ouah	Thai	hoang hoang
German	wau wau	Turkish	hav, hav
Greek	gav	Ukrainian	haf-haf
Hebrew	haw haw	Vietnamese	wau wau

wang wang

hov-hov

boj

Odd words in the OED

The Oxford English Dictionary (OED) is the world's foremost authority on the meaning of words. It was started in 1862 by Frederick Furnivall, who reckoned it would take him three years to complete. By 1884, twenty-two years later, he'd got as far as the word Ant.

It's a complex business, writing dictionaries. For one thing, new words keep creeping into the language. The last year alone has seen the inclusion of hundreds of new words, including those that refer to newly current topics: *fracking, flash mob, selfie, 3D printing* and *Childline*. Then there are those that have only just made it in, but which you'd think would have been included years ago – including *bureau de change, badassery, Discman, family silver, heart-stopper, headmistressy, justice minister* and *whack-a-mole*, among dozens of others.

Now you might think many of those words would be in the dictionary already, but of course they're not there until someone puts them there – and the editors of the OED are very strict about how commonplace a word has to be before it qualifies for entry.

The latest update contained the word *buzzworthy*, which means 'Likely to generate enthusiastic interest and attention, especially in the popular media.' A word whose inclusion, coincidentally, generated both enthusiastic interest and attention, especially in the popular media.

The word with the longest entry in the OED is *run*, surprisingly, because it has so many different meanings. It's closely followed by *red, put, time* and *be*. On the longest-entry rankings, *set*, which topped the list in 1989, has now slipped to seventh place.

The word with the shortest entry is the verb *ysunged*, which we think means 'sinned'. Bizarrely, its entry is so short that it doesn't include any reference to the word actually in use. But, thanks to the wonders of the internet, we've found one – from a version of the Gospels written in the 13th century:

> "Bringeþ him out, þat y se,
> Y preye ou for þe loue of me!"
> "Ich habbe ysunged: merci y crie.
> Þou me help, sone Marie!
> Help me, ȝef þi wille beo,
> Louerd, þat restest on rode treo!"

Take that, Oxford academics! Google 1, OED 0.

What is the longest word in English?

Most of the supposedly 'longest' words in the English language are made up in order to get into lists of the longest words in the English language, such as this one. According to the Oxford dictionary people, the longest genuine words are:

pseudopseudohypoparathyroidism	30	A disorder with similar symptoms to pseudohypoparathyroidism
floccinaucinihilipilification	29	The act of estimating something as worthless
antidisestablishmentarianism	28	The view opposing the idea that the Church of England and the state should be separated

The Oxford dictionaries also list *pneumonoultramicroscopicsilicovolcanoconiosis* (45 letters), apparently a lung disease, but it was almost certainly invented simply to be a long word. Often quoted as the longest are the formal names of chemical compounds which can be almost unlimited in length. Some have been written out with over 1000 letters. But they aren't real words.

The song *Supercalifragilisticexpialidocious* (34 letters) from Mary Poppins is listed in some dictionaries. You're unlikely to find *Lip-smackin-thirst-quenchin-acetastin-motivatin-good-buzzin-cool-talkin-high-walkin-fast-livin-ever-givincool-fizzin* listed, but that's the 100-letter concatenated 'word' from a 1973 Pepsi ad that loads of dads will still remember.

The *humuhumu-nukunuku-a-pua'a* (22 letters) is Hawaii's official state fish, otherwise known as a reef triggerfish. Some say that the name is longer than the fish itself.

Longest place names

Llanfairpwllgwyngyllgogerychwyrndrobwllllantysiliogogogoch in Anglesey, Wales, with 58 letters, is often said to be the longest place name in Britain. In Welsh the name means 'St Mary's Church in the hollow of the white hazel near to the rapid whirlpool of Llantysilio of the red cave'. In fact, the long version of the town's real name of Llanfairpwllgwyngyll (sometimes just called 'Llanfair PG') was made up in the 19th century as a publicity stunt. Nonetheless several shops and the railway station display the sign in full.

To say the name, you'll need to know that the Welsh *ll* is pronounced as the Scots do the *ch* of loch. Make this noise, segueing into *lan – vire – pu* (as in put) *– ll* again *– gwin – gil* (like fish gill), segueing into *ll – go* (o as in dog) *– ger – uch* (with the ch as in Scottish loch) *– win – drawb – u* (as in put) *– ll – llan* (as at beginning) *– ti – silly – o – go – go – go – ll*.

There's a joke about two English speakers asking the person serving them food in Llanfair PG if she can say the name of the place they're in very slowly. 'Certainly,' she says, 'it's M-a-c-d-o-n-a-l-d-s.'

Trying to beat the record for the longest Welsh name, somebody recently came up with *Gorsafawddachaidraigodanheddogleddollonpenrhynareurdraethceredigion*, which has 66 letters against 53 ('ll' only counts as one letter in Welsh) and means 'the Mawddach station and its dragon teeth at the Northern Penrhyn Road on the golden beach of Cardigan bay'. It hasn't taken off.

Longest internet name: The longest internet domain name in the world is probably *llanfairpwllgwyngyllgogerychwyrndrobwllllantysiliogogogochuchaf.org.uk*, which is the name reserved for the upper part of the village. But there are several other contenders for the dubious title of the longest .com domain names, including *thelongestdomainnameintheworldandthensomeandthensomemoreandmore.com* and *Iamtheproudownerofthelongestlongestlongestdomainnameinthisworld.com*.

Longest place name: The longest name in common usage is an 82-letter hill in New Zealand. *Taumatawhakatangihangakoauotamateturipukakapikimaungaho ro-Nukupokaiwhenuakitanatahu* apparently means 'the place where Tamatea, the man with the big knees, who slid, climbed and swallowed mountains, known as land-eater, played his flute to his loved one'.

Longest lake name: There are a mere 45 letters in the Massachusetts lake which revels in the name *Chargoggagoggmanchauggagoggchaubunagungamaugg*, though that does include 9 As and 15 Gs. Locals, who often can't spell it, have simply taken to calling it Webster Lake after the local town.

Collecting the collectors

Shells, stamps, coins, books – we all know people who collect one or more of these items. But what of the collectors of packets of sugar, car tax discs and thimbles? Such people do exist. And they not only have websites, they also have names: for each bizarre collectible, there's an equally bizarre name to describe those who collect them. Here are a few of our favourites:

Aerophilately	air mail stamps and covers
Arctophilist	teddy bears
Argyrothecologist	money boxes
Bestiarist	medieval books on animals
Brandophilist	cigar bands
Cartophilist	cigarette cards
Conchologist	shells
Copoclephilist	keyrings
Deltiologist	postcards
Digitabulist	thimbles
Fusilatelist	telephone calling cards
Helixophilist	corkscrews
Labeorphilist	beer bottle labels
Lepidopterist	butterflies
Lotologist	scratchcards and lottery items
Notaphilist	banknotes
Numismatist	coins
Philatelist	stamps
Phillumenist	matchbox labels
Philographist	autographs
Plangonologist	dolls
Receptarist	recipes
Rhykenologist	woodworking tools
Scripophilist	old financial documents
Succrologist	sugar packets
Tegestologist	beer mats
Tyrosemiophilist	cheese labels
Vecturist	underground and other transport tokens
Velologist	vehicle excise licences (tax discs)
Vexillologist	banners or flags

Pangrams

Pangrams are sentences containing all the letters of the alphabet. The most well known is 'The quick brown fox jumps over the lazy dog', and it's often used to show all the characters in a typeface. Here are some others:

A mad boxer shot a quick, gloved jab to the jaw of his dizzy opponent.
About sixty codfish eggs will make a quarter pound of very fizzy jelly.
Astronaut Quincy B. Zack defies gravity with six jet fuel pumps.
Barkeep! A flaming tequila swizzle and a vodka and Ajax, hold the cherry.
Five jumbo oxen graze quietly with packs of dogs.
Five or six big jet planes zoomed quickly by the tower.
Fred specialized in the job of making very quaint wax toys.
How quickly daft jumping zebras vex.
I have quickly spotted the four women dozing in the jury box.
Jack amazed a few girls by dropping the antique onyx vase.
Jolly housewives made inexpensive meals using quick-frozen vegetables.
Quiz explained for TV show by Mick Jagger.
Six of the women quietly gave back prizes to the judge.
The five boxing wizards jump quickly.
Up at the zoo a roving ox was quickly fed bug jam.
Wolves exit quickly as fanged zoo chimp jabbers.
Woven silk pyjamas exchanged for blue quartz.

How many words in the English language?

The Oxford dictionary people say it's impossible to answer this definitively but suggest that there are at least a quarter of a million distinct English words, with perhaps 20 per cent no longer in current use. It's also believed that English has as many words as French, German and Spanish put together.

The most common nouns in English are, in order: Time, Person, Year, Way, Day, Thing, Man, World, Life and Hand. Ninety per cent of the top 100 words used in English are only one syllable and, despite the rapidity with which new words are coined, the majority of the most popular words we use every day date back to before the Norman Conquest (1066).

The language teacher Michel Thomas reckons that most people only use between 500 and 1,500 words.

Longest and shortest

What is the longest word in English of only one syllable? We can't do better than nine letters. These include 'screeched', 'scratched', 'scrounged', 'scrunched' and 'stretched', as well as 'straights' and 'strengths'.

The shortest word to contain the first six letters of the alphabet is 'feedback'.

Double meanings

Many words in the English language have more than one meaning. Normally, it's easy to tell which meaning is intended by the context. But sometimes it isn't quite so clear. Here are a few cases fraught with confusion:

Worrying: To 'worry' means to be overly concerned, often to the point of desperation. It also means to toy with something, as a cat does when it's playing with a mouse. So when a dog worries a sheep, is it the dog or the sheep that's doing the worrying?

Car parks: A park is a wide open space, often in the form of a garden. To park your car, on the other hand, means to leave it unattended. So is a car park a place where you park your car, or the space in which you leave it?

Sheer insanity: The word 'sheer' means 'transparent', when it's applied to stockings. It also means 'vertical' when it's applied to cliffs. So is sheer insanity transparent or vertical?

No way am I swallowing that, Mr Barrie

See you later, alligator

'Soon' means 'soon', and 'later' means 'later'. So why is it that when you say 'See you later' it generally means the same day, but when you say 'See you soon' it often means some time in the next few months?

Word quiz

1. Only five countries in the world have names of a single syllable. Which ones?

2. What's the first number to contain the letter 'a'?

3. What's the first number to contain the letter 'b'?

4. What's the only number with its letters in alphabetical order?

5. What links the words 'almost', 'begins' and 'chimps'?

6. What's the longest word you can type on the top row of letters on a computer keyboard?

7. Only one number can be spelled using the same number of letters as the number itself. What is it?

8. How does the number sequence 8 5 4 9 1 7 6 3 2 work?

9. The word 'skiing' has two dotted characters in a row. Which place name has three in a row?

10. What links the words 'polish', 'job', 'reading' and 'august'?

11. Can you think of a word that includes six consecutive consonants?

12. What links the words 'scissors', 'cattle' and 'clothes'?

13. What links the words 'cares', 'timelines' and 'princes'?

14. What links the words 'child', 'ox', 'man' and 'woman'?

15. Only one word in English ends in 'mt'. What is it?

16. Only two words in English end in 'gry'. What are they?

Answers

1. France, Spain, Greece, Laos and Chad. 2. One thousand. Or one hundred and one, if you prefer. 3. One billion. 4. Forty. 5. They have their letters in alphabetical order. 6. Typewriter. 7. Four. 8. The numbers are in alphabetical order. 9. Beijing and Fiji are the most well known. 10. They're pronounced differently when spelled with capital letters. 11. 'Watchstrap', 'catchphrase' and 'Knightsbridge' are the most common. 12. They're plural words that have no singular form. 13. They're plurals which become singular when an 's' is added on the end. 14. Their plurals end in -en. 15. Dreamt. 16. Angry and hungry.

Resources for the paperless Dad

MUMS SEEM PREPARED for every eventuality. But – let's be honest – they cheat. Like a portable Tardis, their handbags actually contain the entire contents of a department store.

If you're caught without so much as a piece of paper, don't despair. Here's a handy selection of sheets you can either use directly, or sneakily photocopy in the office when nobody's around.

The template for the Dot game could save you a pencil point or two, the Alphabet Search pro forma may help cut accusations of cheating, while the Hangman outlines ensure everybody's gibbet is constructed identically. We've also included patterns for the spinning helicopter and Flippin' Kipper. If you don't have a pair of scissors on you, what better excuse for finally getting yourself that Swiss Army knife you've always coveted?

There's an aide-memoire for the kids' birthdays, as well as pages for notes and drawing. No pen? Try a quill plucked from a passing goose. And it's a doddle to make your own ink from mashed, boiled walnut shells soaked in vinegar.

The dot game (see page 90)

Alphabet search (see page 68)

Name			
A			
B			
C			
D			
E			
F			
G			
H			
I			
J			
K			
L			
M			
N			
O			
P			
Q			
R			
S			
T			
U			
V			
W			
X			
Y			
Z			

The spinning helicopter (see page 47)

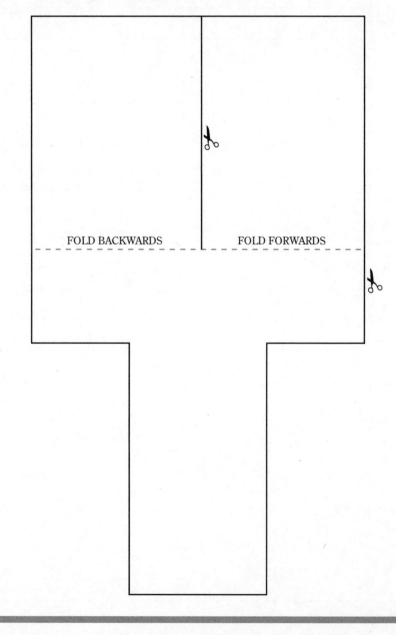

FOLD BACKWARDS   FOLD FORWARDS

Hangman (see page 87)

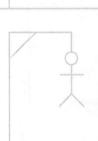

A B C D E F G H I J K L M N O P Q R S T U V W X Y Z

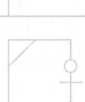

A B C D E F G H I J K L M N O P Q R S T U V W X Y Z

A B C D E F G H I J K L M N O P Q R S T U V W X Y Z

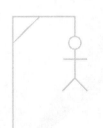

A B C D E F G H I J K L M N O P Q R S T U V W X Y Z

The flippin' kipper (see page 168)

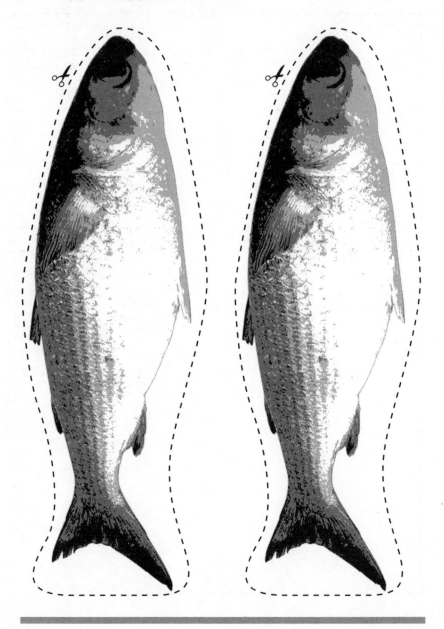

No more than seven folds (see page 4)

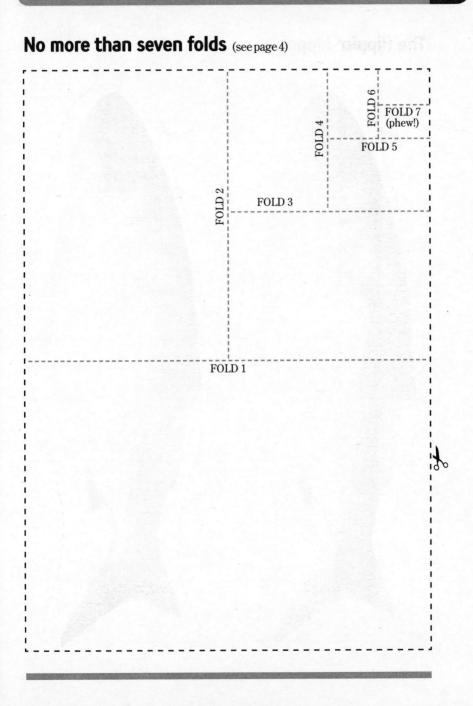

Lined paper

Really blank paper

Your kids' birthdays

Name	Date	What to buy them

...and don't forget...

Your partner's birthday		
Your anniversary		

Other important notes